Scott H. A. Clark
Computing industry expert and best-selling author

W9-ATA-956

PCs

Take charge of your computer
faster, smarter, *better*!

PUBLISHED BY
Microsoft Press
A Division of Microsoft Corporation
One Microsoft Way
Redmond, Washington 98052-6399

Library of Congress Cataloging-in-Publication Data
Clark, Scott H.
      Faster Smarter PC Basics / Scott H. A. Clark.
          p. cm.
      Includes index.
      ISBN 0-7356-1855-0
      1. Microcomputers--Equipment and supplies.   2. Computer networks.   3. Computer software.   I. Title.

   TK7885.4 .C58   2002
   004.16--dc21   2002033733

Printed and bound in the United States of America.

1 2 3 4 5 6 7 8 9   QWE   8 7 6 5 4 3

Distributed in Canada by H.B. Fenn and Company Ltd.

A CIP catalogue record for this book is available from the British Library.

Microsoft Press books are available through booksellers and distributors worldwide. For further information about international editions, contact your local Microsoft Corporation office or contact Microsoft Press International directly at fax (425) 936-7329. Visit our Web site at www.microsoft.com/mspress. Send comments to *mspinput@microsoft.com*.

Acquisitions Editor: Juliana Aldous Atkinson
Project Editor: Aileen Wrothwell
Series Editor: Kristen Weatherby

Body Part No. X08-95124

*For My Parents, With Much Love
and Thanks for Their Unflagging Support*

Scott Clark, 2002

Table of Contents

Part I: Presenting Your Computer

Once you understand how a PC is put together and how it functions, you'll be able to tell whether your computer meets your needs. This part of the book gives a brief history of the PC and discusses the hardware components that make up a PC.

Part II: What Makes a PC?

Now that you are familiar with what makes a PC a PC, it's time to delve deeper into the box. This part of the book explores such important subjects as monitors, hard and floppy disks, the difference between memory and storage, the PC's visual and audio components, and networking hardware and software.

Part III: Presenting Your OS: Windows XP

Hardware is only half the story of what makes up a PC. The other half is software—in particular, the operating system, which functions continuously behind the scenes of your PC. This part describes the Microsoft Windows XP operating system and how you can customize it so it can work faster and smarter for you.

Part IV: No Time for Troubles

Although PCs work well most of the time, things do go wrong sometimes, and you have to be prepared. This part of the book focuses on the most common problems and issues you'll encounter, including resolving hardware conflicts and protecting your computer from unauthorized access from outsiders via the Internet.

Acknowledgments

"Acknowledgment" seems too weak a word to express the gratitude that I feel towards the many people who were part of my life during this project. Some were already here, and knew what they were in for—amazingly, they're still here anyway. Others joined for the duration. Everyone provided support, guidance, love, direction, or food. Some selfless folks even provided more than one of those things, without which my life and this book wouldn't be here.

I'd especially like to thank the refreshingly helpful and professional people at Microsoft Press. Juliana Aldous, the book's acquisitions editor, encouraged me to pursue the project and worked with me to perform the magic that transforms an idea into a vision and, finally, into a table of contents. Project editor Aileen Wrothwell was genuinely invaluable. Aileen spent many hours with me, refining the manuscript. She also provided me with learning experiences which I believe will color and improve my work as a writer from these days forward. Don Lesser, my technical editor, worked to help guarantee that what I tell you is accurate, and Chrisa Hotchkiss, my copy editor, made sure that I make sense and that my English professors won't regret the years they spent on me. To everyone else at Press who contributed, a heartfelt thank you.

Closer to home, my agent, Matt Wagner, gave me this opportunity and I owe him more thanks than I can fit here. I appreciate his experience and his wisdom as much as I appreciate the work. Drew Wadish provided unceasing support through the days of "Sorry, I have to write," and himself contributed significantly to the ideas you'll find here. Friends Mark and Dennis helped keep things at home centered. Don Hash and Kacie Kanemoto went out of their way to make sure I had the available time I needed and Scott Pitts, Diane Manzi, Glynn Alsup, and Jacob Kahla understood.

Thanks to Lori Harris, wherever you are now, for enough reasons to fill 50,000 *cahiers*. Memory is only a mirror, but some things lose little joy in the reflecting.

And thanks to you, dear reader, for the time you'll spend with me and for your interest. I hope we will see each other again.

Introduction

My father called me last week. He's a very bright guy—a former bank president who got bored, went back to school at 50 to get his law degree, and opened his own practice. He's been around computers since they used endless reels of tape for storing information and took up buildings of their own.

"I need your help. I really need to get more out of my PCs. Can you tell me what I have to upgrade and whether I need to buy anything new? I don't have any idea where to begin."

"Dad, we did this just last year."

"Yes, but I'm getting bombarded with ads and articles about new stuff that's out there. LawWidget, that research tool I use all day long, is also coming out with a new version that requires different hardware, or more memory, or something."

As we talked, I was struck by how much my father uses his computers but how little he knows *about* them. He understands the software he uses, definitely. But he's sometimes at a loss when it comes to the physical PCs themselves, because he hasn't *had* to learn about them, and he really doesn't have the time to read any of the 900-page computer books—not even one written by his son—to learn. And he's no dummy. He definitely *wants* to understand, but the resources out there just don't fit his needs and his work style.

I really wanted there to be something out there for my dad and for the women and men like him. So I decided to write it. It's in your hands right now.

This Book Could Be for You

Faster, Smarter PCs won't simply encourage you and my father to buy new hardware. Product reviews in magazines do that, urging you to pull out your wallet even if you don't really need what's "new and improved." What this book will do is help you work faster and smarter with the hardware you have now and with whatever you select in the future. It will help you understand your PC hardware like you already understand the software applications you use every day—maybe even better.

What's In This Book?

I've broken the process down into four parts. Part I, "Presenting Your Computer," will give you a well-rounded understanding of your PC and its components. You'll see, I hope, that what makes the best PC for you isn't simply a matter of putting the latest or "greatest" parts together in a case. What you need depends on the job you want to accomplish. And that's what it's really all about, after all, isn't it? Make the best investment, build your business, get the job done—faster and smarter by getting to know your PC.

In Part II, "What Makes a PC?," you'll start exploring the actual pieces of hardware that work together to make what we call a PC. From how your PC thinks to how it stores and displays information, you'll see that a PC is really more than the sum of its parts. You'll see that all of those parts are necessary to keeping your PC personal and making it useful.

In Part III, "Presenting Your OS: Windows XP," you'll take a look at the operating system (OS) that makes it all happen. Microsoft Windows XP bridges two gaps: between your PC's hardware and you (through the Windows User Interface), and between your PC's hardware and the programs you use (through Windows libraries used by computer programmers). Together, these give you a consistent computing experience that's easy to learn.

Part IV, "No Time for Troubles," gives you a useful, hands-on look at what can go wrong in the PC world and how to prevent (or fix) it. You'll get a good look at the marvelous support and help system that's part of Windows, and I'll introduce you to the user communities where you can get personal answers to your specific needs. You'll also see into the world of viruses and other Internet nightmares; but never fear: Windows is ready. And you will be, too.

Support

Every effort has been made to ensure the accuracy of this book. Microsoft Press provides corrections for books at the following address:

http://mspress.microsoft.com/support/

If you have comments, questions, or ideas regarding this book, please send them to Microsoft Press via e-mail to the following address:

mspinput@microsoft.com

or via postal mail to:

Microsoft Press
Attn: Faster Smarter Series Editor
One Microsoft Way
Redmond, WA 98052-6399

Part I

Presenting Your Computer

This part of the book will give you a well-rounded understanding of your PC and its parts. You'll see, I hope, that what makes the best PC for you isn't simply a matter of putting the latest or "greatest" parts together in a case. What you need depends on the job you want to accomplish. And that's what it's really all about, after all, isn't it? Make the best investment, build your business, get the job done—faster and smarter—by getting to know your PC. Chapter 1, "The Personal Computer," gives you a foundation of where the PC came from, where it is, and where it's heading. In Chapter 2, "The Sum of its Parts," we begin to dig down into the material with an introductory exploration of the hardware that makes up almost any PC. So let's get started...

The Personal Computer

You work with a computer every day and everyone you know calls it a PC. But how well do you understand your PC—and what's so personal about it, anyway? Your computer at home is personal, certainly. You own it; it's yours. Your finances, letters, maybe your journal are stored on it. Things just don't get much more personal. But your computer at work is probably a PC too, even though your company owns it and five different people might share it. A *personal* computer?

Not Your Father's Computer

Part of the reason your computer at work is called a PC can be found in the general history of computers. The days when each desk didn't have a computer on it are becoming distant memories. For me, thinking back to those days is like watching a black-and-white movie. It doesn't really matter how long ago the movie was made; black-and-white just *feels* old. And even when computers started to show up on desks, they were in limited places like banks and insurance companies. Bright green flickering screens provided access to only the most vital customer information. You may even remember having a computer like that on your desk, or on your parents' desk. But there was *nothing* personal about that computer.

Of course, there wasn't supposed to be. In fact, if you had talked to those corporations about letting individual employees influence or customize how computer systems worked, you'd have been shown the door. Companies put computing power into individual hands but controlled and limited every conceivable interaction between employees and computers. And let's not forget that we're talking about 30 years ago. No technology was available to make desktop computers anything more than a front end to a huge central computer that was miles away. We still have computers around today that have this level of power and personality: we call them ATMs.

When the first computers called *personal computers* came on the scene in the late 1970s, the name really meant "not a business computer." Not only did businesses not see any use for them, but they didn't want anything to do with them and their anarchy. Customizing the color of the screen and the sounds the computer made was just silly. But writing your own programs to make the computer do what *you* wanted it to do? "No, thank you!"

It took some visionary people at three companies, IBM, Microsoft, and Apple Computer, to see that a computer you or I could really control—a truly personal computer—was exactly what business had been waiting for.

What Business Do You Have With a Computer?

The revolutionary vision of the folks at IBM was recognizing that the world had room for a small (relative to everything else IBM had ever made) computer. That computer would allow people like you and me to get down to some serious business without the million-dollar price tag that computers traditionally carried. And because people in the mass market do many different things for business, the new computer would have to support a wide set of needs. Designing a computer that could do that was a huge first step toward personalized computing.

The general-purpose or "open" nature of the IBM PC made it possible for many different people (most not working for IBM, incidentally) to recognize businesses' needs and create solutions for those needs. If you had documents to produce, it was no longer necessary to go out and buy a dedicated word processor. You could buy word processing software for your IBM PC. Didn't like how that piece of software worked? No problem—you could buy something from a competitor. Needed to do some accounting, some inventory, some customer profiling and some general calculation? Fine—the general-purpose software called VisiCalc could handle it all (and gave us a new word: *spreadsheet*).

Because it freed businesspeople from the immense cost of buying a dedicated hardware/software solution for every precise task, the IBM PC started a revolution. This "buy just what you need and customize it exactly" stuff caught on a lot faster than even IBM expected. IBM ushered in an era of generalized computing, with diverse tasks being performed on software written by hundreds of vendors—or even by yourself—all on the same hardware. So generalized *meant* personalized. My IBM PC could do what I wanted it to do. Yours could do what you wanted. And neither of us had to pay for a laundry list of features or software we would never use.

Writing a Few Standards

Fortunately for us all, some of those early visionaries also recognized that when things get too personal, anarchy can result. If each of us had his or her own language, not much communication would be happening. As it is with people, so it is with technology.

For software to be written so the IBM PC and its successors could flourish, these computers had to perform in certain, predictable ways, responding to certain, predefined commands. So many key characteristics of the IBM PC were adopted as *standards*. Standard ways of sending information to the video monitor meant that, whatever task you were performing and whatever software you were using, you'd actually be able to see the results. Likewise, standard ways of sending characters to a printer meant that you could print anything your PC could produce.

It's one of those historical ironies that this type of standardization—everybody doing things exactly the same way—was what made the IBM PC family of computers successful as personal computers. By agreeing to restrict the "do your own thing" nature of the PC in some very low-level, fundamental ways, early software and hardware manufacturers could successfully market and sell add-ons to make the PC do just about anything.

If you'd like an analogy, think of television. As long as everyone agrees on how the whole TV thing works, you and I can watch whichever channel we like. It makes no difference whether I'm watching *The Wonderful World of Disney* or you're watching *Friends*. The television works because signals are sent out in certain ways, received by every television in certain ways, and treated in certain standard ways inside the box. So television is more personal—I watch Mickey while you watch Joey—because its underpinnings are standardized.

Of course, the spirit of competition means that everybody doesn't just agree on how things should work. People try alternatives, and sometimes better ways of doing things get devised. The new ways become standards in their turn and are replaced by still newer standards, and so on. Competing or different standards often coexist, too. The choices you make may be greatly shaped by which basic set of assumptions—which standard—most closely fits your needs. This is how we end up with eleventeen different ways to display realistic 3D images on a monitor and why two very different families of computer—the PC family and the Apple Macintosh family—can both be successful.

You'll encounter quite a few different standards in later chapters. For now, I'd just like you to understand this: for technology, agreements between huge numbers of people about how certain things will happen can allow each of those individual people to ultimately have more choices and get down to business in his or her own way.

I Like How You Operate

I mentioned Microsoft a few moments ago. They played a very important role in the development of the PC family—a role perhaps even more important than Intel, the company that manufactures the chips at the center of almost every PC. IBM created an important standard for the PC by selecting Microsoft to produce a piece of software called the Microsoft Disk Operating System, or MS-DOS. We'll explore operating systems in detail later in the book.

Lingo   An *operating system* is a collection of software that controls how the different pieces of hardware in a PC function together.

In brief, an *operating system* is an intermediary between computer hardware and the software applications that let you actually get your work done. Although you may not be used to thinking of it this way, the operating system is actually software, but it's software that bridges the gap between hardware and all the other software—your programs and your data—on the PC. Just as there are standards for how PC hardware works, an operating system establishes some standard ways of interacting with that hardware. Software doesn't have to understand all the hardware in the world. It just needs to understand the operating system it requires.

Let me give you an example. Someone might say that the first version of Microsoft Word, released in 1983, ran under MS-DOS. On the simplest level, that meant that Word could run on any PC that was using MS-DOS as its operating system. That PC didn't have to be made by IBM; many clone systems were out there. Word would still work just fine. How?

Because the different manufacturers of PCs followed the variety of hardware standards you read about a moment ago, Microsoft was able to write an operating system that could reliably communicate with all that different hardware. MS-DOS didn't need to know about any internal differences that existed between a Seagate hard drive and, say, a Maxtor drive. It was enough that

Seagate and Maxtor agreed to certain standards for moving data in and out of their drives, and that MS-DOS understood these standards, too.

Microsoft Word, in turn, didn't have to know the difference between a hard disk, a floppy disk, or a recordable DVD. It just had to know that the operating system, MS-DOS, expected certain commands that meant "here is some data; store it on the device I've selected."

The people who wrote Microsoft Word didn't need to know about the brands and models of hardware that might run their software. In fact, we don't usually even talk about specific hardware "running" software. Instead, we say that Microsoft Word runs under MS-DOS. Any software like Word that ran under MS-DOS would run on any hardware that ran MS-DOS.

The PC: A Team Effort

This collaboration between the PC's hardware and its operating system really got the computing revolution rolling. The operating system eliminated the impossible burden of understanding and accounting for every possible PC component and program that someone might produce. Manufacturers could be sure of success by making hardware that was flexible and compatible with MS-DOS. Programmers could be sure of success by writing software that would work properly because it only talked to the operating system (which took care of all of the software's hardware needs, like saving files and printing). Success wants more success, so products available for the PC diversified and created entirely new markets.

As success spread rapidly and the PC evolved, the number of standards surrounding it went into the hundreds (although you can still count the hugely important ones on two hands). The collaboration between the hardware and the operating system became increasingly important. New hardware, undreamed of even by the early visionaries, came into being to let us do things that nobody thought anybody could ever do with a PC. Here's just a brief list of some of the common tasks we use PCs for today that were considered science fiction just a decade or two ago:

- Take and work with digital photographs that rival film for quality.

- Process thousands of transactions from all over via a single telephone line.

- Allow coworkers worldwide to simultaneously work on the same project while discussing it in real time.

- Edit digital video at broadcast quality.

■ Store a high-quality movie on a 5-inch plastic disc.

■ Teach fully interactive, live university classes with the professor in his or her office and the students all over the country.

■ Compose, perform, produce, record, and distribute your own symphony without leaving your desk.

As new products and capabilities emerged, it fell on the operating system to keep everything working together happily. If you suspect that burden has changed operating systems a lot, you're absolutely right. The PC's operating systems have evolved so much, it can be hard to recognize that they're the offspring of MS-DOS. Some people might even say that the operating system has changed more than the base PC hardware. One type of new hardware may have nothing to do with another, but it all has to work in concert with the basic "guts" inside the PC. Imagine trying to control your digital camera's options if your PC had to pretend it was a floppy disk drive or a printer! And imagine if the only way to get information from one document into another was to type it by hand. The operating system had to grow to solve these problems.

It's All About You: The User Interface

Probably the most significant change in the world of operating systems (at least from the user's perspective) came in 1984 when Apple Computer released the Apple Macintosh computer. The Macintosh was the first commercially released computer that allowed people to interact with it graphically, using the mouse and the icons we're so familiar with now. The part of the operating system that allows us to do that goes by the rather grand name of *graphical user interface*, but everybody just calls it the GUI (pronounced "gooey").

It's now dramatically easier to work with a PC, thanks to GUIs like Microsoft Windows XP. Once you learn how the GUI operates, you'll discover every well-behaved program or tool that works with the GUI works in much the same way. So the GUI really reduces the PC learning curve. And some tasks, like photograph editing, just aren't even practical without a GUI. Because everything is easier to do, we do more than ever before on PCs. Doing more, we are doing more *different* things. So the GUI operating system is a significant part of what makes a PC a personal computer.

At Your Command…   Before the age of the GUI, people interacted with their computers by typing commands on the keyboard. A small blinking block of light, called the *cursor*, showed where the next letter typed would appear on the screen. Let me give you an example. Today, if you want to see the contents of a folder on a disk, you simply double-click the mouse on the icon for the disk, then double-click again on the folder you want to view. In the past, you might have typed a command like this one:

```
dir c:\docs\prfrd\ /p /w /on
```

Figure 1-1 compares using this command with viewing the same folder under Windows XP. Likewise, if you wanted to start Word, you'd type the command **word** and press Enter. For everything you wanted to do, there was a command. And because the system could display only basic text, it was impossible to see on the monitor what a printed document would look like. Changes in formatting were created by typing—you guessed it—commands in the middle of your document. It certainly wasn't an ideal world.

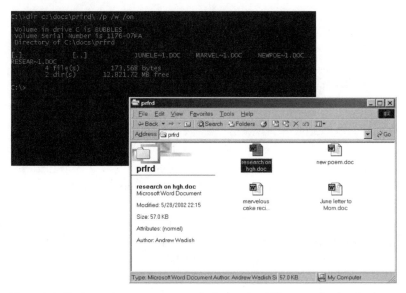

Figure 1-1   On the top is a text screen; on the bottom is a GUI screen showing the contents of the same folder on a disk.

Looking Behind to Look Ahead

It's the operating system (which I'll start calling the "OS," to save wear and tear on your eyes) that really makes all of those things we do with the PC possible and practical. In a very real way, you could say that the OS is the PC. In fact, this is exactly what we do when we say "Word runs on Microsoft Windows XP." It's understood by everyone sharing the conversation that the hardware is present. But because different OS's are available for PC hardware, it's more accurate to think of the OS as one of the PC's vital parts. If you're very visually oriented as I am, you may find the illustration in Figure 1-2 helpful. It shows these interrelationships in a simplified way.

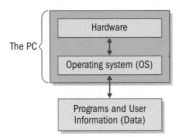

Figure 1-2 A PC is made up of the pieces of hardware and the operating system that work together to allow you to run programs and work with data, from spreadsheets to digital video.

In Part III, you'll start to really get to know your OS, Windows XP, intimately, and I think you'll be amazed by some of what it can do—and what you can do with it. I hope to first help you feel comfortable reading and talking about the many different types of hardware that the OS controls. You'll understand the different tools and tips in Part III much faster after you know what you and the OS are working with.

And because a PC really is many different bits of hardware working as one, that's where we'll start our exploration in Chapter 2. You'll see that the PC is the sum of its parts, and more. As your familiarity with the PC grows, I know you'll start coming up with your own exciting ways to work with your PC faster and smarter.

Key Points

- A PC is a *personal* computer because you can control and customize how it looks, feels, and works to suit your own tastes and your business's needs.

- As the PC evolved, hardware manufacturers made it easier to develop new and better products by adopting certain standards of how the PC would work.

- A special piece of software, called the *operating system*, took the idea of standards further by establishing normal ways for programs and people to interact with the PC hardware.

- Programs were written to do more and to do more *different* things. You only needed to own and understand the software that you chose to use, making the PC yet more personal.

- PC hardware and operating systems have both grown dramatically to help you solve more diverse problems and to further customize how you and your PC interact.

Chapter 2

The Sum of Its Parts

What makes a PC a truly personal computer is the freedom it gives you to choose the tools you use and to customize how they work. And the number of choices out there is staggering! The last time I walked into a computer store, I saw 23 different video cards sitting on the shelves. I found a similar problem in the monitor, modem, and sound card departments. And my local store has 19 different types of mouse devices! But thanks to all those standards you read about in Chapter 1, all of these options work together perfectly, right?

Of course, it's not that simple. A PC is definitely a collection of hardware and software, with everything working in harmony. Like human relationships, the relationships between a PC's parts must be entered into with some care, some knowledge of what you're dealing with, and some foresight of what you'll want down the road. But unlike human relationships, if you select your new widget thoughtfully, it won't jealously insist that you stop using all your other widgets. You can make these good choices; it's not hard. And with a little care, your PC will be much more than just the sum of its parts.

Balanced Integration

These two keys will help you get the most out of your PC:

- Choose PC parts to be compatible with other parts.
- Fine-tune to use the parts you choose to their best advantage.

The rest of this book will make all the details clear, but with these two keys in your pocket, you'll spend a lot less time worrying about your PC.

Using these two keys helps you achieve *balanced integration*—everything functioning together to its combined maximum potential. *Integration* is a familiar concept: dissimilar things working together. And *maximum potential* is familiar, too: working faster, smarter, and better. What about the *balanced* idea? Getting the most out of a PC isn't just setting each piece of hardware for its fastest performance and wiring the pieces together. A PC might actually perform better if you slow down a component or two.

Lingo   *Balanced integration* is my own way of expressing the most important thing to consider when you purchase PC hardware or peripherals—the fact that everything in your whole system must work together in a complementary fashion. By understanding the strengths and limitations of each piece of your PC—which is what this book is all about—you won't spend money for features you can't use, and you won't make purchases which seem economical but which detrimentally affect your whole PC's performance.

So let's take a look at the basic pieces that are part of every PC. Although I'm going to be talking about a standard desktop PC, almost everything you read here is true for notebook PCs too.

The Parts Inside Your PC

If you take a look at any PC, you'll see a beige, black, or silver box with a few lights, a few buttons, and tons of cables. For the moment, let's ignore the cables; they connect your PC with a variety of external devices and with the world at large (we'll talk about all those things in turn). The buttons basically turn the PC on or reset it, and the lights just let you know when part of your PC is busy. That leaves the box. Everything else that your PC is or does is inside that box. There's a lot of hardware packed in there, including chips, cards, disks, slots, and more cables—an abundance of technology.

Even though the technology that's inside your PC today is different from that found inside the original IBM PC you saw in Chapter 1, the most basic components remain the same. Every PC has had a motherboard (or *main board*), a central processor, a storage device, and some smaller cards with specialized electronics on them.

The Motherboard: Backbone for the Bare Bones

Inside your body, your backbone and spinal column do some pretty important jobs. Directly or indirectly, all the parts of your body are connected to them. Almost every physical experience you have gets communicated to your brain through the spine, and almost every instruction your brain sends out passes through the spine. What the backbone and spine do for you, the motherboard does for your PC. All the electronics inside your PC are either part of the motherboard itself or are connected to it through one of a variety of ways.

At the simplest level, the *motherboard* (shown in Figure 2-1) is just a rectangular piece of plastic. Tiny holes drilled into precise places on the board allow microchips and other components to be mounted to the board. These components are all soldered or cemented in place—or both. In most cases, all of the motherboard's components are mounted on one side of the plastic and the connections between them are made on the other side.

Figure 2-1 The PC's motherboard supports the connections between all of its vital components.

The connections between components are incredibly thin lines of copper or gold, commonly called *traces*. All of the electrical signals that move around the motherboard use these traces, which are designed to offer little resistance to the flow of electricity. This point is important for two reasons.

First, electricity moving around inside your PC is how it works. If that electrical movement is hindered, so is everything your PC does. Second, when the flow of electricity is resisted, some of the energy in the electricity turns into heat. Unfortunately, heat is the enemy of almost everything inside your PC. If your PC fan fails, your entire PC could overheat and stop working. (And depending on which parts overheated the worst, it might never work again without major repair. A main processor can actually melt without proper cooling.) So keeping the temperature inside the PC as low as possible is vital, and efficient connections between components play a big role in accomplishing that goal.

Most of the components on a motherboard plug into sockets that are cemented and soldered to the motherboard. This feature allows you to expand your PC's key capabilities as your work demands. For example, sockets make it possible for anyone with the right knowledge and care to replace or upgrade certain components like memory (which you'll read about in Chapter 3) and video capabilities (which you'll read about in Chapter 4). Even a PC's main processor can usually be replaced with a faster model simply by unplugging the old one and plugging in its successor.

Sockets have played an important role in the success of the PC by allowing users to mix and match components from a wide array of manufacturers. As a result, a greater number of manufacturers compete for your business and, in turn, there's more variety in the types of components and equipment available. Of course, for a socket to be useful, components must be made to plug into it properly, so socket design is part of almost all the PC standards I mentioned in Chapter 1.

Many of the sockets on your PC's motherboard are of a special type called *ports*. Most ports make it possible to connect to your PC external hardware like keyboards, mouse devices, monitors, and speakers. You'll get a good look at these in Chapter 8.

The actual microchips on the motherboard can be grouped into two basic types. The first one provides support for a specific feature. Among the most important examples of this type are the chips that control the workings of all (or most) of your PC's storage devices. These chips create what's called the Integrated Device Electronics (IDE) interface, which connects your hard disk, DVD drive, and floppy disks to the motherboard.

Another group of these special-purpose chips might be responsible for sending data to your PC monitor, whereas another might do nothing but support the flow of data in and out of the PC's brain: the *central processing unit (CPU)*. An example of this last type is called the Intel 845, which supports the Intel Pentium 4 processor. These collections of chips go by the lingo *chipsets*, which is a term you'll definitely encounter if you spend much time reading articles about PC gaming. As technology has improved, the functions once provided by several individual microchips have been built into a single chip; for historical reasons, these single chips are still called chipsets.

Lingo   A *CPU*, or *central processing unit*, is the primary computational component of a PC. It's the "brains" of the computer. Each CPU is supported by other processors and specialized circuitry which are collectively known as the CPU's *chipset*.

The second major type of component on your PC's motherboard consists of the many multipurpose systems that support whichever aspect of your work needs them at the time. Chief among these components is the PC's main memory, commonly called random access memory (RAM), for reasons you'll discover in Chapter 3. For the moment, I'll just say that *main memory* is a temporary electronic storage space used by programs. It also holds your data (pictures, spreadsheets, grant proposal letters, and so on) while you're actually working with it. Depending on the support provided by your motherboard's special-purpose chipsets, some of the PC's main memory might even be temporarily used as if it were a dedicated part of your PC's video system.

The PC's main processor is another multipurpose component of the motherboard. Just about all the action in your PC happens inside the CPU. As you're about to see, it is really the computer inside the computer.

Brains: The CPU

Your brain controls everything you do. From breathing, to painting a masterpiece, to dropping your coffee cup, your brain is at the center of it all. It's your central processing unit, if you will. Similarly, the main microprocessor, or CPU, inside your PC is its brain. The PC doesn't do anything that even closely approximates human thinking, but the CPU is nevertheless where your PC does most of its data processing.

The CPU isn't just the PC's brain; it's also rather like its heart. A regular electrical pulse generated by the CPU—called the *clock pulse*, or just the *clock*—determines the speed at which most data manipulation occurs inside the PC. Key parts of the PC, like its memory, look to the CPU clock and perform either on a clock beat or on multiples of beats. The CPU clock keeps everything synchronized so that data moves between components on the motherboard at an expected rate.

This synchronization prevents one component from trying to send data before the receiving component is ready for it (or one component sitting idle, waiting for another to become ready). Either event is a major waste of time.

See Also   *You'll encounter two more manifestations of this type of problem in Chapter 8, although modems, networks, and other major systems inside your PC have their own clocks that aren't linked to the CPU clock.*

The time that passes from the start of a clock pulse to the start of the next pulse is called a *clock cycle*. Until 2000, clock cycles were measured in megahertz (MHz), which is millions of cycles per second. An 800 MHz Intel Pentium III processor thus produced 800 million clock pulses every second. In 2000, Intel introduced the first gigahertz (GHz—billions of cycles per second) microprocessor, also a model of the Pentium III. Now, as I said earlier, the clock has been the *traditional* measurement of "CPU Speed" because a CPU couldn't perform calculations any faster than one tick of its clock. In fact, the first PC performed one basic calculation in fifteen clock cycles. But tradition was thrown out the window when a technique called *pipelining* was developed. Pipelining allows a CPU to perform two or more tasks at once. On average, several instructions can be processed during each clock cycle.

And now, the world of CPU comparisons gets messy. Each manufacturer has its own way of doing pipelining, which each claims is best (and which, naturally, is optimized for that company's CPUs). Additionally, some tasks make better use of available pipelining than others. So a CPU's clock speed and the speed at which it actually performs tasks don't usually match.

For example, one company's 2-GHz processor might perform significantly better—on selected tasks—than a competitor's 2-GHz model. And some tests have shown that a well-used pipeline lets a CPU complete real-life tasks faster than a competing CPU with a higher clock speed. Therefore, you can no longer rely on simple processor speed as a clear measurement of which CPU is fastest. You must pay attention to a variety of real-life tests if you're doing 3D design or complex engineering, and you must be certain that you're getting the most bang for your buck.

The CPU is the closest thing a PC has to a brain; fortunately, it's not brain surgery to fundamentally understand how a CPU works. Modern microprocessors are a great deal more complicated than what you're about to read, but the basics are still true. A CPU is basically a collection of transistors—lots of transistors. The Intel Pentium 4 microprocessor contains over 55 million transistors, in fact, and you can think of each one of them as a microscopic switch that's either on (electricity is flowing through the transistor) or off (no electricity is flowing).

These on and off states correspond to the values 1 and 0, which comprise the binary number system and the binary language your PC understands. By collecting sets of these transistors together, they can be used to represent larger, more useful numbers. Your CPU can move these numbers around, perform arithmetic functions on them, and answer yes-no questions about them. For example, "Is the number in transistor group 'A' larger than the number in transistor group 'B'"? At the lowest level, this moving around of numbers and answering logical questions make up every piece of software you ever use.

Although applications are usually written in computer languages that are easy for us humans to manipulate, your PC understands only *machine language*, which is a basic set of instructions that tell the CPU to manipulate and store values and to answer logical questions about them. When a program is written, it is reduced from the human-readable code its creator uses to the machine language code the PC understands. You start an application, and its code is copied from long-term storage (say, your hard disk) into the PC's main memory, and part of the CPU called the *pointer*, tells the CPU where to find the application's first machine language instruction.

That instruction and usually the next few are copied from main memory into part of the CPU called the *cache*—a small amount of fast memory, which can move instructions into the rest of the CPU far faster than can the PC's main memory. Using the cache to prestage instructions can dramatically reduce unproductive time in the CPU and prevent it from just waiting for instructions or values from main memory. Most modern CPUs have a second bit of cache memory, called a *level 2 cache*, which increases the total cache size and, thereby, CPU performance.

Once instructions are in the cache, another part of the CPU called the *decoder unit* breaks the first instruction down into its simplest parts. The *arithmetic logic unit (ALU)* then begins to execute the instruction, using special collections of transistors called *registers* to temporarily store values on which it needs to perform calculations, as well as the end result. When each instruction is complete, the ALU tells the CPU's *control unit* (think of it as the director of this little drama) that it's done, and the control unit asks the pointer to provide the location of the next instruction. Performing billions of these instructions each second, the CPU runs the program.

All PC CPUs also contain two other special parts. The *floating-point unit (FPU)* can perform amazingly fast calculations on fractional numbers—something that the ALU isn't designed to do comparably well. The clock, which I mentioned earlier, is like the PC's coxswain, keeping the beat for the rest of the computer.

Storage Devices

I mentioned earlier that some of the chips on your PC's motherboard provide the PC's main memory. Part of your PC is also responsible for storing all those applications, data, and files when you're not actually using them. These storage devices aren't part of the motherboard as RAM is. (RAM chips can be unplugged easily, and they are still commonly considered to be a part of the motherboard.) They do connect to the motherboard directly by means of flat, wide connections called *ribbon cables*. The actual storage devices get mounted in your PC's main case, and are of three basic types.

The type most familiar to everyone, and which is found inside every PC, is called a hard drive or *hard disk*. You'll learn a lot of useful information about this topic in Chapter 5, so I'll just introduce the basics. Hard disks are sealed boxes that contain several hard metal platters mounted together on a spindle, a bit like a stack of records in an old jukebox. There is one major difference, however: between each platter is a tiny bit of space in which a metal arm can move without touching the platter below or above it.

At the end of this arm (and there is one for each platter inside the hard disk) is the *read/write head*. In the jukebox analogy, it's a little bit like each record having its own sound arm and needle. But, as the name implies, read/write heads don't just "play" back what's stored on the platters; they can also store ("write") new material and erase old material, too. The read/write heads change magnetic material embedded on each platter, and the patterns of changing material can be interpreted by the PC as programs, data, or Microsoft Windows XP itself, which is stored on your PC's hard disk.

The platters in a hard disk spin at incredible rates: 7200 to 10,000 revolutions per minute (RPM) in current drives. As you might expect, the faster the platters spin, the faster the content on them can be retrieved. (In truth, it's not quite that simple. Other factors, including how fast the read/write head can accurately move, help determine the performance of hard disks, but we'll look into that in Chapter 5 and Chapter 12). Because of the air movement caused inside the disk drive when the platters are spinning, the read/write heads are able to literally float over each platter surface.

A hard disk can fail for many reasons, but in the past, a common cause was the read/write head accidentally touching the actual platter. At those speeds, a more accurate way to describe this kind of touch is to say *crash*, so the term we use generically for a hard disk failure was born. Notable exceptions exist, but what we call a hard disk is usually permanently fixed inside your PC. You don't often use hard disks to move data around.

The next most common type of storage device in today's PCs is the *floppy drive*, which stores data on floppy disks. They got their name because instead of having hard platters, floppy disks consist of a plastic casing with a flexible ("floppy") plastic disk inside. At the simplest level, floppy disks and hard disks work similarly; floppy drives also use magnetism to store data on the special material that usually coats both sides of each floppy disk.

Two big differences do exist between floppy disks and hard disks, however. First, just like the recording heads in a tape recorder, the read/write heads in a floppy drive actually touch the disk's magnetic material. The flexibility of the disks makes this a much more forgiving process than it is inside a hard disk. Second, the average performance of floppy drives is about 1/150 that of a good hard disk, and their standard capacity is roughly 1/75,000 that of a 100GB hard disk. Therefore, floppy disks are impractical for most uses today, and their continued presence in PCs is of largely historical value.

Some PCs don't have a standard floppy disk at all. Instead, they have one of several varieties of high-capacity floppy disk drives, like the Iomega Zip drive (at roughly the capacity of 178 standard floppies) or the LS120 SuperDisk drive, which can read and write to standard floppies but which, when used with special disks, can store about 85 floppies' worth of content. Still other PCs are used exclusively as workstations on large networks and might not have any type of floppy drive at all.

The third variety of storage device your PC almost surely has is *optical storage*: a DVD or CD drive that uses laser light to read (and write, with recording drives) information from 5-inch plastic discs. A DVD can store about 1/15 of what a good hard disk stores, and a CD holds about 1/10 of one DVD.

Unlike floppies, however, CDs and DVDs are more than large enough to move a useful quantity of content around. Their near ubiquity means that you can store information on a recordable CD disc and take it to almost any other PC in the world, and you'll find a compatible CD drive waiting to read the information back. Although the world of recordable DVDs is still evolving, regular play-only DVD drives are everywhere now, letting you watch movies on your laptop or play amazing games with huge amounts of full-screen, quality video.

For a standard desktop PC, all three types of storage device plug into the motherboard. Standard floppy disks generally have their own ribbon cable and plug into a dedicated socket that is part of the *floppy drive controller*: a collection of special-purpose components on the motherboard that manage the entire process of reading from or writing to a floppy disk, right down to turning the motor on and off.

In some older PCs, a small magnetic tape drive used for backup storage could plug into the same cable as a floppy disk and would be controlled by the floppy disk controller. The larger floppy disks, hard disks, and optical drives share a different connection, called the IDE interface: a collection of specialized components on the motherboard, which serves the needs of the high-speed, high-capacity storage devices that connect to it.

Tip   Unfortunately, the more you work with your PC, the more likely you are to eventually run out of storage. How much storage is enough? The answer depends on how you use your computer and what you want from it now and tomorrow. Here's an excellent guideline: if you think you'll use your PC for more than just e-mail, when you're buying storage, buy the most you can comfortably afford. You shouldn't necessarily buy the biggest, fastest disk. But when you're considering the total cost of a PC, look at what you can spend on the whole package, figure out which portion you can spend on the hard disk, and find out how much storage costs. Then buy the largest disk you can obtain within your budget.

Adapter Cards

The fourth major part of the PC that lives inside the main case is a collection of chip-covered cards that plug into the motherboard and basically do everything that the motherboard doesn't. These go by various names like adapter cards, plug-in boards, expansion cards, add-in cards—you get the idea.

The cards themselves are of many different types, providing a variety of services. Your PC might have cards to run the monitor or to allow you to watch television on the screen. You might have a card to provide network support or digital sound, or even a modem if the motherboard doesn't have those electronics built in. In some instances, you might determine that the ports the motherboard provides either aren't numerous enough or aren't fast enough, and you can install a card to give you more or faster versions of almost anything your PC can do.

PC Standards: Checking Your PC's Bus Schedule Support mechanisms provide different ways for adapter cards to connect to and share information with your PC's motherboard. For example, add-in cards plug directly into the motherboard through specialized slots near the back of the PC so that the cards can have their own external connectors too. (This functionality is useful for modem cards, which need to plug into the telephone line, sound cards, which plug into speakers, and so forth.) Collectively, these slots share a data superhighway called a *bus*—a special electrical path to the PC's main memory and its CPU. Buses facilitate efficient, direct access to your PC's key resources, such as memory.

Today, three different adapter, or expansion card buses coexist: the Advanced Graphics Port (AGP) bus, which is amazingly fast; the Peripheral Component Interconnect (PCI) bus, which is normal speed; and the Industry Standard Architecture (ISA) bus, which is amazingly slow. Each bus has its own unique connector and slot, and adapter cards plug into one of them. Each type of bus/slot comes with its own set of capabilities, limitations, and controlling hardware. Together with the physical connector specifications, these capabilities define each bus standard.

The Parts Outside Your PC

In addition to the components you'll find inside almost every PC case, you'll find two outside every PC: the keyboard and the mouse. Perhaps because these are the parts of the PC we interact with intimately, different varieties exist for every type of user.

The Keyboard

In addition to the traditional PC keyboard, keyboards are available for people with a lighter or heavier touch. The incidence of repetitive stress injuries (RSIs) from typing has skyrocketed, causing a lot of pain and costing a tremendous amount in suffering, medical bills, and lost productivity. *Ergonomics*—the study of how our bodies interact with our tools—has led to a variety of angled keyboards designed to reduce the impact of all-day typing on the wrist. Split keyboards have been developed, which are designed to perfectly match the natural at-rest positions of human hands on a tabletop.

If you're not quite average, a split keyboard can be angled to fit your hands' greatest comfort. If you're even more unique, you can buy a keyboard that is completely split into independent halves that can be placed anywhere on the desk. And vertical split keyboards allow you to type with your hands positioned thumbs-up, as if you were about to shake someone's hand.

Probably the most unique keyboards are called *chording* keyboards, like the Infogrip BAT. These keyboards have just a few keys at the tip of each finger of one hand. Combining the slightest of finger movements, a user can type anything, making it possible for someone with near-paralysis to use a PC.

Note   Wired and wireless radio-powered versions are available for almost all these types of keyboards.

The Mouse

The mouse, as you probably know, is a small handheld device that controls the movement of a graphical pointer on the PC's screen. The mouse has traditionally been a mechanical device. Desktop movements of the mouse cause a large ball on the mouse base to roll; tracking the speed and direction of that rolling generates the signals the mouse sends to the PC to control the screen pointer (or mouse cursor).

A major revolution occurred in mouse design with the appearance of optical devices. These types have no rolling ball, but instead use technology from the world of digital photography to quite literally "look" at the desktop under the mouse and "see" when and where the mouse has moved. Optical mouse devices are a great deal more accurate than their mechanical ancestors, and they never need maintenance or cleaning (which their mechanical counterparts need regularly).

Sadly, discomfort and repetitive stress injuries caused by using a mouse have become common, too, so ergonomic versions have largely replaced the old-fashioned square rodent. The contoured mouse now embraces either the right or the left hand. In addition, a mouse with a third, programmable button is popular. Fairly ubiquitous now, the mouse-with-wheel is a popular, useful innovation that reduces the need for large, sweeping mouse movements by letting users scroll through documents at the touch of a finger.

An upside-down mouse, usually called a *trackball*, provides another alternative. In this kind, the ball that traditionally rolls around between the mouse and the desk has been moved up top, and the user rolls it directly with the fingertips. It's not necessary to move the trackball base at all. Like keyboards, PC mouse devices come in both wired and wireless varieties.

Customizing the Keyboard and the Mouse Early PC keyboards had 83 keys. Today, 101 keys are more common, and 150 keys are also available. Most of these extra keys are programmable. You can use them to type special characters you select or assign them to sets of instructions—called *macros*—which perform tasks. For instance, you could program one of these keys to go online, launch Microsoft Internet Explorer, open Microsoft Outlook, and check for e-mail. Press the key, and the programmed actions happen one after the other.

You can also customize a keyboard's settings without adding programmable keys. Select Control Panel from the Start menu, select Printers And Other Hardware, and then click Keyboard. Now you can personalize how long you need to hold down a key before it repeats, and how fast each key repeats. You can also personalize languages and keyboard layouts, as discussed in Chapter 11.

To personalize how your mouse works, select Control Panel from the Start menu, select Printers And Other Hardware, and then click Mouse. Now you can change how fast you need to double-click the mouse to have it "see" a double-click rather than just two single clicks; you can reverse the functioning of the main mouse buttons so that you can use a mouse with the left hand and still use your strongest finger for most mouse clicking; and you can choose how fast the mouse will move across the screen. Chapter 11 discusses other ways to modify mouse behavior.

The wired versions of keyboards and mouse devices plug into the motherboard via one of two PS/2 ports, named after the model of IBM PC that first featured them. Keyboard and mouse connectors are now made in standard colors—purple for a PS/2 keyboard and green for a PS/2 mouse—to help users plug the right device into the right port. (Otherwise, both PS/2 ports look the same.) Some motherboards allow a keyboard or mouse to be plugged into either port; in this case, the ports might be colored the same, or they might be marked with half/half colors.

Revisiting Balanced Integration When I spoke of balanced integration at the beginning of this chapter, I said that one way to get the most from your PC is by selecting compatible and complementary components. I introduced the idea of balance early in this chapter because balance among the most basic of your PC's parts is crucial. Many people pay endless attention to the big touchy-feely parts of the PC, like the monitor, but pay little heed to what's inside the box. Nothing stifles the power of a top-of-the-line CPU like an underpowered video card or slow or insufficient memory. Nothing will destroy your enjoyment of digital music and video like a slow hard disk and a tinny sound card.

In addition to balance within your PC, balance between you and your PC is also important. You can't write the great American novel if your hands are too sore to type. Good balance means putting components together so that their strengths are beneficial to the rest of the PC and their limitations don't drag you down. To empower you to make the best choices, the next seven chapters each focus on one individual part of your PC, giving you the understanding—and the tools—to be a smarter user, a more selective consumer, and a more productive you.

Key Points

- Balancing the strengths of each part of your PC will give you the best computing experience. The limitations of one component can degrade the performance of many others.

- Understanding the parts of your PC and how they work will empower you to make the PC-related choices that are best for you.

- Every PC is made up of four fundamental parts: a motherboard, a main microprocessor (or CPU), one or more storage devices, and support for a variety of adapter cards.

- A CPU is like your PC's brain. It's the place where your PC performs calculations and controls the movement of data.

- PC storage devices are of three different types: hard disks, which are usually mounted permanently to the PC's case and provide large, fast storage; floppy disks, which can move small amounts of information between PCs; and optical discs, which are slower than hard disks but can move large amounts of data between PCs.

- Hard disks, optical disks, and large-capacity floppy disks generally connect to the motherboard through the IDE interface, which is a collection of special-purpose electronics on the motherboard that pass commands to the drives, instructing them to read or write data.

- Special keyboards and mouse devices can accommodate the needs of people with repetitive stress injuries and can even prevent injuries.

Part II

What Makes a PC?

In Chapters 1 and 2 we spent a little time looking at where the PC came from, why it's called a personal computer, and why it matters. We also started exploring what's inside every PC box, or case. At this point, you should know that what makes the PC a powerful tool is its ability to be adapted and personalized to fit your needs.

The next seven chapters will build and strengthen the foundation of your understanding of the PC. The path we'll take moves from the inside out. We'll start with a look at the PC's memory; we'll conclude Part II by mastering Windows networking, finding you and your PC connected to everything else. And with Microsoft Windows XP Internet connectivity, I do mean *everything* else. It's a world of resources to help you work faster and smarter.

Chapter 3

Working with Memory

Memory is probably the most useful and least understood resource available to your PC. It's a limited resource, but it's infinitely reusable. At any given moment, you could run out of memory. But you'll never have to buy a new collection of memory because you've slowly depleted your available supply, as if memory were really like a scratch pad or a sticky note. And once you use some memory, you don't have to move on and use different memory, as if memory were really like an unpainted house or a canvas.

Why all the analogies, anyway? The conclusion I've come to is that folks have decided that memory is one of those complicated parts of the PC. People who do know a lot about memory seem to turn to the endless list of "it's like…" because they figure you don't really want to know, and you don't really have the time to get it.

All of which is nonsense, as you'll soon see.

What Is Memory?

Memory is the electronic space where your PC works. It is a collection of specially designed microchips that plug into your PC's motherboard (and a few other places), which the PC uses to store your programs and your data temporarily while you're using them. I say *temporarily* because memory is different from *storage*—a difference that lots of people miss. While your PC is powered on and you're running an application, the code that makes the application work is in memory. If your PC suddenly turns off, everything in memory is lost forever.

But you know from experience that you don't lose software every time you suffer a power outage, and you can keep data for years by saving it in files. You don't lose programs and files because they're kept in storage—on your hard disk. When you start an application, it's simply copied from storage (your hard disk) into memory. When you open a file, a copy of the file goes into memory, and you work with the copy that's there. When you make changes and save the file again, the data is copied from memory out onto your hard disk—from memory back to storage.

Normally, you can't lose the work you've saved to storage even though everything in memory is lost when your PC turns off. Similarly, when you close a file or quit a program, any work you saved to storage is kept—as is the program you were running. Any data you don't save is removed from memory and is gone. Of course, you can still lose data you've saved due to a hard disk crash, but generally you can consider it "permanent."

Lingo   *Memory* is the electronic workspace your PC uses to process and manipulate data. *Storage* is the "warehouse" where data and programs are kept for "the long haul."

You don't need to understand how memory works electronically to get the most from it. What is useful is having two other bits of knowledge: how the PC uses memory and why memory comes in a variety of types.

How a PC Uses Memory

Entire books have been written about the full story of how the PC uses memory. Fortunately for you *and* for me, this isn't one of them. (Nothing is worse than writing a book you'd never choose to read!) The full story of how a PC uses memory is, as Victor Borge said about the history of the piano, "quite uninteresting." What's important about memory is that memory and the CPU work together to make the PC a "thinking" machine.

Bits and Bytes

Your PC doesn't communicate in the same way you do—but like you, it has a language. I'm not talking about all the different computer languages you hear about, like C#, C++, or Perl. Those are just specialized human languages that make it easier for you to tell the computer what you want it to do. The only language your PC understands is a binary machine language consisting of two numbers: one and zero.

This is because your PC is one of millions of *digital* computers. Put simply, your PC works with specific and regulated amounts of electricity, which you can think of as being either on or off. The physical microchips that provide your PC's memory are actually just huge collections of transistors and capacitors. The capacitors function like bottles of electricity that can be either full or empty.

Whenever a capacitor is given a bit of electricity to hold (the bottle is full), we symbolize that with the number one. Whenever a capacitor is holding no charge, we symbolize that with the number zero. Everything in your PC comes down to ones and zeros. Just as human language gathers letters into groups of sounds and groups of sounds into words, the PC organizes all the ones and zeros together into chunks. The most basic chunk of one-or-zero values your PC uses is a short string of only eight of those values. These eight values (ones, zeros, or a combination of the two) collected together are called a *byte*. Each of the eight values that make up the byte is called a *bit*.

Bytes make up the building blocks of everything your PC accomplishes. What sets one byte apart from another is how they are used. The right collection of words is a Shakespearean sonnet; the right collection of bytes is a photo of Rover. Your PC must use bytes properly to make sense of them. Try to look at a photograph by opening it with an application designed to edit electronic music, and you won't see your pooch or hear any glorious melodies; you'll get nothing at all, because most modern software will politely refuse to work with an inappropriate collection of bytes.

When you talk about your PC's memory capacity, you're talking (roughly) about how many bytes it can work with at any given time. (As you'll see, your PC might be able to work with far more bytes than are strictly available in its memory chips.) The original IBM PC had 640 kilobytes (KB) of memory—meaning that it had the capacity to store roughly 640,000 bytes in its memory chips at once. We often use the shorthand letter *K* to indicate 1000 of something, and you'll encounter that symbol throughout this book.

Another bit of shorthand you'll see often is *MB*, which means *megabytes*, or millions of bytes. If your PC has 256 MB of memory, its memory chips have the capacity to handle roughly 256 million bytes at once. And your PC's memory chips are usually just called RAM, pronounced like the name of the animal. *Random access memory (RAM)* simply means that your PC can instantly access any byte that's held in it, without first looking through all the bytes that are being used. So 256 MB of RAM is the same as 256 MB of memory. (Remember, though, that RAM has nothing to do with your PC's storage capacity. RAM, or memory, is just the temporary electronic space your PC uses to work.)

To give you a frame of reference, the Microsoft Word file that contains the text and pictures of this chapter uses about 921,000 bytes (that's 921 KB). A high-quality digital photograph generally fits in a file that holds 6 million bytes (6 MB). As you open multiple files, your PC must have enough memory to hold the code of the application you're using to view the files, plus all the bytes in the files themselves.

Why Are There Eight Bits in a Byte?   You might be wondering why a byte consists of eight bits, rather than one, or 12, or 8000. The answer is based on one important use of bytes: to represent human letters in a way that the computer can understand. Well before the IBM PC premiered, other computers were using collections of bits to represent letters (and, in bigger collections, words). Because a bit can have only one of two values, the number of different letters you can represent with one bit is only two—which is far too few to be useful. Two bits together have four possible different values: 00 01 10 11.

But there are a lot more than four different letters, and don't forget about punctuation, too! To represent all 52 letters of the alphabet (uppercase and lowercase), plus the 10 Arabic numbers from zero to nine, plus a few reasonable bits of punctuation, it takes the 128 combinations you can get from a series of seven bits.

Anyway, this way of mapping human letters and punctuation to the values of different collections of bits is called a *character set*. The most famous character set is the American Standard Code for Information Interchange (ASCII), and it uses the set of seven bits that I just mentioned. When the IBM PC was developed, IBM decided to use a collection of eight bits. This would provide 256 possible combinations and allow IBM to extend ASCII to include a variety of foreign characters, drawing symbols, and other goodies. IBM's extended ASCII was born.

Memory Types for Every Need

Your PC uses several different types of memory to support its different needs. For example, RAM, which you've started to learn about, is flexible and changeable. Within the RAM family, lots of different types exist. Your PC also uses read-only memory (ROM, rhymes with "Tom") to store permanent information that can't be changed. ROM also comes in several types. This section takes a look at these different types of RAM and ROM. You'll likely encounter them when you buy or upgrade a PC, and you'll definitely come across them in articles and reviews of PC hardware innovations and options.

Dynamic RAM

Your PC's main RAM is a specific type of memory called *dynamic RAM (DRAM)*, shown in Figure 3-1. By design, immediately after data is sent to this type of memory, the DRAM (pronounced "dee-ram") begins to lose, or "forget" it. To solve this rather significant problem, a bit of circuitry called the *refresh* reads and rewrites the value of every DRAM capacitor (which I'm going to call a *cell*, just for simplicity and because you might hear that term).

Figure 3-1 DRAM provides the main memory for all modern PCs.

How fast do DRAM cells lose their contents? That rate is part of the specifications you'll encounter when you purchase memory. It's measured in nanoseconds (one billionth of a second), written *ns*. A DRAM chip that is rated at 40 ns refreshes its values once every 40/1,000,000,000 of a second. And you thought you had a short memory!

As it turns out, the shorter a PC's memory is (that is, the faster its capacitors lose their charge), the better the memory (and the more expensive) because a DRAM chip's refresh rate is also the fastest speed at which the bytes it's storing can be modified. Faster RAM is better because it enables your PC to perform tasks ever-faster. This speed is one of the reasons why the memory used for high-end video cards is so expensive (as we'll see in Chapter 4). For applications that perform complex calculations, like the drawing of photograph-quality 3D models, the speed of a PC's main memory can make a tremendous difference.

Because early DRAM was not the fastest boat in the harbor, new types of memory had to be developed. Aside from certain shared characteristics, like refresh rate, one DRAM module might be distinguishable from another based on a few key features. Sometimes buying memory feels a little bit like buying a car. You might not be sure which features you want, but you can be sure the salesperson will know what he or she wants to sell you. So let's put all of the jargon and features in their place. You can be comfortable in the world of DRAM in just a few minutes.

Synchronous DRAM   *Synchronous DRAM (SDRAM)* is the most common type of RAM in PCs today, but SDRAM isn't one specific type of DRAM. Instead, it's a family that includes the original—now old-fashioned—SDRAM, and several newer, faster offspring. If you find memory modules for an amazing price that are simply identified as SDRAM, the low price is most likely because these are antiquated chips. Today's power-memory SDRAM goes by the name double-data rate (DDR) SDRAM, which is illustrated in Figure 3-2.

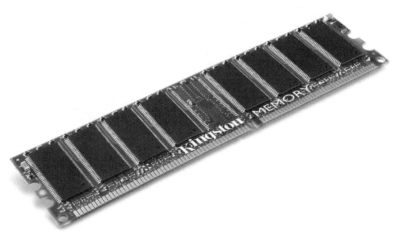

Figure 3-2 DDR SDRAM is the most recent innovation in mainstream PC memory.

DDR SDRAM   *Double-data rate (DDR) RAM*—properly called *DDR SDRAM*—was something of a revolutionary development. To explain why, I need to digress for just a moment and talk about clocks. If you listen to an old pendulum clock or a wristwatch, you hear the familiar tick-tock sound. The timepiece actually makes two sounds—one tick, one tock—each second. The PC's system clock doesn't make any sounds, but it "ticks" and "tocks" electronically, so to speak. In fact, the PC clock is just an electrical circuit that regularly switches from passing a higher voltage to a lower voltage and back again. One complete cycle (low-high-low) of voltage changes is the pattern that defines a clock cycle.

So what does all this have to do with SDRAM? It's like this: Whereas regular SDRAM works on full cycles, DDR SDRAM, shown in Figure 3-2, works on half cycles. That is, it can store or retrieve a value with each "tick," and it can store or retrieve a value with each "tock." This double-data rate, which leads to much greater speed, gives DDR its name. I've illustrated this idea in Figure 3-3.

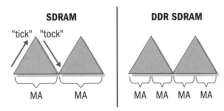

Figure 3-3 SDRAM accesses memory contents on each full clock cycle; DDR SDRAM works on half cycles, making it twice as fast.

A PC must have both a motherboard and central processing unit (CPU) designed to work with DDR SDRAM to benefit from this potential. This requirement is a bit of the balanced integration I introduced in Chapter 2. Recall that I mentioned pipelining, which at the simplest level is a way to break CPU instructions down so that several instructions can be executed in parallel (meaning that several instructions are completed, on average, in each tick of the clock).

Some processors, including the Intel Pentium 4, do pipelining tasks so that the CPU benefits from the double-speed potential of DDR SDRAM. If we say that "at once" means a single tick of the system clock, we can say that the Pentium 4 can perform two (or more) tasks at once. DDR memory can also perform two tasks at once, in this sense, so this type of pipelining and DDR are a great team. Other types of pipelining work differently and use DDR's capabilities less efficiently.

When you select DDR SDRAM, you must consider more than just your CPU, however. The world of DDR is full of even more jargon intimately related to its performance. Terms like *PC1600*, *PC2100*, and *PC2700* are just the latest in what will surely be a long line of lingo. The numbers tell you the maximum speed at which the memory modules can move data. The PC1600 can move 1.6 billion bytes—that is 1.6 gigabytes (GB)—of data per second; PC2100 can move 2.1 billion bytes (2.1 GB) per second, and so forth.

Unfortunately, these numbers—chosen to be impressive, not informative—don't really tell you what you need to know. You need to know whether a given model of memory will work with your motherboard. So here's a bit of translation.

When You See DDR SDRAM Labeled...	Look for a Motherboard That...
PC1600	Has a system bus (or front-side bus) speed of 100 megahertz (MHz) and a 200 MHz data rate.
PC2100	Has a system bus (or front-side bus) speed of 133 MHz and a 266 MHz data rate.
PC2700	Has a system bus (or front-side bus) speed of 166 MHz and a 333 MHz data rate.

Most modern motherboards are capable of supporting several different bus speeds, depending on which CPU and memory you install. You'll want to carefully coordinate these three pieces of hardware when you make a purchase.

To Check or Not to Check   Each basic flavor of DRAM comes in two varieties: error checking and nonerror checking. Because memory chips today are exceptionally reliable, it's not absolutely vital to purchase the error-checking variety for most applications. If you're setting up a large server or a system for engineering design, however, you'll want to spend the extra money to have RAM chips that will look after themselves. Two classes of error checking are available.

The first type, called *parity*, is the older of the two. Memory modules that use parity are capable of detecting when the value stored in a memory location is not what it should be. The second type, called *Error Checking and Correction (ECC)*, is newer.

As the name Error Checking and Correction implies, ECC memory can actually repair mistakes, which enables your program to keep functioning. ECC or parity DRAM can be used only on a motherboard that supports it. It's unusual for a motherboard to require either parity or ECC, but some high-end, multiple-CPU systems do.

Video RAM

Specialized memory for high-end and 3D accelerated video cards is sometimes called *video RAM (VRAM)* or *Windows RAM (WRAM)*. We'll look at this type of memory more in Chapter 4, but its primary feature is its ability to respond to read or write requests from more than one part of the PC at once. In this way, part of the VRAM can be putting a complex 3D image on the screen while another part of it is already in the process of receiving the data necessary to generate the next image that should be shown. This functionality makes for some dramatic performance improvements, leading to more lifelike animation.

Static RAM

Yet another type of RAM, quite different from DRAM, is called *static RAM (SRAM)*, and it's a lot faster than dynamic RAM. Therefore, SRAM is used in CPUs for the cache memory that you read about in Chapter 2. SRAM uses complex combinations of transistors to store its contents.

Because of its design, SRAM maintains its values so long as power is applied to the SRAM module. SRAM contents don't slowly drain away like DRAM contents do, so SRAM never has to be refreshed. Sending the correct set of signals to a group of transistors changes their stored value instantly. So why isn't every bit of your PC's memory provided by SRAM? Cost—SRAM is many times more expensive than even the most expensive DRAM. It is best used in small quantities for special purposes where absolute performance is mandatory.

Read-Only Memory

ROM is another type of memory used in every PC. The data stored in ROM can never be changed. When it is created at the factory, it already contains the values it's expected to maintain, and it keeps those values even when the power is turned off. Because of this, we say that ROM is *nonvolatile* memory (as opposed to RAM, which loses its values when power is lost, and so is *volatile*).

If it can never be modified, what good is ROM? The fact that it works the same exact way time after time is useful for two reasons. First, a ROM chip takes up a lot less space than would all of the full-size transistors and diodes and other electronics necessary to wire comparable permanent functions. Second, ROM chips make it possible for a manufacturer to use the same basic design for different products. Your VCR and your DVD player, for example, might have remote controls that are exactly alike, except that in one, the ROM chip contains instructions for controlling the DVD player.

In a PC, regular ROM was originally used to store the most fundamental instructions required to get your PC working when you turned on the power. These instructions form the *basic input/output system (BIOS)*, which controls the PC from the moment power is applied until the PC's operating system can be accessed from a storage device and made to start up. Today, your PC's BIOS is not stored in this kind of ROM. Instead, a special kind of ROM is used which, paradoxically, can be modified.

Electrically Erasable Programmable Read-Only Memory

This specialized ROM goes by the name *electrically erasable programmable read-only memory (EEPROM)*. I'll admit, the name doesn't make a lot of sense on its own, because it basically means changeable unchangeable memory. But the name fits because that's exactly what EEPROM is. Normally, EEPROM behaves exactly like ROM. You can turn the PC's power on and off repeatedly, and the values in EEPROM won't change.

However, EEPROM chips are designed with a controller which, after receiving a specific series of instructions, allows the data stored on the EEPROM to be changed. This set of instructions is usually sent to the controller as electrical signals generated by a small program you run. EEPROM is now used to store your PC's BIOS code because it's sometimes necessary to update that code to support new technologies. Then a motherboard manufacturer that updates its BIOS can just post the new code on its Web page. You can download and save the code to a bootable floppy disk, restart the computer using that disk, and then run the program you downloaded.

SmartMedia cards and CompactFlash (shown in Figure 3-4) are specialized EEPROM cards, known by the collective term *flash memory*. Each of these cards uses proprietary methods to store and modify data in memory that maintains its contents, even when the card is removed from its host PC or handheld computer and power is lost.

Figure 3-4 A CompactFlash card contains a specialized type of EEPROM memory chip.

How Much Memory Is Enough?

After deciding which type of memory to purchase for your PC, you need to determine how much memory you need. But how do you decide? The "correct" answer depends on what you've got and what you want to do. First, looking just at memory, how much is enough?

Consider What You've Got

Think about the hardware and software you own. The principle of balanced integration says that if you've purchased a fast CPU and motherboard, it makes no sense to purchase just a tiny bit of memory. Because the PC uses memory to temporarily store everything it's working on, you need to have enough memory to complement the power of your CPU. If you don't have enough actual memory, your PC will attempt to compensate by using a system called *virtual memory*, which is much slower than the real thing. You'll never reap the benefits of that amazing CPU if you don't give your PC enough electronic elbow room.

Also consider your video card (or the video system built into your mother-board). With some video support, the cost of the card or the motherboard has been reduced by not providing any dedicated video memory. In that case, the memory needed to put images on your screen (more about this in Chapter 4) will come from your PC's main memory. In essence, part of your main memory will be set aside and dedicated to video-specific tasks. Naturally, dedicating some of your memory to one task removes it from the available pool of RAM. If you start out with too little memory in the first place, this is a recipe for disaster.

Now, if you've purchased a lot of high-end, fast-performance hardware, you're likely the kind of person who's going to push your PC to its limits. So having taken the actual hardware into consideration, let's look at the software you intend to run.

Consider What You Want to Do

Every piece of software you run, including your operating system, has a set of *minimum system requirements (MSR)*: a short list of the resources your PC abso-lutely must have for the product to work. (Mind you, I didn't say work *well.*) Always focus on the word *minimum* when you're looking at the requirements of the tools you want to use and the software you want to run.

Let's consider Windows XP for a moment. Its minimum system requirement for memory is 64 MB of RAM. And it will run in that amount of memory, no question. But four times the memory—256 MB—costs only about $20 more at the time I'm writing this. Twice as much memory again, 512 MB, costs only another $35, and you'll get vastly more than your money's worth from that pur-chase. Windows XP will work better the more memory you give it.

But the amount of memory Windows XP is actually using is memory that other applications can't use at the same time. So it's not sufficient to look just at the MSR for Windows XP. Think about how you intend to use your PC. Will you run a word processor? Will you edit pictures and insert them into the term papers you're writing? Will you take advantage of your broadband always-on connection to the Internet and run MSN Messenger in the background at all times? Each piece of software you use has its own set of MSR. So, although few people do it, you could sit down and add up the MSR for the applications you know you'll want to run simultaneously and then use that as a baseline.

Some companies, like Microsoft, actually provide useful recommendations, like indicating that the MSR for Microsoft Office XP, running under Windows XP, is 128 MB of RAM, plus a minimum of an additional 8 MB of memory for each Office program you're running. You should still consider these bare minimums. Certain types of software require notably more memory than do others: AutoCAD 2002 requires 128 MB of RAM; Adobe Photoshop requires 128 MB; and popular video games often require 64 MB of RAM each.

If you'd like a rule of thumb, I generally use the same one for memory that I use for storage devices: buy the most you can comfortably afford.

How Is Memory Distributed?   Memory is sold in modules that plug into your PC's motherboard. You might be able to install between one and eight memory modules, but some restrictions generally do apply. Modern motherboards allow you to install memory modules one at a time; older motherboards might require that you install modules in pairs or even in groups of four. Naturally, you can install only the type of memory your motherboard supports.

In addition, once you purchase your first memory module, you'll probably have to purchase the same type of module for all modules you add—or you'll have to stop using the older modules and upgrade to a newer type. For example, if you use error-checking memory (either ECC or parity), you must use only ECC or parity RAM from then on.

Also consider the amount of total memory your motherboard will support, or the amount of memory it will support in each module. If your motherboard has two memory sockets and can handle up to 1 GB of RAM, you might have to start over to upgrade to your PC's max. Because nobody makes a 768 MB module, you'll need to obtain two 512 MB ones. Finally, if you purchased a PC that came with a proprietary type of memory, like *RDRAM*—a type of DRAM manufactured by a company called Rambus—your motherboard might support only that type of memory. If the company has gone out of business or has moved on to newer technologies, it could be expensive to upgrade that PC's memory later.

Windows XP Memory Management

How does Windows XP manage the memory we give it? If an operating system doesn't properly allocate memory to applications, they won't run well. And if each application isn't given its own protected memory space, your word processor could write data into the memory being used by your financial calculator, with disastrous results. Further, if the memory a program is using isn't released when that program exits, other programs can't use that memory. So you could end up with plenty of memory installed and no applications running, but no memory available to run anything. Fortunately, Windows XP provides a solution: virtual memory.

Virtual Memory

When you can't give your PC all the physical memory you'd like, virtual memory takes up the slack. It allows the PC to use blank space on a storage device as if it were memory chips. In other words, space on your hard disk becomes an extension of your PC's RAM.

Here's how it works. When Windows XP is first installed, it checks how much physical memory is installed. It then creates a hidden file on your primary hard disk (usually your C drive) that is 1.5 times the size of your actual RAM. So on a PC with 512 MB of RAM, Windows XP creates a 768 MB file, usually called the *swap file* or the *paging file*.

As the applications you run require more memory, Windows XP analyzes which parts of program code and data in memory have been accessed the least recently. Then it copies that code and data into the paging file on your hard disk. The memory that code or data was using is released so that your RAM-hungry application can use it. This process repeats as your software requires additional memory. Should your applications need the data or the code that was relocated to the hard disk, it is moved back into RAM, swapping places with other, least-recently-used code or data there. Data is swapped back and forth as needed.

As you'd expect, virtual memory is a lot slower than physical RAM. But with your Windows XP virtual memory settings chosen wisely and properly balanced, you can easily get better performance from your PC than you would if it were strictly limited to the physical RAM installed.

Maximize Your Virtual Memory Performance

Windows XP provides a number of tools and settings you can use to tweak the best performance out of your virtual memory. Because disk storage is so much slower than physical RAM, the most important factor to consider is whether you have enough RAM in the first place. If you don't, your PC will be moving data to and from virtual memory a lot. If your hard disk sounds like it's having a conniption and everything on your PC screen is updating very slowly (or if the entire PC seems frozen), you're likely *thrashing* your way through virtual memory.

As usual, the bottom line is all about balance. If you want your PC faster, you need to think smarter about how it's configured. So, once you've determined that you do have sufficient physical RAM for most of your needs, you can use the following techniques to fine-tune your virtual memory performance.

Selecting a Hard Disk

If you have more than one hard disk in your PC, you should store the swap file for your virtual memory on the fastest one. You'll learn how to make this determination in Chapter 13. A point to consider now, however, is that you'll get the best speed if your swap file is on a different hard disk than Windows XP and all of its operating system files. Normally, you'll want Windows XP on your fastest disk because its files are accessed continually. Having your swap file and Windows XP on the same disk can lead to thrashing if you rely heavily on virtual memory.

A better solution is to move the swap file to a different disk, even if that disk is a little slower. If you are truly hard-pressed for virtual memory performance, you might need to consider upgrading your secondary (or third, or fourth...) disk to a faster model that is better-suited for hosting the swap file.

Dividing the Swap File Between Several Drives

An alternative way of increasing virtual memory performance—sometimes dramatically—is to put part of the swap file on each of several disks. Consider a PC that your company is using as a low-end file server for documents everyone shares. Such a PC might be equipped with six hard disks. If the PC has 1 GB of physical RAM, its swap file should be 1.5 GB, according to Microsoft's recommendations. Skipping the first disk, which contains the operating system, you could configure one 300 MB swap file on each of the remaining five disks. Windows would treat this like a single large swap file, but with a major difference.

> **Note**   Because the swap file is actually five files on five different disks, Windows could theoretically be reading from or writing to each of those disks simultaneously. Your overall virtual memory performance wouldn't be five times better than what you'd get from using a single disk, but it would be considerably faster. (Of course, if one of your disks is a lot slower than others, don't use it for even *part* of your swap file. Similarly, if you have two disks and one is quite slow, you might experience better performance by placing the entire swap file on only the single, fast disk.)

Placing Virtual Memory on Different Partitions

Partitioning is a way to divide up a single physical hard disk so that it behaves like multiple disks. With partitioning, you can take a single 100 GB hard disk and make it function like you've actually got two 50 GB disks (perhaps a C and D disk drive).

However, partitioning isn't magic. It doesn't turn one disk into two, and it doesn't add additional read/write heads to the disk, either. Because all of a partition's space is together, partitioning one disk into two disks is like dividing it in half. The read/write heads will have to make large (read, "slow") movements each time you access data first from one partition and then the other.

Caution   Separate physical disks can do different work at the same time, so a swap file on multiple disks works fast. But splitting a swap file between partitions just guarantees that your disk will be thrashing. It's one of the best ways to ruin your virtual memory performance. (You'll learn more about partitions in Chapter 5.)

Key Points

- Memory is the electronic space where your PC works. Your operating system, the applications you run, and the data you work with are stored in memory while you're using them.

- Memory works like the rest of your PC, by converting real-life information into a series of ones and zeros, which make up the binary language the PC can understand and manipulate.

- Each of the individual ones and zeros that are used to represent information is called a bit.

- Bits are grouped together into sets of eight, which are called bytes. The byte is the basic block of data in the PC; 1024 bytes is called a kilobyte (KB); roughly 1 million bytes is called a megabyte (MB); roughly 1 billion bytes is called a gigabyte (GB).

- Main memory inside your PC is called random access memory (RAM). Your PC also contains read-only memory (ROM), which contains code and data that can't be changed.

- Your PC should ideally contain enough physical RAM to support all the programs and data you commonly use simultaneously.

- Windows XP provides virtual memory, which uses space on a hard disk to supplement the physical RAM in your PC as needed.

Chapter 4

Results You Can See

Getting results depends on seeing the right answer, and seeing—as far as the PC is concerned—depends on a monitor. With everybody using a monitor, you might think that you shouldn't have to think much about selecting one. But when it comes to *video* (by which I mean PC monitors and the hardware that makes them work), you've got choices aplenty. The bulk of this chapter will help you differentiate between all those choices. You'll understand how PC video works, so you'll know what to look for to make it work best for you.

A lot of the most important choices aren't even related to the monitor itself, but focus on the video card that gives a monitor its marching orders. But don't think that discovering monitors first (which we're going to do) will put the cart before the horse. Think of it as getting the big picture before you start working with the details.

Monitors: A Window on the PC

Almost all of us who use a computer depend completely on our monitors, but few of us pay much attention to them. Lots of folks don't put any more thought into selecting a monitor than choosing a can opener. That's too bad, because there's a lot of productivity to be had (and a lot of physical pain to be avoided) by making the right choices. To get in on those benefits—to see your PC better—you just need to see monitors a little differently. Let's start with a quick look at how monitors do their thing.

How Monitors Work

Monitors come in two basic types. Traditional TV-like monitors use analog displays, but flat panels use both analog and digital displays. Let's dig into the world of monitors by seeing them all as members of these two different camps: analog displays or digital displays.

Using More than One Monitor with Windows XP If you've ever dreamed of having more digital desktop space, you'll be happy to learn that Windows XP can support up to 10 monitors simultaneously. (Earlier versions of Windows supported only two.) So if you're working with multimedia, tracking investments in real time, or performing any number of other tasks, you can basically provide yourself with as much display space as your eyes can reasonably handle.

One of the nicest aspects of using multiple monitors under Windows XP is that everything is automatic. Windows XP detects each video card and each monitor, and it's a snap to choose which monitors you want to use, and how you want them configured. The Windows XP Display Control Panel allows you to drag monitors around virtually, so you can effectively line them up any way you like.

You can also extend the use of multiple monitors to your notebook PC. Dualview, a mobile feature of Windows XP, lets you configure a second monitor not merely as a duplication of your notebook's screen but as an *extension* of it. As you can with your desktop, you can drag objects right off your notebook's screen and onto the second monitor's extended desktop. If you've got a lot of work to accomplish at home or on the road, believe me, it's a really great bit of technology!

Analog Displays: Technology Born from Television

An *analog process* involves continuously changing signals, whether we're talking about photons from a star or neurotransmitters. If you have a lamp in your home that's on a dimmer, that's an analog process; as you turn the knob, the amount of current flowing to the bulb gradually increases or decreases. Graphically, the whole idea of "analog" looks like the sine wave in Figure 4-1. And *analog displays* are the first of the two main types of PC monitor.

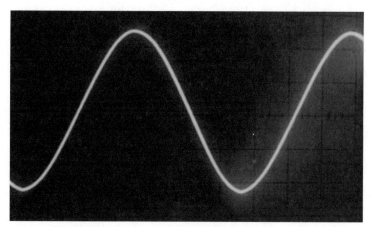

Figure 4-1 Analog signals can be metaphorically represented by a sine wave.

Analog displays work by responding to continuously changing signals from your PC. This technology was born with the color TV set. Indeed, most analog displays are just expensive televisions. Because they're the greatest in number, we'll look at these first. We'll then take a look at what I think of as a hybrid technology: analog flat screens.

CRTs: The PC TV   Most of the analog displays out there are *cathode ray tubes (CRTs)*. Like your television, a CRT monitor is just a big glass tube and some electronics. You can see a simplified illustration of how the CRT fits into a monitor case in Figure 4-2.

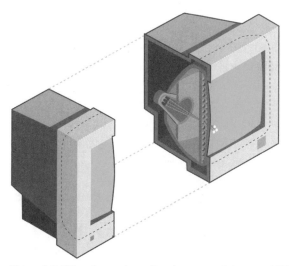

Figure 4-2 This cutaway shows the placement of the actual CRT inside a monitor case.

At the narrow end of the tube, three electrical circuits called *electron guns* produce electrons that shoot out in a stream. As Figure 4-3 shows, the three streams of electrons travel straight out of the guns toward the wide end of the CRT—the part we call the screen. Electromagnets or other circuitry focus the beams into narrow spots and deflect the beams, guiding them so that they point in an orderly fashion from one side of the screen to the other (say, from the viewer's left to right). At the far side of the screen, the beams turn off, the magnets adjust themselves, and then the beams turn back on, directed again at the left side of the screen, but slightly lower than before.

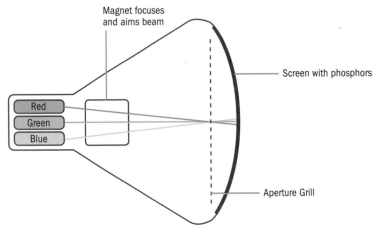

Figure 4-3 The location of electron beams is controlled by electromagnetic fields.

The magnets cause the electron beams to sweep from side to side, moving slightly lower each time, until they reach the lower right corner of the screen. At that point, the whole system resets and the beams start again at the top. From the upper left corner to the lower right corner, we call one full sweep of the screen one *frame* of video.

Our human eyes can't see the electron beams, however, so what we see on the screen isn't light produced by the electron guns. Instead, the inside of the "screen" of the CRT is coated with a substance that glows when it's stimulated by electrons. This special material is called a *phosphor,* and lots of different types abound. One common type makes children's toys and adults' wristwatch hands glow in the dark. In a CRT, streams of electrons stimulate the phosphors to glow. Like the hands on a glow-in-the-dark watch, the phosphors glow brighter if they're stimulated more (by a stronger stream of electrons), and they don't fade to black immediately. And that's of prime importance, because the images we see on a CRT are formed one spot at a time.

CRT phosphors glow just long enough to give us the illusion that the entire screen is glowing evenly, as the electron beams sweep from side to side, top to bottom. It's important that they don't glow any longer, or the image the electrons need to paint in one frame would blur with the image from a previous frame. The first spot of phosphor is just about to fade to black by the time the electron beam is back in the upper corner, ready to stimulate it again.

What I've just described is exactly how a black and white TV works (except black-and-whites have only one electron gun). Realistic shades of gray are obtained by sending a stronger (more stimulation, lighter spot, closer to white) or weaker (less stimulation, darker spot, closer to black) electron beam. Our brains put all of the spots together and convince us that we're seeing whole, stable images, as we do when we see frames of motion picture film. (The similarity is where the phrase *frame of video* comes from.)

Color CRTs are, of course, a bit more complicated, and they do have the three electron guns I mentioned in the first place—one for each primary color of light that we see: red, green, and blue. Color monitors also have either a *shadow mask* or an *aperture grill*—a thin piece of metal covered with tiny holes—that sits between the electron guns and the screen. The electron beams strike the screen phosphors only after passing through the holes. This makes for a sharp-edged and controlled spot. Why is it necessary?

In a CRT that's black and white (also known as *monochrome*, for one color), each spot of phosphor is a single dot that glows at some level of gray to white. In a color CRT, each spot is actually made up of three different phosphor spots, called a *triad*. In each triad, one spot glows red, one glows green, and one blue. The electron beam that controls red hits the red spots; the electron beam for green hits green spots, and so forth. By varying the strength of each of the three beams, infinite colors are formed.

If a triad is hit with a strong red beam and nearly no green or blue beam, that spot will glow red. With more power given to the blue beam, the spot would be more purple. Full power on all three beams causes the triad to glow evenly, and all three primary colors mix to form a spot of white light. This is an analog process because the strength of each electron gun can vary infinitely (at least in principle).

Now, each spot of light on the screen (called a *pixel*) is tiny to begin with; the space between triads is called *dot pitch* and is measured in hundredths of millimeters. The color spots in each triad are smaller still. (Incidentally, the size of each triad is called the *spot size*.) The aperture grill or shadow mask helps to precisely position each electron beam to strike the phosphors exactly right. If it didn't, you'd get fuzzy spots of light with soft edges, and television and your PC would look more like a watercolor painting come to life. Keep these ideas of dot pitch and spot size in mind; we'll encounter them again in a moment.

Running this entire show is your PC's video card or motherboard video circuitry. Most video cards convert the digital data inside your PC into analog signals that tell the CRT how strong a beam of electrons to shoot at each spot in each phosphor triad. Although it does take a little time to initially convert your PC's data into analog signals, the video card has circuitry dedicated to this task. In general, analog is a fast way to run a monitor.

Combining Flat Panels with Analog Video   Flat panels don't work at all like CRTs. And, although flat panels are increasingly compatible with analog video, they are by nature digital beasts. In a CRT, the electron beams can be infinitely adjusted, a bit like the flow of water out of an adjustable hose nozzle. However minutely you adjust the strength of the flow, you could always adjust it even more minutely if you had a precise enough means of control. Arithmetic works the same way—no matter how many times you divide a number in half, you can always divide it in half again. Infinity is a supremely analog concept.

But flat panels are not. You'll soon see that flat panels are more like your PC's (digital) CPU than they are like a CRT. The increasing number of analog flat panels you see today are actually hybrids, created for economic reasons. As a class, they're a family of flat panels that can receive analog control signals. These analog signals are then quickly converted back into the digital control signals the flat panel actually needs.

In short, digital data in the PC is translated into analog signals that are sent to the flat panel, which converts them into digital data. It's not the best idea because it can take too much time if you're someone who demands top performance from your PC display. People think of flat panels as an improvement over CRTs, but many analog flat panels can't display animation or video as well as a CRT can. All that time spent converting signals makes the display fall behind. It can't keep up with the stream of video flowing out of the PC. Chug a glass of water and some of the water won't make it to your stomach; you can swallow only so fast. An analog flat panel has its own version of the same problem.

Sadly, the troubles don't stop there. When the video card converts the PC video data from digital to analog, a little precision is lost. When analog instructions are initially converted to digital instructions, the converter may change an instruction from say, "50.0% red, 20.25% green, and 29.7% blue" to "50% red, 25% green, and 30% blue." Then, when the digital converter in the flat panel receives the instruction, it may introduce its own approximation. The result is a color spot that is not the same as that sent by your video card.

Unseasonable delays in processing the video stream and imprecise color are not a recipe for great success. Returning to the idea of balanced integration for a moment, I urge you to consider this sort of issue before you purchase an analog-only flat panel. If you edit photographs, watch movies, play amazing games, or make similar demands of your PC's video potential, you might be disappointed with the result. Fortunately, there is an alternative.

Passive- vs. Active-Matrix Flat Panels Don't confuse the difference between analog and digital flat panels with the difference between passive- and active-matrix flat panels. Whether a flat panel is active or passive has nothing to do with whether it's analog or digital. *Passive* or *active* refers to the different ways a panel puts a spot of color onto the screen and maintains it there. Passive panels aren't precise when turning pixels of a given color on or off. Turning a pixel off generally has the effect of turning those around it off, at least partially. Passive-matrix panels tend to produce muddy color and fuzzy, slow-to-respond images. An active-matrix panel offers sharper, cleaner, higher contrast and brighter, more intense color images. Overall, this active-matrix system performs much better, and digital active panels do a great job with multimedia, animation, and video.

True Digital Flat Panels

I divided this discussion of monitors the way I did because analog and digital are really the two basic camps out there. Some flat panels are analog, but *all* CRT's are analog, so it made sense to talk about CRTs first because most of us are most familiar with them. What I said about CRTs—about signals of different voltages coming from your video cards to control what the monitor displays—is, in brief, how all video circuitry works, so it's a good foundation to build on. But flat panels are becoming increasingly common—indeed, almost ubiquitous.

Figure 4-4 This all-digital flat panel is state of the art.

You might recall that I said analog flat panels came into being largely for economic reasons. By making that distinction, I meant to imply that analog panels didn't come first. Flat panels were originally digital. The economic problem is that a digital video card has always been an expensive commodity—partly because PCs have traditionally used analog video cards, so everybody's already got one. If you buy a new analog monitor, you just plug it into your existing analog video card and you're set. If you buy a new digital flat panel, you've also got to buy a new digital video card, increasing the cost considerably, particularly since you might end up throwing out your older, perfectly good analog card.

Because the prices of flat panels were already high relative to CRTs, early digital panels had a small market. Therefore, few companies produced digital video cards to support the panels, with two results. First, prices were driven still higher. Second, companies came up with their own ways of doing digital, which were at first compatible only with specific digital panels. Good old supply-and-demand on the rampage.

> **Note**   To make their products commercially viable, flat-panel makers eventually added the analog-to-digital conversion capability so that anybody with a video card could use a flat panel. Flat panels have subsequently dropped in price dramatically and have shown up on the desktops of executives and kids alike.

I'd now like to acquaint you with the strengths of the all-digital approach, and I'll show you how flat panels work at the same time. I'm going to be talking only about active-matrix flat panels because of their superior quality. (See the sidebar "Passive- vs. Active-Matrix Flat Panels" for more information.) I'm not evangelistic about much, and I almost never proselytize. But I will say that my own all-digital SGI flat panel is the one part of my PC I'd want to protect in one of our famous West coast earthquakes.

LCDs: From Your Wrist, with a Twist   Up until now, I've intentionally avoided talking about *liquid crystal displays (LCDs)* so as not to burden you with technical minutiae. But there's a time for everything, and now's the time to discuss LCDs.

Liquid crystal is a liquid that sometimes behaves like a solid. When exposed to an electric current, the molecules of the liquid crystal either twist up or untwist and line up in an orderly fashion, depending on which type of liquid crystal you're using. Light passing through the liquid is bent by the twisted crystals. By making a sandwich of polarizing filters with liquid crystal between them, light is allowed to pass completely through the sandwich (when the twisted molecules bend it to pass through the polarizer) or not (when the molecules untwist so they stop bending the light waves).

LCD watchmakers place a mirror behind a liquid crystal sandwich so that light is reflected, except in places where an electric charge causes the molecules to unwind. That prevents the light from bending so that it can pass through both polarizers and be reflected by the mirror, so the electrically charged areas look black.

For More Than Just Telling Time: LCD(isplays)   The liquid crystal in most displays untwists when charged with electricity. By varying the amount of electricity sent through the liquid, you can make the molecules untwist more or less—thus letting more or less light through. If you have a white light source behind the LCD sandwich, you can create different levels of gray in exactly this manner.

Now, if you set up an electronic grid so that you've got circuitry controlling the twistiness of a tiny bit of liquid crystal, with row after row of these bits organized into columns, you've got the makings of a display. Each space in the grid where a row and column meet is a bit of liquid crystal you can independently control. Each of these spaces controls the appearance of a single spot of light on the screen, so each is called a pixel, exactly like the spots of light on a black and white television.

To get color, you just do more of the same. First, add more electronics and divide each liquid crystal space on the grid into three independent spaces, called *subpixels*, side by side. Insert an array of microscopic color filters into the sandwich so that a triad made up of a red, green, and blue filter is aligned behind each set of the three LCDs. By independently sending electricity to untwist the liquid crystal behind each filter, complex colors are made up of the primary red, green, and blue filtered light. As with a CRT, these triads of color are so small that we perceive single pixels, not independent triads of light. Because each LCD subpixel is of a definite size, the images on LCD panels can be much sharper than those on CRTs, where electron beam focus is not perfect and variances in the screen's phosphor might make any given spot glow more or less, bleeding into its surrounding pixels.

As you might suspect, the electronics that make all this work need to be unbelievably small. In fact, for each pixel on a panel, three transistors (and capacitors) must be etched onto a plate of glass. On the flat panel I use, that's almost 5 million transistors! Because they are so small, they're hard to make reliable. If some of a panel's transistors don't work, the entire panel has to be scrapped. Scrap enough of what you're trying to make, and the few you actually get to sell are going to be expensive, to offset your scrapping losses. This is what happened to flat panels—until recent innovation reduced the number of faulty transistors, panel prices were astronomical.

Capacitors Made the Difference The capacitor associated with each subpixel is part of what makes an active-matrix panel so much better than a passive panel—which doesn't have them. Each capacitor holds the precise charge that is supposed to be sent to the part of the triad it controls. So once the three subpixels are given their "untwisting" orders, they each stay untwisted exactly the right amount. As a result, active-matrix colors are bright and well-saturated, not muddy and unreliable like the product of passive models.

What's So Special About Digital?   Earlier, I said that flat panels are digital beasts by nature. That's because the technology that makes them work is intimately related to the digital world. All the circuitry that controls the panel's millions of transistors is digital, designed to respond to discrete (specific) electrical signals. These discrete digital signals can be graphically represented as a square wave, shown in Figure 4-5. Unlike a CRT, which can respond to a continuously changing electrical voltage and produce a spot of color that is more or less bright, an LCD panel responds only to precise instructions.

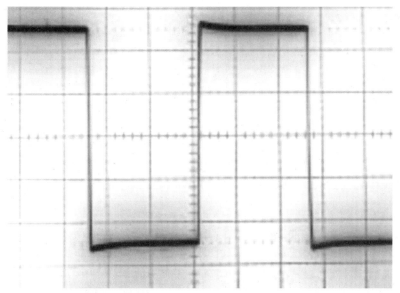

Figure 4-5 Digital signals operate at specific voltages and jump from one voltage to another, as opposed to the smooth, continuous analog signal wave shown in Figure 4-1.

By design, a CRT is able to handle imprecise instructions like "gimme some red, some green, and a little blue," but an LCD panel expects to hear "I need exactly this much red, this much green, this much blue, and I need it right now!" When an LCD panel is configured to accept a traditional analog signal from an analog PC video card, it has to go through all the shenanigans of converting "gimme some" into precise commands. That takes time and reduces performance.

When a digital panel is driven by a compatible digital video card, no time and precision are lost to translation. Everybody speaks the same language from the start, and it makes for efficient, accurate "conversations." Today, several digital flat-panel standards have evolved, and a number of companies are producing video cards that are either all-digital or can produce analog or digital output. Some, running Windows XP, can even produce both at the same time.

Feature Differentiation

Whether you're using a CRT or a flat panel, a number of features are common between all video monitors (and their supporting video cards, for that matter). These are the specifications that get thrown in your face whenever you read product reviews or shop for video hardware. Conquer these, and you're set.

Resolution: Dot's What It's About!

The most common specifications you'll encounter when looking at video hardware are the three factors that define the sharpness and precision of the video image you'll see: resolution, dot pitch, and spot size. Unfortunately, the term *resolution* means one thing for printers and a different thing for video. To make matters worse, the term is used collectively to refer to three different factors, one of which is also called *resolution*. But I must claim innocence; this is how the word gets used. To clear things up, for the remainder of this chapter, I'll use the term strictly to refer to the number of pixels displayed horizontally and vertically on a PC monitor. But first, let's look at dot pitch and spot size.

Which Pitch Is Which?

Strictly speaking, *dot pitch* is a diagonal measurement (hence, the "pitch" concept) of the space from the upper left corner of either the red, green, or blue subpixel in a pixel's triad to the upper left corner of the same subpixel one column to either side and one row above or below. (See Figure 4-6 for an illustration of this concept.) This factor is crucial to the image quality of CRTs. (Dot pitch isn't really relevant to flat panels.) Because the phosphors on a CRT actually glow, a small aura of light surrounding each subpixel makes them seem to blend into solid colors, the way watercolor paints blend on paper.

Figure 4-6 Dot pitch refers to the distance between pixels on a screen.

   In addition, the glowing of each whole pixel helps make images on a CRT seem smooth and continuous. However, if too much space exists between pixels on the screen, that effect is defeated. Your eyes will be straining, and your brain will be struggling constantly to ignore the black space and try to put the little dots together into the coherent pictures and text they're supposed to be. A good monitor's dot pitch is in the neighborhood of 0.25 millimeters (mm). A dot pitch of 0.23 mm is considered excellent; most people find 0.28 mm and above to be uncomfortable.

   Problems can arise if dot pitch is too small relative to other factors, too. Although this rarely happens—the precision of a small dot pitch is expensive to manufacture, so it's always well balanced with other monitor characteristics—a monitor that has gone out of adjustment can produce blurred or muddy images if its dot pitch is small and its spot size grows too large.

Spot Size and Focus

Spot size (also known as *focus*) is just a measurement of how precisely a monitor's electron beams can be focused to strike a single subpixel. If the electron beam is not finely focused, it will strike too large an area on the screen, stimulating the phosphors not only in the subpixel it's supposed to target, but also those around it. Poor beam focus plus a low dot pitch leads to washed-out colors and muddy images on-screen.

Unfortunately, bright colors on the screen are best achieved with high-power electron beams, which tend to bleed into the areas around their actual target subpixel. This is where aperture grills and shadow masks shine (or prevent shining, to be technically accurate). The physical holes in the mask prevent the high-energy beam's superfluous electrons from striking the screen. The electrons pass through with sharply defined edges, not a haze of unintentional particles.

> **Note**   Like dot pitch, the concept of spot size doesn't really relate to LCD flat panels. The light you see on an LCD screen is just the panel's backlight passing through colored filters and shining through an array of tiny liquid crystal "windows." The color that each window lets through to your eyes is not affected by the color of the pixels or subpixels near it.

On some monitors, spot size is a user setting that you can customize to your taste. Generally, spot size is set at the factory, and your monitor will need professional repair if an adjustment must be made.

> **Caution**   The CRT inside a monitor produces its electrons by generating extremely high voltages at amperages that could easily kill you and could certainly throw you across a room. You can open up your PC to upgrade hardware or add components at will, but *never* open up a monitor. Even an old monitor could be dangerous because cathode ray tubes and capacitors store voltages and maintain them for a long time. If you're not actually a trained video technician, don't open a monitor even just to see what it looks like inside. *You could die*.

Resolution: What It Means, Whatever It Means

Dot pitch and spot size have little to do with flat panels, but resolution applies to every kind of monitor. In the world of video, resolution refers to the number of pixels you can see horizontally and vertically. On most flat panels, resolution is therefore fixed. If your flat panel is like mine, it has a resolution of 1600 by 1024, or 1024 rows of pixels with 1600 pixels in each row. The higher the resolution, the smaller the pixels, and the smaller the pixels, the sharper the image and the smoother the curves. The result? Text is easier to read, and graphics and pictures are sharper.

On a CRT, resolution has the same meaning, but it works a little differently because of the nature of the beast. With respect to a CRT, we usually speak of the *maximum resolution* it can produce. That's because the glowing quality of CRT pixels makes it easy to configure pixels to function in groups. By doing so, the apparent size of each pixel is increased, and it actually looks like there are fewer pixels on the monitor. This is why a CRT can display a full-screen image at 1024 by 768 resolution one moment and display a full-screen image at 640 by 480 the next.

Most modern monitors are capable of working at a variety of apparent resolutions, depending on which settings are chosen for your video card in the Windows XP Display Properties dialog box, shown in Figure 4-7. If you set your CRT to 800 by 600 resolution and its maximum resolution is 1600 by 1200 pixels, the video card will treat groups of four pixels—two pixels horizontally and two vertically—like a single pixel. The minimum-sized spot of light you see on the screen will be four times larger than the monitor's actual spot size.

Figure 4-7 The Windows XP Display Properties dialog box lets you fine-tune your display settings.

Reducing a CRT's apparent resolution is particularly useful for people with reduced vision because all of this combining of pixels means that everything on the screen appears to be four times larger. Of course, you might not fit as much on-screen at lower resolutions, but it's a tradeoff. Better to work with less but see all of it clearly.

Color Deep as the Ocean

The next major video characteristic we'll consider is called *color depth*: the number of different colors that can be simultaneously displayed on the screen. Like resolution, color depth is a factor of how your video card works with your display. A relatively new CRT monitor should be able to display as many colors as the video card supports. Because a CRT is an analog device, it can send out electron beams of any strength to stimulate the red/green/blue subpixels any way you want.

Flat panels, digital beasts that they are, are preset to display only certain colors. In practice, flat panels commonly display as many colors as CRTs, but a digital video card and flat panel can usually produce more accurate colors. As I mentioned earlier, this is because signals (voltages) often vary between the video card and the monitor, and precision is simply not an analog device's game.

With CRT or flat panel, the number of colors that can be displayed is determined by a setting on the Windows XP Display Properties dialog box. This setting changes nothing in the display; it changes a lot in your video card.

What Is the Color of One Byte?

In fact, the color depth setting tells your video card how much memory to use to store the color of each pixel on the screen. This measure is normally expressed in bits, so you'll often hear about 8-bit color, 16-bit color, and 32-bit color. To explain what that means, let's look briefly at how a video card manages the images on your screen—whether it's a CRT or LCD.

Every pixel on your display is associated with one or more spaces in RAM. We call this concept *mapping*, and say that the display is mapped to memory. In most cases, the memory in question is dedicated memory on your video card itself. Sometimes, your PC's main memory is used instead.

Recall from Chapter 3 that the IBM extended ASCII character set provides a way of mapping real-life characters with values the PC can manipulate. Extended ASCII uses the value of a single byte, eight bits, to represent each of its real-world characters and symbols. Because each bit can have one of two possible values (zero or one), eight bits give us a total of 256 possible combined values ($2^8 = 256$). So extended ASCII can represent 256 different characters.

What ASCII does for characters, your video card's color depth setting does for pixels. If the video card sets aside one byte (again, eight bits) to store the color of each pixel on the screen, it can store 256 different color values, each of which represents a color on-screen. Because we live in a colorful world, more different colors equate to more realistic color images, but 256 doesn't show the world in an accurate light. By using more than just 8 bits, more color values can be stored and more colors displayed. A color depth of 32 bits is capable of generating 4.2 billion different colors, which is more than capable of digitally showing us an accurately colored world.

What a Refreshing Experience!

The next video specification we'll look at, the monitor's *refresh rate*, causes even more eyestrain and headaches than poor resolution. Unlike the refresh rate of memory that we encountered in Chapter 3, a monitor's refresh rate is measured as the number of times each second the entire image on the screen (one frame of video) is "repainted" by the moving electron guns. Because CRT phosphors fade, a slow refresh rate can easily make a screen image seem to pulse or flicker. This flickering plays havoc with your eyes and brain; if you get a headache after sitting at your PC for a short time, you're probably the victim of a low refresh rate.

Fortunately, most modern CRTs can work at a variety of refresh rates. How fast is fast enough? In general, the best setting for your monitor is as fast as possible. Most people will get eyestrain from any refresh rate under 72 hertz (Hz), which means the monitor image is repainted 72 times each second. For technical reasons, 60 Hz is often selected as the default refresh rate. Unfortunately, it's far too slow for almost anyone to use comfortably for long. To check and modify your monitor's refresh rate, follow these steps:

1   Open the Windows XP Display Properties dialog box.

2   Click the Settings tab.

3   Click Advanced.

4   Click the Adapter tab, and then click List All Modes to display the List All Modes dialog box, shown in Figure 4-8.

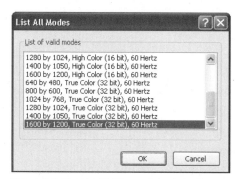

Figure 4-8 The List All Modes dialog box allows you to customize your PC display's refresh rate.

If your *adapter* (another bit of lingo that means video card, in this case) is set to Optimal, you can probably leave it there. The card will detect the fastest refresh your monitor can produce and will select that refresh rate. If it says Adapter Default, you can probably do better unless you have an older monitor.

Select the fastest refresh rate option in the list. Click Apply, and instruct Windows to apply the setting without rebooting when you're prompted. If the screen suddenly looks bizarre, don't worry—Windows XP will revert to your previous setting in a few seconds and all will be well. Try the next fastest refresh rate in the list until you find yourself using the fastest rate your monitor supports happily.

Try This! If you want to see your monitor flashing as it refreshes, try this cute trick if your monitor is set to a relatively slow refresh rate. Sit facing your monitor, and then turn your head to the side as far as you can while still being able to see your monitor in your peripheral vision. While looking at the monitor out of the corner of your eye, rapidly move your eye up and down two or three times. For reasons I'm not qualified to explain, most people can clearly see their CRT monitor flickering at refresh rates under about 75 Hz. One way of determining which refresh rate is fast enough for you is to increase the rate until you can't see this flicker as clearly. (By the way, if you know why this trick works, I'd love to hear from you. Feel free to contact me in care of Microsoft Press.)

Full Motion Video Considerations

If you'd like to view high-quality video (either motion pictures or animation) on your PC, you'll want to consider two important issues. First, don't use an analog-only flat panel because you won't get the performance you want. If you want the flexibility of an analog flat panel, select one that also supports one of the standard all-digital interfaces.

Second, you'll want a monitor that can support as high a refresh rate as possible, to eliminate any vestiges of flicker. This is a point for balanced integration, however. The video card you select must support the monitor's fast refresh rate, and must also be powerful enough to produce a steady stream of video for you to watch. In fact, the video card you select to support the monitor is almost as important as avoiding analog-only flat panels.

Video Adapters: What They Are, What They Do

The number of different video cards available today probably matches the number of models of monitor. Unfortunately, the number of people who are capable of producing new and profound ways of handling PC video is a lot smaller than the number of people who want to make money in that industry. This is good and bad. It's good because we benefit when a certain video processor becomes so ubiquitous, software developers start writing their programs to make special use of the processor's unique abilities.

On the other hand, it's bad because it's that much harder to select the video card that's best for you when they all look alike. Advertisements and product reviews commonly focus on a video card's processing engine, so if the same engine is used to run 20 different cards, how can you possibly tell them apart? Do any of them really work differently, or is this truly just an example of product packaging gone mad?

As it turns out, all video cards are not created equal, even when the labels on their packaging advertise the same brands of processor. The video processor is key to most of what a video card does, but that isn't the whole story. Today's video cards have their own CPU, memory, and even buses. Video-card memory is selected for its speed and, at the high end, its ultra-high refresh rates. Video data moves so fast that you might say it doesn't move into and out of memory, it just moves *through* memory. The PC's main CPU still runs the show, but the video card's own graphics processor does a lot of the work.

Video cards have one (or both) of two different types of processors (CPUs) built into them. The first type, usually called a *graphics processor unit (GPU)*, works in conjunction with the PC's main CPU. The two processors do the necessary rendering and memory management together. A GPU is an independent beast, designed to rapidly perform the sorts of calculations used in rendering high-quality video images—especially 3D images. It doesn't have to be controlled by the PC's main CPU. Instead, it automatically processes all video-related tasks on its own and sends the result to video memory and the display.

The second type of video card CPU is a *graphics accelerator*. It waits for the PC's main CPU to tell it to perform a specific set of video operations, and then it does its thing. The PC's CPU doesn't have to perform the calculations itself, but it does have to be a more intimate part of the overall video process, giving the graphics accelerator all of the necessary marching orders.

Which type is superior? The answer depends on your needs, of course. A GPU's speed can be amazing, but only if you run software that does a lot of 3D rendering and animation. If you don't, the special features—by which I mean the *expensive* features—of the processor will never be used, and it won't provide much faster video than would a graphics accelerator. So before you buy a high-powered GPU, make certain that you'll actually use it.

The last major thing video cards do depends on whether the card is digital or analog. If the card is digital and your flat panel is too, the card simply sends digital data directly from video memory out to the panel. Zoom! But if your video card is analog, before anything can be sent to the display, the digital data first has to pass through a digital-to-analog converter (DAC). This circuitry reads all of the ones and zeros stored in video memory and changes them into the variable analog voltages a CRT can understand. And the faster those values are converted, the higher the refresh rate the analog video card can provide.

Feature That!

When you start comparing the capabilities of video adapter cards, you'll be putting together all the specifications we've already discussed (dot pitch, spot size, and so forth) with a couple of others. Each card's packaging usually contains a matrix that shows the different resolutions, different color depths, and different refresh rates the card supports. The matrix might look something like this:

Resolution(s)	Color Depth(s) Bits	Refresh Rate(s) in Hz
640 × 480, 800 × 600, 1024 × 768	4, 8, 16, 24, 32	60, 72, 75, 80, 85, 100
1280 × 1024	4, 8, 16, 24	60, 72, 75, 80
1600 × 1200	8, 16	60, 72

Incidentally, you wouldn't want to buy this particular video card (if it existed). It would be considered woefully underpowered by today's standards. In general, a good video card will support refresh rates of at least 85 Hz at its highest resolution, and should provide realistic, "true color" 24-bit color depth at the same resolution.

What this matrix does show you, however, is that card features are a tradeoff. It takes memory and processor power to support higher color depths, or higher resolutions, or higher refresh rates. If you're going to do extensive editing of 2D photographic images, you would probably want to spend your money on a card that has more memory (to support the most realistic color depths) and high resolution, rather than paying for an expensive 3D GPU on a card with lower resolution. On the other hand, if you do photorealistic 3D rendering, like that done for engineering or architectural purposes, you'll probably find yourself buying the top-of-the-line card anyway, with a large dedicated video memory and super-high refresh rates.

Because most video cards provide some enhanced support for 3D graphics, you'll commonly encounter something called the *polygon draw rate*, which means how many polygons can be put into video memory in 1 second. Although other factors come into play, a big part of how well a video card performs its 3D magic is how many polygons it can draw in a second. (The more polygons it can draw, the smoother and more realistic an image. If you're adding animation to the 3D mix, polygons must be drawn very fast, indeed.)

Another expression of this capability is called *fill rate*, which doesn't focus on polygons specifically but, instead, refers to how quickly a video card can render a full-screen 3D image. One of today's top-of-the-line GPU cards can draw 136 million polygons per second—of course the video card alone costs $1500. It's a lot of money to get the most out of a $49 video game, but you know what they say: do what you love.

Video Standards

Recently, new video standards have been introduced at such a fast rate, it's been hard to keep up. I'd like you to be familiar with the most common standards, however, so that you'll be able to make better feature comparisons, overall:

- The *Video Graphics Adapter (VGA)* standard calls for a screen resolution of 640 by 480 pixels at 8-bit color depth (256 colors). It's the granddaddy of today's video standards.

- The *super VGA (SVGA)* standard extends the maximum screen resolution to 1280 by 1024 at color depths of up to 24 bits (16.7 million colors).

- The *ultra extended graphics array (UXGA)* standard ups the ante to 1600 by 1200 pixels at 24 bits.

- The *enhanced extended graphics array (EXGA)* standard pushes video to 2580 by 1920 pixels.

You'll also encounter variations of these, especially in the world of flat panels, where UXGA+, SVGA+, and other varieties exist. These aren't exactly standards, but are proprietary enhancements of the standards designed to provide better performance. As flat panels and high-quality theatrical digital video have increased in popularity, a standard called *SuperWide*, introduced by SGI, brings a motion-picture-wide screen resolution of 1600 by 1024 into the mix.

DVI   The most recent major innovation in video standards has been the move to all-digital video. Currently, two Digital Video Interface (DVI) standards have emerged. DVI-D supports only an all-digital connection. DVI-I (for *integrated*) supports either an all-digital or an analog-to-digital connection. DVI-D can provide High Definition Television (HDTV)–quality video at a resolution of 1920 by 1080, and certain implementations of DVI-D can perform at up to 2048 by 1536 pixels—a resolution called *quad extended graphics array (QXGA)*.

Microsoft DirectX One good way to bring superior video performance to everybody—not just to people who own a specific video card—is for an independent source to come up with a set of well-optimized tools: ways of doing common jobs. The source can then make these tools available to everyone so that new products will use them, and everybody wins.

Microsoft DirectX is just such a set of tools; DirectX 8 is the latest version at the time of this writing. In fact, DirectX tools don't just enhance video. Audio also benefits. Within the DirectX family of tools, DirectDraw and Direct3D make it easier for game manufacturers (and other software makers) to provide fast graphic rendering using code that is highly optimized. GPU manufacturers tune their hardware to be particularly efficient with DirectX code, and the combination is some lightning-fast productivity (if you consider playing a video game to be productive).

Key Points

- Monitors are either analog or digital. On a desktop PC, the display—called a *cathode ray tube* (CRT)—has traditionally been analog. On notebook computers, flat-panel displays have traditionally been digital. Today, while CRT's remain analog (except for a very niche few), flat panels may be digital or analog.

- PC CRTs are basically high-quality television sets. They use three electron guns—one for each primary color (red, green, blue)—to paint images on the screen.

- Flat panels are more like old-fashioned digital watches than they are like CRTs. Liquid crystals allow varying amounts of the panel's backlight through colored filters, producing spots of light on the screen.

- Video adapters come in both digital and analog varieties. Some provide support for both types of display.

- Video adapters come with their own memory, in which graphic images are stored and sent to your screen.

- Video adapters may come with a GPU, or graphics processor, which can dramatically increase the card's 3D performance (and its cost).

- When selecting a video adapter, it's important to consider the refresh rate, dot pitch, and resolutions the card can provide.

Chapter 5

Saving What's Important

Nothing is as frustrating as losing something important, especially if what you happen to have lost is the product of hours of work. In part, computers make it easier to get work done—but then you've got more work available to lose. With all that memory, you would think it would be hard to lose something on the computer. Isn't memory storage?

Storage vs. Memory

As a matter of fact, it's not. As you read in Chapter 3, PC memory is volatile: turn off the power and everything in memory is gone. To really benefit from your work, you need to be able to store it when you're done working with it. Memory doesn't provide this capability, and it would be too expensive to use for that purpose even if it did. Storage is the solution. Unlike memory, which provides a *temporary* place for programs and data to reside while you're working, storage devices provide permanent (and semipermanent) places for your work, your programs, and everything your PC needs to operate.

Basically two primary types of storage devices are available today. The type that has been around the longest is a group of products that use magnetism to store data, programs, and so forth. This type includes floppy drives and hard drives as well as tape drives. The second major type of storage is optical; it uses light in one way or another to store its content. In this chapter, you'll look at both types of storage, and you'll learn about some great features of Microsoft Windows XP that make using and managing storage easier than ever before.

Several things differentiate both types of storage from memory, but the key factor is that unlike memory, these storage devices are all *nonvolatile*. If your PC's power is turned off, anything stored is preserved. When you turn the PC back on, it's all there.

Also unlike memory, data doesn't get moved to storage just because you're using it. If you type a letter into your word processor and save it, your work is copied from memory into a file in storage. A *file* is an electronic version of a document, whether it's a letter, a novel, or a photograph. Every properly written program and application that runs under Windows XP will *always* ask whether you want to save your work before it allows you to close (and destroy) anything that's unsaved.

With all of this in mind, let's take a look first at magnetic storage and then at optical storage. We'll see how each works and when each is the right tool for the job.

Good Storage Habits What happens if you store your work and then you can't find it again? Your first line of defense against losing data is Windows XP's directory or folder system. When you save your work for the first time, the Save As dialog box displays. From here, you can use the various drop-down lists and buttons to navigate to the location on a storage device where you want the file to be stored.

It makes sense to save your documents within the My Documents folder (the default), but if you save every document you create there, two things will happen. First, you'll have to search through literally thousands of documents to locate a given file. Second, every time you want to open a document, the application you're using has to read in the entire contents of the document's home folder and process the list of files it finds there. That's a major productivity sinkhole if you have thousands of files in an endless list.

Fortunately, you can keep far better track of your documents. Within any well-designed application's Save As dialog box is a powerful button near the upper right that allows you to create new folders: it has the image of a folder with an asterisk (*) on it, as highlighted in Figure 5-1. Here's how to make the most of this feature.

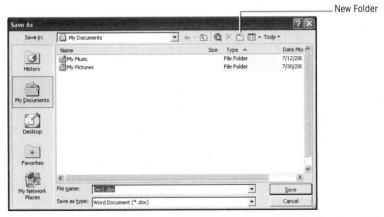

Figure 5-1 The New Folder button allows you to create a new folder for files from within the Save As dialog box.

Think about the kinds of documents you're most likely to create. (Notice in Figure 5-1 that Windows XP has already provided empty folders that it suggests you use for your pictures and multimedia files; you need not use these, but they are available if you want to do so.) When you click New Folder, Windows XP creates a folder and lets you give it a name. Once you do that, Windows will show you the contents of that new, empty folder. Type the file name you want to use for the data you're saving, and it's instantly put into that new folder. Simple as that!

You can also create *nested folders*—folders within folders—but you don't want to take that too far, of course, or you can make it just as hard to find your work.

Try This!   Windows provides a way for you to search for documents based on their contents. The Windows XP Indexing Service allows you to search for documents based on what's inside them, and it's easy to use. It's part of the Windows XP Search feature, accessible by selecting Search from the Start menu. The Search Results window opens, as shown in Figure 5-2.

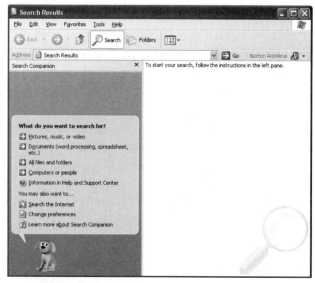

Figure 5-2   The Windows XP Search features are powerful and customizable.

If you've never used Search before, click Change Preferences in the left pane, then click With Indexing Service (For Faster Local Services). The Indexing Service will use idle PC time to scan the files on your local computer and analyze their contents. It builds a catalog of this indexed information, making searches even faster—rather than searching the actual drives for all files containing the word *psychobabble*, for example, it just looks for that word in the catalog and displays the indexed results.

If you find it impedes your PC's performance, you can turn this feature back off just as easily. Just click Change Preferences in the Search window and disable Indexing.

Hard Disks: Magnetic Storage for Everyone

The primary source of storage in any PC is its *magnetic storage*—the hard drive or drives. Over the years, their capacity has exploded and their price has imploded. As storage costs dropped, hard drive technology kept improving, and drive capacity went through the roof. In a box smaller than the average paperback novel, we can now store the contents of thousands of novels.

Drive speed improved too, in three ways. First, the IDE bus was upgraded to allow for dramatically faster data transfer rates. Second, the speed at which drives spin increased, reducing a property called *latency*, which is the dead time a PC has to wait for a location on the disk to spin under one of the drive's read/ write heads. Finally, the act of increasing drive capacity indirectly increased drive speed. All of this is great. But how do hard drives work, anyway?

How They Work

The story of how hard drives do their thing goes back to primary school. Remember how, if you pick up a paper clip with a magnet, the paper clip *becomes* a magnet, and can pick up other paper clips, until you've got a whole chain? Remember that the north and south poles of two magnets attract each other, whereas two north or two south poles repel each other? At the simplest level, that's how hard drives work. They take advantage of three neat facts of magnetism:

- Certain metals can be magnetized.

- Magnets have polarity (that is, a north and a south, or positive and negative pole).

- Electricity flowing through a wire creates a magnetic field, and a magnetic field around a wire generates electricity.

Let's take a quick look at each point. First, certain metals can be magnetized. You know that from the paper clip trick. The natural magnet in your hand induces a magnetic field that affects the iron in the steel paper clips. Many iron (or *ferrous*) molecules become tiny magnets, so the attraction of the original magnet is essentially emulated or mimicked down the chain of clips. As it turns out, the material that coats each platter inside a hard disk is—you guessed it— ferrous. It can also be magnetized. And because of the special properties of this type of ferrous material, once a bit of it is magnetized, it holds that magnetic charge for years.

Second, magnets have polarity, which means that when one magnet is brought near another one, it's either going to attract the second magnet (the two polarities are opposite) or it's going to try to push that second magnet away (the two polarities are the same). Conveniently, the fact that magnets have two—and only two—possible polarities fits in nicely with the fact that computers are binary, and have, at the lowest level, only two possible values for data.

Theoretically, then, an array of eight magnets could be used to represent a byte of data, if we say that one magnetic pole symbolizes a zero and the other a one. And that's exactly what we do, not with an array of eight magnets, but with a platter covered with ferrous material that makes up billions of microscopic magnets. But how do you "read" and "write" magnets?

That's where the third neat fact of magnetism comes in—a relationship exists between electricity and magnetism. That's how all the electricity we've built our lives with is generated. An electrical generator is just a set of huge magnets spinning fast inside a (huge) coil of copper wire. The moving magnetic field caused by the magnets induces a flowing electric current in the wire coil. Do it on the scale of Hoover Dam, and next thing you know, you're powering the American Southwest. Do it on the scale of a hard disk, and next thing you know, you're reading data.

A hard disk's read/write head is really just a tiny coil of wire on the tip of an articulated arm. As the drive surface spins and passes by the read/write head, the magnetic polarity of the material on the platters induces a flowing electric current in the wire coil. The flow of that current is changed by whether the microscopic magnetic areas of the disk—they're called *domains*—has one polarity or the other. The hard drive's rather complex and *very* sensitive electronics monitors those electrical changes in the read/write head, and translates the changes into the bits—ones and zeros—your PC uses to "think."

To ensure that every drive will work with every PC, hardware standards were adopted that specify how that translation will take place, and which kinds of messages the hard drive can send back to the PC. Your PC's operating system—Windows XP—imposes its own standards, too, in the form of a *file system*, which dictates how all of the billions of magnetic domains will be organized so that data can be reliably retrieved.

See Also   *You'll learn a lot about the different Windows XP file systems in Chapter 12.*

When it's time to write data to the disk drive, the process works in reverse. Bits of data flow from your PC's main memory through the IDE interface (which I introduced in Chapter 2) into the hard drive's own electronics. There, the binary data is converted into electrical signals that flow through the read/write head's wire coil. These signals—which are much stronger than those induced by the magnetic domains—turn the read/write head into an electromagnet. The magnetic fields it creates actually change the polarity of the magnetic domains on the disk platters—"writing" those ones and zeros to the disk drive.

Feature Primer

Like cars, hard disks have their own set of characteristics, or *features*, which distinguish them from each other. In this next section, you'll get a good look at the important ones.

Drive Types

At the most fundamental level—in the automotive world, perhaps the level at which a car has either an internal combustion engine or a diesel engine—mainstream PC drives fit into one of two types: IDE drives, which you've already learned about, or Small Computer System Interface (SCSI) drives. SCSI drives are found in the PC world, but they're far more commonly found on network servers and Apple Macintosh computers. Because SCSI drives are relatively uncommon in the PC world, we won't concern ourselves with them. Suffice it to say that SCSI devices require their own interface, which is rarely part of a standard PC's motherboard, and they are always more expensive than IDE drives because their market is smaller and their drive electronics are more complex.

Drive Capacity

After its type, a drive's capacity is its most obvious feature. A good desktop PC comes with storage around 100 gigabytes (GB) in capacity, and a good notebook PC comes with between 30 and 60 GB of storage. As you've already been advised, you should buy the most storage you can comfortably afford, balancing that expense with the cost and value of the other components of your PC. (Of course, if your PC is of good speed and good memory size and you're just upgrading to a larger hard disk, buy the biggest one you can budget.)

Drive Speed

Drive speed involves three factors. The first is *rotational speed*. A drive's platters can rotate at either 5400 or 7200 revolutions per minute (RPM). Rotational speed definitely affects the cost, so don't be surprised to find a significant difference in the cost of two 100 GB drives if one spins at the lower speed and one at the higher. The faster rotation means that everything about the drive must work faster. If this were not the case, the drive's read/write heads would take in data faster than the electronics could process it, and the "lost" data would have to be reread every time that data was lost. Nightmare. Balanced integration is an important factor within PC components as well as between components.

The second factor that fits within the aegis of speed is a drive's *transfer rate*: the maximum speed at which data can stream from the drive out to the PC in short bursts. A drive's transfer rate is the speed at which the drive *might* perform under certain ideal conditions. Naturally, you can expect better performance in general from a drive with a higher transfer rate than from a drive with a slower transfer rate, but don't expect to get the 100 megabytes (MB) per second the box promises every time you read your e-mail. A more realistic factor is a drive's *maximum sustained transfer rate*: the highest rate at which the drive can continuously perform. This, too, is a maximum, not an average. The average performance you'll get from a drive is based on a number of factors, which you'll read about in Chapter 13.

A far more useful and reliable factor of drive speed is its average *seek time*: how many milliseconds (ms) it takes, on average, for the drive to find any given location on disk. An excellent access time is 3.6 ms, but 8.9 ms is far more common. Seek time is a reliable comparator of disk performance because it incorporates aspects of all the other speed factors. To seek to a given disk location, the drive must be spinning, and it must be reading data from the drive to verify the location of the read/write head. Seek time is also more reliable than other speed factors because hard disks now contain cache memory that can skew other read factors.

Drive Cache

Most hard drives today have a little bit of memory built into them. This memory functions as a *cache*—a *temporary* temporary holding place, if you like—where data from the disk is stored before the PC needs it. How does the disk know what the PC is most likely to need? It turns out that on a well-organized hard drive, the bit of data a computer is most likely to need next is the bit of data that immediately follows the last bit of data it needed. So what's a well-organized disk? Chapter 12 will tell all.

Of course, as I've said before, to get the most from your PC, all these factors need to be in balance. If you're going to be configuring a network server, you need to purchase drives with the lowest possible seek times so they'll work like lightning. If you're going to be editing digital video, you'll want to pay more attention to the sustained transfer rate and the drive's memory cache—those factors are vital when you're trying to get stable, reliable streaming video off a hard drive. On the other hand, if you spend a lot of time working with hundreds of small files, rotation and seek time might be most important to you because they'll give you faster access to all the little bits and pieces you'll be needing.

These considerations are important, because you'll definitely pay for any high-end or high-quality feature you want, and it makes no sense to spend money for something you'll never use.

The Disk Cleanup Wizard The Disk Cleanup Wizard in Windows XP is a handy graphical tool that steps you through the process of eliminating useless stuff on a disk drive. To access it, from the Start menu, select All Programs, then Accessories, then System Tools, and finally Disk Cleanup. When the wizard first runs, it will automatically scan your primary hard drive looking for junk. What's junk? The kind of stuff you're never going to miss, such as the following:

- Temporary files that should have been automatically deleted, but weren't

- Files downloaded to your PC while you surf the Internet

- Files in your Recycle Bin that haven't yet been permanently deleted

When Disk Cleanup is done scanning, a window like the one shown below appears to show you the drive capacity that it can free up by deleting the junk it's found. After you've selected the content you want to delete, Disk Cleanup prompts you just to make certain you want to proceed. Click Yes, and the junk is gone and that disk space is available again.

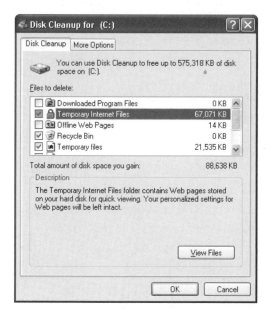

Optical Discs

The second major class of storage devices is *optical*—devices that do what they do through light. There is, in fact, a third class, which is a hybrid of the two technologies—it's called *magneto-optical (MO)*—but it's something of a white elephant today. Optical technology has reached a combination of price, capacity, reliability, and ubiquity such that magneto-optical devices are fading from the scene. For the sake of our discussion, when I'm talking about optical storage, I'm talking about truly optical storage—storage that uses the power of light alone to read or write data: CDs and DVDs.

Lingo   You might have noticed that the spelling of *disc* in "optical disc" is different from what you're used to seeing. Standard practice has evolved so that, generally, when you're writing about magnetic storage, you're talking about *disks*, and when you're writing about optical storage, you're talking about *discs*. If you ever find yourself writing about storage, it's important to look like you know what you're writing about. Plus, it's one of those "expertise checker" things that give people a secret chuckle when they see it misused. Enjoy.

How CDs and DVDs Work

Although someone could easily fill a book with the differences between how CDs and DVDs work, they are much more alike than they are different. We'll be taking a look at how these optical technologies are similar because it tells you just about everything you'll need or likely want to know. As we proceed, I'll just point out a few important differences.

To understand how optical drives work, forget everything you've read in this chapter about magnetic storage. Other than bits going in and coming out, optical drives have almost nothing in common with magnetic drives. But they have a lot in common with each other. CDs and DVDs don't use magnetism, domains, read/write heads, or anything ferrous to store data. They do use metal, but the metal in these discs is nothing like the platters of a hard disk.

Instead of being a coated solid platter, optical discs contain a thin sheet of metal foil that is sandwiched between two protective plastic layers. If you touched the surface of a hard drive, you'd likely damage the material severely—merely opening the drive case would expose the disk drive to so much dust, it would probably never work again anyway. But if you touch the surface of a CD or a DVD, you're just touching the plastic coating. The part that actually stores the data—the metal foil—is safe inside. Severe scratches on a disc's surface could render it unusable, but scratch-repair kits now exist and optical drives have sophisticated error-correction technology that can make it possible to read even a badly scratched disc.

Scratch That If you've ever purchased a recordable CD, you might already know that you should always wipe the disc from the center outwards, *never* in a curved pattern around the disc. Why? Error correction.

Data is stored on an optical disc sequentially—that is, each bit of a file is followed by the next bit of the same file, until all the bits are stored. Then an end-of-file indicator is stored, after which the first bit of another file can be stored.

If a linear scratch (say, crossing from the disc edge to its center) damages the disc, error correction will likely make it possible to reconstruct the few individual bits that the scratch damaged from the bits that come before and after it. (And in the case of an audio CD, the damaged bits will most likely just be ignored—you probably won't hear the difference.) Because the scratch is linear and the data is stored around the curve, a scratch of this type is unlikely to destroy a huge succession of bits.

A curved scratch, on the other hand, could destroy an entire file, or many files, making error correction useless. Curved scratches are most likely to occur if you wipe a disc in a curved manner. Thus, always wipe linearly from edge to center.

Now, let's look at how data is read from a CD or DVD. In the case of both types of drives, a small laser is used to provide the optical source (the light) required. The laser light is shined through a lens that focuses it and aims it at the metal foil inside the plastic disc. Depending on the condition of each tiny spot on the foil where the light hits, the light is either reflected back through the lens at a bit of "receiver" electronics, or else is not reflected (it's diffused) back.

These two conditions—reflected or not—are the optical disc's analogue to a magnetic drive's domain polarity and your PC's ones and zeros. These truly microscopic areas on the foil are called *pits* or *lands*, respectively, depending on whether that spot of the foil has been dented (so the light doesn't reflect) or not (so it does). As the disc spins, these pits and lands come under the eye of the drive's lens. And the pulses of light they send back to the drive are translated into bits and bytes that are usually moved into your PC's memory across the IDE interface—the same interface shared by your hard disk.

How are the original CDs and DVDs manufactured? Not with a laser, as you might suppose. They're actually pressed. A master disc is made and the raw foil that will be sandwiched inside the optical disc is compressed, a process that creates the pits and lands I mentioned a moment ago. In this way, optical discs are more like old vinyl LPs than they are like magnetic storage. (Optical discs also store their data in one long, spiral track, like LPs do; magnetic drives consist of many tracks arranged in concentric rings.)

Naturally, the process of creating optical discs is precise, which is why CDs were originally so expensive. Now that CDs and DVDs can be manufactured for pennies, you might expect their price to drop. You'd be wrong.

Rewritable and Recordable Discs

How data is written to a recordable CD or DVD is a much more complicated matter, and here, huge differences between the two types of disc emerge. If manufactured discs are pressed, how, then, is data stored on recordable discs? In brief, the pits and lands must be created *optically*. While an optical drive is reading data, its laser operates at a low power level. The light-sensing electronics are sensitive and precise; it doesn't take much light to do the job.

Lingo   When I use the term *light*, I don't necessarily mean visible light. CD drives use light in the infrared range of the spectrum; DVDs generally use a red laser beam, and drives using blue lasers are being developed that can increase DVD capacity by a factor of four.

However, to create pits and lands requires so much energy that if you remove a recordable CD or DVD from its drive immediately after it has been recorded, it will almost always feel warm. A variety of methods are used for making the necessary pits and lands, but they all involve the laser beam creating an area of intense heat at a precise spot—one spot for each binary *bit* of data you want to store—on the disc. This heat changes the molecular structure of either the foil inside the disc or of a special dye or crystal material that coats that foil.

As a result, nonreflective spots (pits) are created on the disc to contrast with the disc's perfect, reflective natural state. The unaltered spots still reflect light back and become the disc's lands. By flashing the laser on and off as the disc spins over the lens mechanism (at speeds up to an excess of 8900 RPM), bit after bit—one or zero—is recorded to the disc.

In the case of recordable CDs and DVDs, it's a one-time process. Once the disc is altered by the drive's laser, that's it. Optical discs have an estimated life of 90 years, and the data won't fade or change over that time. Discs given the name *rewritable*, however, are made in such a way that—by setting the laser to an even higher power level—data written to them can be erased, and new pits and lands can replace the ones previously present. Currently, rewritable CDs and DVDs should be able to be erased and reused roughly 999 times.

Speed Factors

When you're considering the purchase of an optical drive, you'll want to consider two factors: maximum speeds and drive cache memory. While a hard drive's cache memory is most useful for reading data, an optical drive's cache is vital when it comes time to write (or record, if you prefer) data. This is so because an optical drive sometimes writes data faster than a PC can consistently provide it to the drive. When that happens, an error called a *buffer under-run* occurs, and the disc is usually useless (unless it's rewritable, of course). It's exceptionally annoying to take the time to record a CD or DVD, only to have the process fail near the end because your PC got busy with receiving e-mail or something similar.

Although I strongly recommend using your PC for nothing else while you're recording optically, new optical drives use their memory cache to increase the size of their write buffer. In this way, the PC can send data to the drive when it has processor power available, and the drive will read that data from its memory cache, rather than directly from the PC. If the PC gets busy and stops sending data for a fraction of a second, the optical drive still has data in its cache memory to write. A buffer under-run occurs only if the PC is busy for so long, all the data in the drive's cache gets recorded first.

As you'd expect, recording faster means that data moves out of that drive cache faster, too—so consistent, high-speed recording relies on a larger cache. At the time of this writing, it's uncommon for drives to have a cache of 8 MB or more. Unless your PC is seriously underpowered for the drive you're trying to use—balanced integration, again—a cache of this size should be more than sufficient for today's highest drive speeds.

And what are those speeds, in fact? When it comes to read speeds, it's common to see numbers like 54X. The *X* is a fudge factor. Its presence indicates that this particular drive can read data up to 54 times faster than the rate data is read from an original-style audio CD, which is 150 kilobytes (KB) per second.

When it comes to writing data, *X* still means *times*, as it did back in primary school. Currently, the newest recordable CD drives can write at speeds up to 20X and rewrite at speeds up to 8X. DVD writers—of which there are several, incompatible formats—can currently write or rewrite DVD data at 2.4X and read it at 8X.

DVD Recordable Formats

Although basically only two different types of recordable CDs exist—a write-once format (CD-R) and a rewritable format (CD-RW), numerous DVD formats exist, and no clear, single winner has yet emerged at the time of this writing. The format that appears to be the winner in terms of technology, compatibility, and cost is called DVD+RW, but it is unclear whether this format will ultimately prevail. This format's high compatibility—you can create video DVDs that will play in any newer DVD video player—presents a considerable threat to copyright (because if you can create, you can copy). Consequently, a lot of DVD drive manufacturers are developing technologies that are far less compatible, such as DVD-RAM, DVD-RW, and DVD-R.

Rewritable (DVD-RW) and write-once (DVD-R) formats have a number of faults, relative to DVD+RW. First, while a DVD+RW disc can be used like a hard drive or giant floppy disk—a little data written today, a little more written tomorrow, a single file erased and replaced with an update, and so forth—the DVD-RW format forces the erasure and rewriting of the entire disc to effect even the most minor change. This can hardly be seen as convenient.

Also, DVD-RW does not support error correction, significantly increasing the likelihood that slight damage to the disc will render it useless (whether a scratch is linear or otherwise). This factor also means that small defects in the disc's surface or even the most minor flickers in the process of writing to the disc will likely be unrecoverable. The DVD+RW format is currently 2.4 times faster than the rewritable format supported by DVD-RW. The DVD-RW format also supports only a reduced-quality video encoding, which will guarantee movie studios that end users won't use the drives to duplicate copyrighted material. And did I mention that DVD+RW drives and media are significantly cheaper than those of the other formats? Well, they are. Which format is best for you?

Key Points

- Memory and storage are quite different. Memory is a temporary workspace where data and programs are kept while you and your PC are using them. Storage provides a long-term means of maintaining data in the form of files.

- Storage is of two basic types: magnetic storage like hard disks and floppy disks, and optical storage like CDs and DVDs.

- Hard drives generally connect to your PC through the IDE interface.

- Hard drives read data by using an electromagnetic read/write head to sense the changing polarity of a magnetic material on the disk's platters.

■   Hard drives write data by reversing the process, sending electrical impulses into the read/write head, which actually change that magnetic material's polarity in tiny regions called domains.

■   Optical drives use a laser beam to read or write data. For reading, the beam is focused on tiny spots on the disc. Depending on whether the beam is reflected back to a receiving sensor or not, each spot on the disc can be interpreted as a binary one or zero.

■   Reflective spots on an optical disc are called lands; nonreflective spots are called pits.

■   To write data, optical drives use their laser beams set to a high power that physically alters a material coating the disc's base. These changes form reflective or nonreflective spots, producing the optical disc's version of binary ones and zeros.

Chapter 6

Increasing the Volume

Few issues in the computing world have been more controversial recently than those concerning digital *content*: video, images, and sound. The discussions about these issues have centered largely around the question of who owns content. Under today's laws, if you buy a CD or a DVD video, you own it, but you can't make copies of it and share them with friends. You can share the original with friends, although at the time of this writing, there is legislation heading for the U.S. Congress that would make that illegal. In the past, the U.S. Supreme Court soundly rejected arguments that would have restricted the public's right to exercise some level of control over content. So why are the same arguments back? Why are these arguments moving to the newspaper's front page and increasing in volume?

These questions are important because the answers will likely change many of the entertainment and educational opportunities that we take for granted. All these controversies and challenges to public rights stem from one distinction: the difference between analog and digital. In this chapter, we'll take a look at why this distinction is one of the most significant technological contrasts of all time, especially with regard to digital sound and music. Understanding how digital content works will give you the power to really enjoy and benefit from it, personally and professionally. That same understanding will better equip you to be a participatory citizen, able to join in all the discussions that will affect your future, one way or another.

Speaking of Digital

You've probably noticed that when you make a copy of a cassette tape, a little bit of the quality of the original sound is lost, and a little bit of tape noise is introduced, even if your recorder has all the latest bells and whistles. Every time you make a copy of a copy, the process is repeated until, 14 generations down the road, most of the quality is lost. The reason is that the signal that gets laid down on an old magnetic audiocassette is a continuous, analog signal. Its qualities vary continuously, like the sine wave I showed you back in Chapter 4 (repeated again in Figure 6-1 for your convenience).

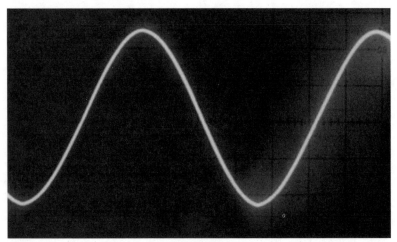

Figure 6-1 A sine wave has an electrical value that varies continuously over its period (the time it takes for the entire wave to repeat itself) and its amplitude (the maximum and minimum values for the wave).

Because the recording on an old cassette is analog and continuous, the only way to make a copy is to play the tape and have another recorder "listen" to the continuously changing signal. If the recorders' electrical environment is noisy, the recorder doing the copying will do the best it can to lay down what it "hears," but nobody's hearing is perfect—not even a machine's. If you've got good quality recorders, the first-generation analog copy probably sounds close to the original—so close that most people won't notice any difference. But the effects of a machine's bad hearing are additive. When you start making an analog copy of a copy of a copy, the quality quickly erodes. At some point, if you really want to hear what was recorded, you'll end up going out and buying the original.

This was, in fact, exactly what the producers of music (and later, movie and TV) programs were counting on. When the courts defeated their original attempts to make it illegal to tape *anything*, they reassured themselves with the sound (excuse the pun) knowledge that copies wouldn't proliferate too far, and anybody who wanted a really good copy would just buy one. This was especially true in the world of video where a VCR's inherently "poor vision" was much more obvious than a cassette recorder's "poor hearing." (Eventually, a copy-defeat scheme was devised for video which made it impossible to duplicate protected videotapes if you were one of the tens of millions of people who *didn't* own a time-base corrector. We'll talk about video copy protection briefly in the next chapter.)

When consumer digital audio premiered in the form of the compact disc (CD), nothing changed. The sound quality of CDs was as good as or better than that of LP records—at least, to most ears—but cassette tape recorders had the same hearing impairment they always had. The ever-increasing quality of home and car audio equipment started to make even the small flaws in a first-generation tape audible, so people slowly began to purchase their own CDs when they wanted high-quality music. Eventually, the first automobile and portable CD players emerged, around 1984, and CD popularity really took off. A decade later, everything changed. In September 1995, Hewlett-Packard introduced the first consumer-affordable digital CD recorder.

Oh, there were problems. A recordable CD could hold only about 70 minutes of music—fully 20 minutes less than the most popular length of audio cassette. The recorders were originally more than twice what an excellent cassette tape deck cost. The blank media also cost roughly twice what a high-quality blank cassette cost—and early CD media could be used only once. Blanks were hard to find if you didn't have a computer store in your neighborhood. Recorded CDs originally wouldn't play in regular CD players, and so forth. But none of these problems changed the most important development in the history of consumer audio: CD copies were perfect.

The Trouble with Digital

So what's the problem? In all likelihood, a perfect copy of an audio CD is probably going to inspire listeners to do just one thing: listen to it. Reputable evidence proves that people who originally have a copy of a CD they enjoy do eventually purchase it. But they don't *have* to purchase it to own the full-quality experience of that CD, and there's the rub. Put frankly, nobody cared that you could copy stuff when all those copies were inferior. But when you and Mega-MusicMillionaires, Inc., can produce CDs of equal quality—well, that's threatening. And so, we have all of the controversy and legal challenges I mentioned earlier.

Content providers take the view that while you might own the physical CD or DVD, they own what's on it—forever. Knowing that the American public will not refuse to buy entertainment, they have taken an approach of "Play by new rules, or we'll take our content and leave." So the rules are changing because technology has made it possible to do something today that nobody anticipated the last time "the rules" were written. The digital world is inherently a perfect world, so a digital copy is a perfect copy.

Let's look at an example. If you take one of your old cassette recordings and feed it into your computer, you can record it onto a CD. Of course, that CD recording will have all of the tape noise and deterioration that your 20-year-old tape does, but let's simplify things and pretend for a second that your tapes are nearly perfect. If you make a copy of the CD for a friend, that copy will be—bit for bit—an exact duplicate of your original CD. How?

The CD player in your computer doesn't "listen" to the sound and send it out for recording; it reads the digital bits on the disc—reading them multiple times if necessary to guarantee it's read them perfectly—and that stream of bits flows to your CD recorder, which burns them to a blank disc, one bit at a time. The whole process of turning those bits into music you can listen to (digital-to-analog conversion) is bypassed. This is called *digital audio extraction.*

Although many of the first-generation computer CD players couldn't do it, today's computer CD drives can perform flawless digital audio extraction at many times the CD's normal play speed. You can copy 70 minutes of CD music in about 4 minutes—and even faster if you save the digital sound to your hard drive, rather than writing it to a blank CD.

How Digital Sound Works

But what is digital sound in the first place? For that matter, what is sound? As I said once before, the world we live in is an analog world, and sound—as part of that world—is an analog thing. Sound is nothing more than the movement of a pressure-wave through the air. When I speak, my lungs push air out of my mouth, past my vocal cords. My vocal cords vibrate and change the flow of that air, and my lips and tongue shape the flow even further. When the air finally gets outside my body, the vibrations and shaping of it are passed on to the air in the room between you and me, like the ripples of a pebble tossed into a pond.

Eventually, the waves of vibrating air—*sound waves*—reach the surface of your eardrums, which vibrate. That causes changes in your auditory nerves, which your brain interprets, giving you your sense of hearing. The process is much the same if the sound source is an instrument like a piano or violin. The instrument's string vibrates, and these vibrations propagate as sound waves through the air around the instrument to the ears of the audience. A microphone is nothing more than a sensitive "electronic ear" that detects the moving sound waves much the way your eardrums do.

The flow of speech from our bodies or music from an instrument is a continuous thing, and sound waves propagate as continuous, ever-changing signals. Because that's the definition of an analog signal, sound is analog. Sound waves are measured by the *frequency* with which they cause the air they pass through to vibrate. These vibrations are measured on a scale called *hertz*, after Gustav Ludwig Hertz, a German physicist whose work with electromagnetic waves paved the way for the early development of radio.

A measurement of 1 hertz (abbreviated Hz) means that the moving wave (in this case, a sound wave) is causing one vibration per second. The slower the vibration, the lower (more bass) the pitch of the sound; the faster the vibration, the higher (more treble) the pitch, or tone. Humans can hear sound waves from between 20 Hz up to 20,000 Hz (which is usually written as 20 kHz, or 20 kilohertz). Of course, if you're hearing a sound that is at all complex, you'll be hearing hundreds of frequencies at once.

The vibration *frequency* of a sound wave causes additional waves to be generated at frequencies that are directly related to the original frequency (called the *fundamental*). Because of this close relationship, these secondary waves are called overtones, or *harmonics*—they exist in harmony with the original wave. Harmonics give body and depth to a sound and are the basis of *timbre* (pronounced "tambur"), which is the jargon for why a piano doesn't sound like a trumpet or a cell phone.

So much jargon—frequency, fundamentals, hertz, timbre! But sound and hearing are pretty complicated things. Fortunately, doing some really amazing things with digital audio doesn't require a Ph.D. in either acoustics or psycho-acoustics. What you've just read and what you'll find in the rest of this chapter will set you well on your way.

From Analog to Digital: A Journey of 44,100 Steps

You know that sound is an analog wave, and you know that our ears respond directly to the stimulus of those waves and we hear. But computers don't have ears. A microphone might work a bit like an electronic ear in the way it also responds directly to sound waves, but your computer can't do anything with the signal that comes out of a microphone—that's an analog signal, too.

Note   That analog signal is measured in voltage, not frequency, because a microphone directly converts the frequencies of an analog sound wave into the corresponding, continuously changing voltages of an analog electrical signal.

To bridge from our analog world to the PC's digital world, we need an analog-to-digital converter (ADC). A lot of analog-to-digital conversion happens around multimedia, but when analog sound waves are converted to digital signals, we call that process *sampling*.

Unlike our brains and bodies, the PC doesn't do anything continuously. Everything that happens inside the PC or in the peripherals and networks attached to it happens only occasionally. Those "occasions" might take place 2 million times a second, but they don't happen all the time. The natural, analog world is like infinity—continuous forever. The digital world is like trying to count to infinity: no matter how many times a computer's clock subdivides a second, it will always be possible to divide that second further and process more in the same time. At no speed is a computer ever working continuously.

The process of making analog audio something a PC can digest is, then, the process of sampling—taking a little clip of sound here, a little clip of sound there. Each *clip*, that is, each sample, has a numeric value that represents an encoded form of the sound frequencies the PC encountered during that particular clip. Sampling turns sound into numbers. Because numbers can be processed and stored digitally, sampling turns analog sound waves into digital data. That data can later be fed through a digital-to-analog converter (DAC), sent to speakers, and turned back into sound waves: *digital sound*.

If the PC gets enough clips of sound fast enough—if the *rate* of its sampling is high enough—the quality of the digital sound will closely approximate that of the original analog signal. But what's fast enough, and what's reasonable? The digital audio industry has come up with a standard answer, at least for compact discs: a sampling rate of 44,100 times per second produces analog-quality sound. Where did they get that number?

Remember earlier I said that human ears can hear sounds in excess of 20,000 Hz? The actual number is closer to 22,050 Hz, which is a frequency that is exactly half of 44,100 times per second. If you want to accurately sample an analog wave, you've got to sample it at least twice as fast as the fastest frequency in that wave. So if you want to capture sound in the full range of human hearing—up to 22,050 Hz, you've got to use a sampling rate of 44,100 Hz, or 44.1 kHz, as you'll usually see it. In PC audio applications, this is referred to as *CD Quality Audio*, and lower sampling rates of lesser quality are also available.

Sound Bytes

Sampling rate is only part of the total digital audio picture. How big is a sample? Am I talking about 44,100 bits of sound? In the case of CD Quality Audio, a single sample is made up of a number that is 2 bytes (16 bits) long. The more bits contained in each sample, the more realistic the digital sound will be—at a sufficient sampling rate. Combine 44,100 samples per second with 16 bits per sample, and you get a high-quality stream of digital audio. Do the math, and it turns out that an audio CD should be able to store about 70 minutes of two-channel (stereo) music—which it does. Thus, 44,100 samples per channel per second times 16 bits per sample equals the roughly 700-megabyte (MB) capacity of an audio CD.

Certainly, it is possible to use more bits to encode each sample, but the disc capacity required has been completely unreasonable until recently. The forthcoming *DVD Audio* standard uses 24-bit samples (taken at 192 kHz) to provide the highest quality of digital audio ever. That's great, but it requires the capacity of a DVD to be useful. A total of 192,000 samples per second, per channel combined with a 3-byte sample size comes out to about 60 minutes of music fitting into a DVD's 4.6-gigabyte (GB) capacity. A compact disc could hold only 10 minutes of music at that sampling rate and bit depth.

When you record digital audio—that is, when you sample analog audio—you tell the PC which sampling rate you want to use, and which bit depth you want for each sample. Again, 44,100 samples/sec combined with a 16 bits/sample depth provides audio quality equal to commercial CDs. In other words, this sample size and rate provides a digital sound that is as accurate to the original analog sound as commercial CDs are. A poorly recorded or noisy original piece of music doesn't miraculously improve in quality just because we sample it at CD Quality Audio. All we actually get is a CD-quality accurate recording of the noise.

Just as you can increase the sampling rate, you can reduce it. You'll be reducing the range of frequencies that you can sample, but that might not affect the quality of your recording, depending on what you sample. Audio of the spoken human voice can be successfully recorded at a sampling rate as low as 11 kHz, because the human voice fills the frequency range from 50 Hz to 5 kHz. (Most adult speech occurs right around 4 kHz, in fact.) Twice that frequency would be approximately 10 kHz. The digital audio industry went with 11.025 kHz because it multiplies nicely up to the standard 44.1 kHz sampling rate used for CDs.

You can also reduce the bit size of each sample, but that change will affect the quality of the digital sound, regardless of the sampling rate you choose and regardless of what you record. As with an 8-bit photograph, 8-bit audio might sound "blotchy" because an insufficient number of bits is being used to store the numerical value of each sample. Again, 16 bits gives us the quality of CD sound to which we're accustomed.

Windows XP Sound Recorder   You can take a look at the sorts of options available to you for recording and editing digital audio on your PC using software provided with Microsoft Windows XP. From the Start menu, select All Programs, Accessories, Entertainment, and finally, Sound Recorder. When the program starts, you will see the dialog box shown in Figure 6-2.

Figure 6-2 Sound Recorder is a useful tool provided with Windows XP that allows you to record, edit, and store digital sounds.

With a sound file loaded, from the File menu, select Save As, and then click Change at the bottom of the window. The Sound Selection dialog box, shown below, opens, which gives you options for saving a set of digital sound samples—collectively just called a *sample*—at a given sample rate and bit depth using a chosen encoding method. The Format box lists the encoding methods that Windows XP supports. Of these, PCM is the most common because it's the format used for compact disc audio. Many other formats exist, chief among which are the Windows Media Formats (two versions) and the MPEG3 audio format.

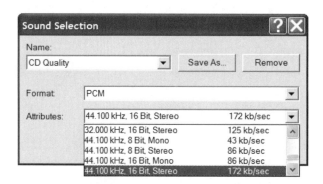

The Attributes drop-down list also shows the approximate amount of space the saved sample will require at each sampling rate and depth. The most frequently used options for the PCM format are shown in Table 6-1.

Table 6-1 PCM Format Options

Sample Rate (in kHz)	Bit Depth	Channels (Stereo/Mono)	Data Space per Second
11.025	8	Mono	10 kilobits (kb)
11.025	8	Stereo	21 kb
11.025	16	Mono	21 kb
11.025	16	Stereo	43 kb
22.050	8	Mono	21 kb
22.050	8	Stereo	43 kb
22.050	16	Mono	43 kb
22.050	16	Stereo	86 kb
44.1	8	Mono	43 kb
44.1	8	Stereo	86 kb
44.1	16	Mono	86 kb
44.1	16	Stereo	172 kb

See Also   *We'll play around with Sound Recorder in Chapter 11, "Your* Personal *Personal* Computer."

What's a Sound Card?

A *sound card* is a card that makes sounds—and I'm not being sarcastic here. The term *sound card* is something of an historical one because many PCs today have all of their support for audio provided by circuitry built onto the motherboard. If the technical specs for a new PC include the rather dubious phrases *Integrated Audio* or *Audio Support*, the motherboard provides all of the system's sound support. Your speakers plug directly into a socket on this system's motherboard, and you're all set. Integrated audio became all the rage about a year ago when it became cost-effective for motherboard manufacturers to provide basic audio capabilities as a feature of their own product. Before that, a PC could make only a few annoying buzzing, beeping sounds unless you installed a sound adapter card into it.

How does a sound card do its job? Sound cards are relatively simple devices that convert digital signals into analog waves—they're digital-to-analog converters. Most sound cards can convert the other way too, turning an analog input into digital sound. It was originally the job of each piece of software that needed to produce sounds to know how to communicate with each proprietary sound card available. But these days, the job of making a sound card work belongs to the operating system: Windows itself.

Microsoft has developed a number of audio methodologies that it incorporated into DirectX, the collection of multimedia tools you read about in Chapter 4. Games and other audio-enhanced software use DirectX to talk to Windows XP, and Windows XP uses its hardware driver library to talk to whatever audio card or support your system contains. This arrangement allows for the best of both worlds. Cards can be proprietary and provide cutting-edge audio capabilities, but card manufacturers provide Windows drivers that establish standard ways of accessing a card's potential.

Your PC's overall audio capabilities, whether built-in or provided by an adapter card, fall into one of two different camps. Part of the sound card hardware manipulates *digital audio* signals. This includes CD audio, music clips that you purchase over the Internet, the audio portion of a digital video, *streaming audio*, and even the music and beeps that make up the Windows XP system and startup sounds. This same part of the audio card provides your PC's audio recording and sampling capabilities.

Lingo   *Streaming audio* is sound that is transmitted over the Internet to your PC live, as you listen to it.

The second part of practically every audio card is a *Musical Instrument Digital Interface (MIDI)* synthesizer. In its latest incarnations, this device uses specially crafted samples of the sounds of music instruments to place an orchestra inside your PC. Let's take a look at the key features of each of these parts.

Digital Audio

As you might expect, a large part of a sound card's total circuitry is devoted to the sampling and converting of all that digital data. Most of a card's capabilities are part of a single chip or chipset, called the *digital signal processor (DSP)*. A number of these exist, and each is proprietary. Along with basic sampling and DAC/ADC capabilities, a sound card's DSP provides a number of tools that are useful for modifying the quality of the card's sound.

Chief among these tools is *equalization*—the ability to enhance certain frequencies of sound and subdue others. If you happen to like a lot of bass boom in your music, you can simply equalize the sound card's overall output to boost the lowest frequencies. Although most sound cards come with a proprietary equalizer, the Microsoft Windows Media Player (shown in Figure 6-3) includes an equalizer (EQ) that will work with whichever sound card you have installed.

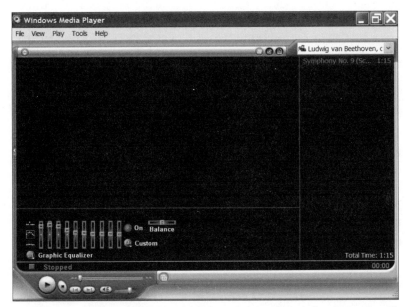

Figure 6-3 The Windows Media Player provides a digital audio equalizer that works with any Windows XP-supported sound card.

The drop-down menu to the right of the equalizer sliders gives quick access to a variety of EQ presets, customized for different genres of music—rap, techno, rock, country, and more, including special settings that provide the best sound quality from streaming audio over a standard 56K modem connection.

Another major characteristic of a sound card's DSP—and something of a recent development in the digital audio world—is its support for certain types of three-dimensional (3D) audio effects and multitrack emulations like Dolby Digital. 3D audio effects modify the sound wave, altering phase and other characteristics of it to trick your ears into thinking that two speakers are actually four or more, with you at the center. This feature is particularly popular in video games—you can hear the bad guys sneaking up behind you or a spaceship flying above you.

Dolby Digital, on the other hand, is a high-quality proprietary system that uses up to five actual speakers and a subwoofer to provide true 3D sound. The sound source—usually the audio track of a DVD movie—must be encoded as a Dolby Digital soundtrack, and the special hardware on the sound card simply decodes the Dolby instructions, sending certain sounds to certain speakers. High-end sound cards can provide an optical digital connection for use with a

DVD drive's optical audio output. Combining these capabilities, your PC can provide a home theater experience right at your desktop.

At the more professional end of the scale, sound cards can provide support for the special connector used by digital audio tape (DAT) recorders. Because DAT is used in most recording studios, this connection makes it possible to get studio digital music off a DAT tape into your PC where you can edit it and send it back to DAT without any loss of quality. Producers of digital video also use this connection to transfer high-quality audio and music from studio DAT recorders to the PC, where they will be combined with digital video and output to a recordable DVD. Today's $200 sound cards put tools at your fingertips that would have cost you well over $100,000 just five years ago.

MIDI

The second major component of any modern sound card is its MIDI synthesizer. MIDI allows multiple synthesizers (and some other devices) to be connected together in a long chain. What's special about MIDI—and the primary factor that separates it from the rest of the digital audio your PC can produce—is that MIDI doesn't transmit music. It transmits musical instructions.

Instructions to turn notes on and off, change the quality of sound played, and many other characteristics are shared in the form of messages over 16 standard channels (up to 256 channels, today) that can operate independently, each producing its own type of sound. A message might be *System-Exclusive*, meaning that its content will be acted upon by only one MIDI synthesizer in the chain, or it might be a general message that all interconnected MIDI devices will obey. Instructions are also channel-specific, so certain note instructions can be sent on one channel and played with an oboe sound while other instructions are sent on a different channel and played as a flute.

All these instructions are stored in MIDI-format files, saved on proprietary disks or on a PC. MIDI files are tiny compared to digital audio files because the actual music isn't saved; only instructions for producing music are saved. A piece of music I composed a couple of years back fits into a 50 kilobyte (KB) MIDI file. The CD Quality Audio version of that music being performed takes up about 200 MB of disk space!

All of the MIDI instructions are managed by a piece of software called a *sequencer*. The sequencer keeps all 16 channels of MIDI instructions synchronized to a clock, and a good sequencer provides high-quality editing capabilities. If you connect a MIDI keyboard to the MIDI port of your sound card, most recording sequencers can capture a live performance exactly as you play it.

However, any mistakes in a live performance can be edited and corrected in the MIDI file. When the edited file is played, the "live" performance will be perfect.

Moreover, you can record a different live performance to each of the channels in a MIDI file, and the sequencer will play back all channels at once, with each channel's notes sounding like whichever instrument you select. That allows one person to play many different instrumental parts; when played back, the piece will sound like an orchestral ensemble!

The Windows Media Player includes a play-only sequencer. If you've ever surfed to a Web page and heard instrumental music playing, you've listened to the Media Player. It downloads the small MIDI file when Internet Explorer is opening the Web page, then automatically executes the MIDI instructions—which cause your sound card's synthesizer to play.

For the first 15 years of MIDI, most synthesizers produced a proprietary collection of sounds. But today, most mainstream MIDI synthesizers (including those provided on PC audio cards) adhere to a *General MIDI (GM)* standard. Included in that standard is regulation of which sounds (often called *patches*) a synthesizer will produce and their order in a numbered list. Thus, GM instrument number 1 is always an acoustic piano; instrument number 69 is always an oboe, and so forth. Better synthesizers produce better-sounding pianos and oboes, but a piece of music written to the GM standard and played on GM hardware sounds as much like what the composer wanted as possible. Synthesizers continue to provide proprietary sounds, of course, but these are accessed separately from the GM sounds, using different instrument numbers.

Many MIDI synthesizers—particularly those built into PC audio cards—support the use of software-based sound patch libraries, or *sound banks*. Consequently, the synthesizer can play new or customized sounds that are downloaded into the synthesizer by software. For example, you can purchase a collection of high-quality piano sounds, guitar sounds, or steam train whistle sounds on disk. Once loaded into the synth, these new sounds are immediately available to enhance a performance or composition.

How are these sounds made? In general, multiple digital audio samples are taken of each note the original instrument can play. These samples are combined by the computer during playback, depending on the characteristics of the "note on" instructions sent over the MIDI channels. In high-quality synthesizers, the result is remarkably hard to distinguish from the original.

Any sound that can be digitally sampled—which is to say, any sound that can be heard—can be fed into a MIDI synthesizer's sound banks and associated with one or more musical notes. You could even take the sound of your own voice and map it to the notes of the synthesizer. You could also use percussive samples, like the sounds of drums, cowbells, and triangles, load them into the synthesizer, and provide yourself with a complete MIDI drum kit. Of course, these samples need to be short. If you want each note on a synthesizer to sound like a choir singing that note, you need to have a small sample of a choir singing a note—not an opera.

MIDI has been an important development for musicians and composers. A composer can sit alone at home and command the attention of a complete symphony (or, of course, a chorus of cowbells). Musicians can now produce demo tapes of their work without the expense of paying others to play. Film students can join forces with music students and produce professional-quality video with a complete, original orchestral score. All of it gets mixed inside the PC and then written to a recordable DVD. You can take the sound of your children singing, combine it with a MIDI performance of the same song and digital home video, and create a gift that no grandparent would ever forget.

See Also   *We'll start to talk about how to make this kind of magic in Chapter 7.*

Quality Concerns and Compression

MIDI is great, but even the best MIDI synthesizers don't sound quite like the original acoustic instruments. MIDI can give you a performance of a violin concerto, but it can't give you a performance of Itzhak Perlman. MIDI can't immortalize a famous speech or your daughter's first words. And you can't compose a piece of MIDI music and have your PC perform it and burn it automatically to a CD to share with friends—except on a select number of higher-end sound cards. Digital audio can do all of those things MIDI can't, but digital audio has its limitations, too. And the biggest of these limitations is, literally, *big*. CD Quality Digital sound files are simply huge. The chart in Figure 6-4 shows how digital audio files compare with others.

When you start taking 44,100 samples per second at 2 bytes per sample, it adds up fast. Naturally, you can use fewer samples and reduce the size of each of them, but then you don't have CD Quality Audio anymore, and somewhere along the line, you're going to notice the difference if you try to save disk space this way. You've got to use a sample rate that's twice as fast as the highest frequency you want to record digitally. Some instruments' notes (and, especially, their harmonics) will be lost. You're trading quality for size.

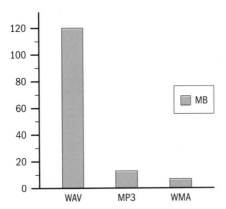

Figure 6-4 This simple chart compares the size of a CD Quality Digital audio file with other versions of the same audio.

I'm sure you intuitively understand some of the reasons why size is a problem. Although storage space on your PC isn't nearly as expensive as it once was, it's certainly not free, and it's definitely not infinite. If you have a 100 GB hard disk, you could store about 140 CDs on it (making the false assumption that Windows XP and your applications don't take up any room—which they do). Maybe that sounds like a lot of music to you, but most of us who play around a lot with digital audio are amazed at how quickly our hard disks fill. Traditional *WAV* audio files (by which I mean audio files that are encoded using a certain scheme and that traditionally have a .wav extension in their file names) often don't compress much in Windows compressed folders.

So what's a music lover to do? If you can't reduce the sample rate or sample size without losing quality, and you can't compress, what's left?

Lossy Compression Is Key

What's left is a different kind of compression for digital audio files. Two major types of compression exist. The first type is used by Windows Compressed Folders (which produce files with a .zip extension), and it's *lossless*. That means that, the way the compression is done, no data is lost, and when you decompress the file, what you get back is the exact, original file. But this method doesn't work well for WAV files because WAV is a pretty efficient, compressed algorithm to begin with.

The other type of compression is called *lossy*, which means that to compress the file, data is actually thrown away. You can never reconstruct the exact original file from a file that's been lossy compressed. But what good is lossy compression if you're throwing away data? Isn't that the same as reducing the sample rate, or shrinking the sample size?

In a word, no. There's a lot of data in your standard, everyday digital audio file that isn't important because you can't hear it anyway. That's the data that gets thrown out in lossy compression. The different lossy compression methods use quite a few tricks about human hearing to discard the data that represents stuff you'll never hear in the first place. Let me give you an example.

When there's a spot in a piece of music where certain frequencies are really loud, whether it's trumpets, a synthesizer, or Laurie Anderson's electric violin, your ears are going to hear only those frequencies. Sampling that music at 44.1 kHz is fine, but that process saves room (in acoustics lingo, it's called *bandwidth*) for all the frequencies you could hear—whether you're going to hear them or not. Much more efficient is sampling the music at the normal 44.1 kHz, and then throwing away everything that the listener can't hear. If you do just that, you can easily reduce the size of that music's digital audio file from huge and ungainly to merely big. If you apply additional techniques that strip out unnecessary data, you can shrink the file from big to manageable.

So this is exactly what you do. How much compression you actually get from these methods is variable, because the result directly depends on the nature of the sound you're trying to compress. Recall that the human voice generally uses only about 5 kHz of frequency bandwidth. But an audiobook on CD stores that speech in 44.1 kHz of bandwidth. Throw away everything that's not used, and your file size drops—not just by a factor of 9 (44.1 rounds up to 45, divided by 5, giving you a factor of 9), but by a good deal more. Naturally, music doesn't compress nearly as well, and if you try to force it into ever-smaller packages, you will start discarding sound that you would have heard, and your quality will suffer quickly.

What, Exactly, Is MP3? MP3 is the previous generation's state-of-the-art format for storing (lossy) compressed digital audio on the PC. Its name comes from the Motion Picture Experts Group (MPEG), the folks who came up with most of the standards for putting video (and audio) onto DVDs. And it's called MP3 by folks like us because its formal name is MPEG Layer-3 Audio. MP3 was the first really popular format for compressing audio because it was the first to provide near-CD-quality sound from files that were small enough to store and move around.

With MP3 files and a typical digital subscriber line (DSL) connection, it's possible to share an entire CD in minutes. Some people began to share content so much that all the controversies I mentioned at the start of this chapter began. There's no question that, used responsibly, MP3 is marvelous. Portable CD players and DVD players often now support MP3 files, which means that you can fit several hours of sound onto a CD and take it anywhere you want to go. Although MP3 doesn't provide perfect CD-quality sound, the format is well-suited to the portable environment such as the gym, where you're not expecting to have perfect speakers, perfect acoustics, or a perfect listening experience.

I said that MP3 is the previous generation's top-of-the-line music compression format because the Windows Media Audio (WMA) format has made tremendous strides. As you'll see in the next section, it provides music at a better quality than MP3 from files that are smaller—and it's designed to help content owners relax, too.

Windows Media Player

Windows Media Player has been around since Windows 95. Although the name is still the same, it's now more of a one-stop-shopping media tool than it ever used to be. Windows Media Player 8, the version that comes with Windows XP, is an integrated tool that can take care of just about anything you'd want to do with digital audio. (Media Player also plays MIDI files, but you need separate sequencing software or hardware to create and edit them.)

What sorts of things might you want to do? Well, how about copying your favorite songs from CD to your notebook computer so you can listen to them on the road without carrying all those discs around? How about relaxing while soothing colors dance in front of you as you sip a glass of something pleasant and let the stress of work slip away? How about burning your own music CDs at high speed without buying any expensive software?

Windows Media Player (which I'll call "the Player" for short) does all of that, as well as running almost any multimedia you encounter while surfing around the Web, cataloging your music library, even storing song lyrics. The Player is a great tool. When you first start it, it'll look something like what you see in Figure 6-5. Its exact appearance depends on your screen resolution, and whether you or anyone else has run the Player before and changed its settings—and there are quite a few of these. You can even change the Player's "skin" (appearance) so that it looks different from what you get out of the box.

Figure 6-5 Windows Media Player puts all your digital content at your fingertips.

To select a new appearance for your Player, just start it (from the Start menu, select Programs, Accessories, and then Entertainment), and select the View menu to make sure you're looking at Full Mode. Once there, select Taskbar from the View menu and click Skin Chooser. You'll see a window like that in Figure 6-6.

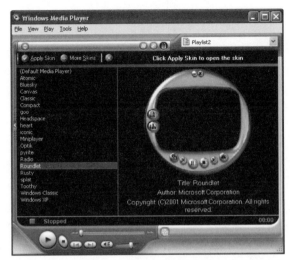

Figure 6-6 Changing the Player's skin is really easy, and it helps make your PC feel just a little more like yours.

Here you can choose from the installed skins and click Apply Skin in the upper left corner of the window. Your Player will switch to Skin Mode, and you'll see a small window in the lower right corner of your screen, as in Figure 6-7. Just click the button in the center of that window to open a menu that will take you back to Full Mode or to other options. Naturally, some skins are easier to navigate around than others.

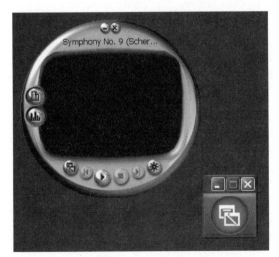

Figure 6-7 After you select a skin for the Player, you'll find yourself in Skin Mode.

One of the great features of the Player is the way it can automatically catalog all of your media into a library—again, it's all about working smarter, putting all of the good stuff where you can get to it faster. Whenever you copy from a CD, that content is automatically added to your Media Library. You can also have the Player search your entire PC for digital media, which it will organize for you. This strategy is a lot faster than using the Start menu's Search command when you're trying to find a piece of music or a snippet of home video.

Adding all of your media to the library is easy, too. From within the Player, select Search For Media Files from the Tools menu, or just press the F3 key. The Search For Media Files dialog box shown in Figure 6-8 will open. Click the Advanced button to display all of your options.

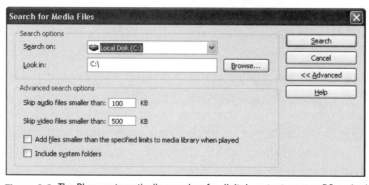

Figure 6-8 The Player automatically searches for digital content on your PC and add it to your Media Library.

Two of the four Advanced options are especially useful. You can have the Player perform all of the media on your PC for you automatically if you just want some background music—but all of the Windows system sounds are stored in digital audio files, too. Fortunately, most of these are small files, indeed, and by excluding small audio files (say, files smaller than 400 KB—a setting I recommend over the 100 KB default), you'll prevent all the toots, whistles, plunks, and booms from being cataloged and played as though they were your favorites.

Similarly, excluding video files smaller than 1000 KB will make sure that a performance of all your home movies doesn't get interrupted with a short video clip on how to benefit from WidgetWare's Carbuncle Digitizer. Set your options and verify where you want the search performed, and click Search. When the process is complete, you'll see that the Player has found a place for all of your digital stuff, as in Figure 6-9.

Figure 6-9 The Player's Media Library automatically categorizes your digital content—here, my Windows XP sample music has been sorted by artist.

Note Even though your digital content will be organized into several different categories—each song by album, artist, and genre, for example—don't worry that your disk space is vanishing. The Media Library is just a cross-index. It doesn't copy or duplicate any of your files. It just makes them easier to find.

Ripping CDs and a Replacement for MP3

The Player has been able to play CD audio for many years now, and a great relief it was to those of us who just hated the different CD player tools out there at the time. Windows Media Player 8 goes a step further than earlier versions and lets you copy CD music directly to your hard disk without the need for any third-party software. The distinction here is key: older versions of the Player let you play CDs on your PC, but it used to be necessary to buy extra software—which usually cost over half of what you paid for all of Windows XP—to actually copy CD music to files on your hard disk, a process called *ripping*. The digital audio extraction I mentioned earlier is a form of ripping.

The Player provides high-speed digital audio extraction much faster than the regular music-playing speed. Combine this with the Player's built-in CD-burning capabilities, and you can copy a CD to your PC and write it back to a new CD in mere minutes—some nice new capabilities. Imagine you're responsible for your company's marketing plan and you've just received an express delivery of a CD with the music commissioned for the campaign. You've got a meeting with the directors 30 minutes from now, and you need to be able to give each person a copy of the music to review. No problem; in fact, you have two options. You can easily use the Windows Media Player to copy the files from CD to your hard disk, and from there to the company network server. Then you need only tell everyone where to find the files, and your job is done. Or you can use the Player to quickly copy the entire CD onto new, blank CDs which you can distribute at will.

Windows Media Audio: MP3 for the Future

When you use the Player to copy CD tracks to hard disk, it defaults to storing the music in a Microsoft compressed format that has some really neat features. The Windows Media Audio (WMA) format provides CD-quality audio at higher fidelity than MP3. It also uses a sufficiently clever compression algorithm that it can provide this improved quality from files that are smaller than MP3 files—sometimes half as large. Not that surprising, when you consider that MP3 has been around for about 10 years.

Windows XP still provides support for MP3 through optional MP3 Creation Packs available from Microsoft or third-party vendors, but unless you've purchased a portable MP3 player, it's hard to imagine why anyone would choose the MP3 format over WMA. The WMA format makes music sound better, and it takes up less storage space or Internet transfer time. Content sharing is easier, and WMA is favored by recording artists because it provides optional protection of music files so that copyrighted content doesn't get used illegally.

Compression and Re-Compression   I said earlier that lossy compression is the key to efficient and economical storage of digital audio, and that's true. The WMA format is the state of the art, and it's a tremendous boon to consumers and content producers alike, but you need to use it and any other type of lossy compression (including that used for JPG image files) wisely.

Every time you save a file using lossy compression, more data is lost. That's the nature of the beast. If you copy an original CD to your hard disk, lossy compression is used to store the digital audio (unless you manually select one of the Microsoft WAV file formats, which create huge, uncompressed files). If you burn those files to a CD and then later copy them back to your hard disk, the files will be put through a lossy compression pass again as they're saved to your PC. Each time you repeat this cycle, some data is lost. As with antiquated audio cassettes, if you copy a copy of a copy of a copy enough times in this way, you'll absolutely notice the difference eventually.

Key Points

- The proliferation and popularity of many different types of digital content has caused controversies, likely to remain unsolved for some time, regarding the ownership and control of that content.

- With each successive analog copy of some original content, quality suffers.

- Every digital copy of digital original content is perfect.

- The sound we hear is analog; it is a continuous wave of energy (pressure, specifically).

- Digital sound is created when an analog sound source is sampled and encoded into numbers that can be represented and stored as ones and zeros in the PC.

- To sample analog sound at a high level of quality, it is necessary to use a sampling rate that is at least twice that of the highest frequency of sound you want to convert to digital audio.

- CD Quality Audio uses a sample rate of 44.1 kHz, and a sample size of 16 bits.

- A sound card is an adapter (or electronics on your PC motherboard) that does the job of converting digital data back into audible sound. A sound card also includes a MIDI synthesizer that can play instrumental music.

- Files can be compressed without losing any of their original data (lossless compression) or by methods that actually throw away data that is not important (lossy compression). The MP3 and WMA audio formats achieve their sound quality and small file size through lossy compression.

- The Windows Media Player is a single piece of software, built into Windows XP, that can provide nearly all of your digital content needs, including playing, burning (recording), and copying audio CDs, playing streaming content from the Internet, and managing all of your digital media in an organized library.

Chapter 7

From Your Vision to Your Product

Twenty-five short years ago, no one expected great artistry from the PC. Graphics were just parlor tricks. Technology improved, but it was still our own brains that did most of the work, putting the jagged spots together into something coherent. Even today, video can't begin to produce images at a level of detail higher than what our eyes can see, but we can take digital photographs at a resolution as high as the photosensitive molecules of physical film. What's the benefit of that to you and your business?

Your Vision: Introducing Digital Imaging

If you work or play with digital photography, you already know that it's an exciting world. The digital still camera, scanners, and digital video are tools that appeal to professionals and to plain, everyday folks, too. We usually refer to this whole industry as *digital imaging*, a crossover between the PC and pictures. It's an industry that has touched most of us. Anyone can purchase a digital video camera for under $500 and produce amazing images. Sales of digital still cameras have skyrocketed, and scanners have dropped in price so much, they're often freebies with a new PC.

The history of digital imaging has been a striving for perfection—trying to capture the world as we already see it. And digital imaging has gone through a series of steps, all leading from "Boy, that sure is fuzzy and tiny" to "Wow! What professional film did you use for that picture?" But why bother? What's wrong with film? Nothing. Film is great. But the PC can edit and manipulate images cheaper and easier than film processors can. The problem has been that film just looks better. All those molecules of light-sensitive chemicals are so small, film has had a much higher resolution than digital cameras could provide.

Digital Revolution

But digital cameras now have resolutions as high as 35mm film. Digital has caught up with film's ability to record what we see. High resolution and editing ease have become an unbeatable pair. With the right camera and software, seeming photographic miracles are now possible. Your vision can now exist entirely in the digital world, whether your vision is of your child in the backyard or aliens on Mars. It's exciting: you can do on your PC what only studios could previously manage. The creative freedom of digital imaging is that, now that we can finally digitally capture the world as we see it, we can just as easily create a world we've never seen. It does still take skill and talent to create seamless digital manipulations, sure. But for the first time, this is a world that any of us can work or play in.

Digital Cameras

Before you can take a picture of your friend in ski gear and transform it into a picture of your friend looking very silly in ski gear on the beach in Tahiti, you need a picture of your friend and a picture of Tahiti. How does digital imaging put the pieces together? It starts with you taking a quality photograph in the first place. The quality of a digital photo depends on your talent as a photographer, naturally, but also depends on several technical specifications. These differentiate one camera from another, just as different brands, speeds, and grades of film are differentiated.

How Digital Photography Works

A digital camera and its "film" are one, and that's the first important point to remember. In traditional photography (which is the term I'll use for taking pictures with a camera and celluloid film), you've got your camera and you've got your film, and they have nearly nothing to do with each other. Not so with digital. Digital cameras naturally have a lens and shutter, and many have a physical *aperture*. This is a diaphragm that regulates the amount of light that enters the camera when the shutter opens. Many digital cameras don't have a physical aperture, but use a setting known as *gain* to approximate the dual functions of an aperture and selecting a different film speed.

Instead of film, a digital camera uses a *charge-coupled device (CCD)* a bit of electronics that is sensitive to light. A CCD is made up of microscopic receptors which produce and store an electric current when they are struck by light, as represented in Figure 7-1. At the simplest level, these receptors send out more or less electricity depending on whether they are struck by more or less light. As photons of light hit the receptors, they continue to store energy.

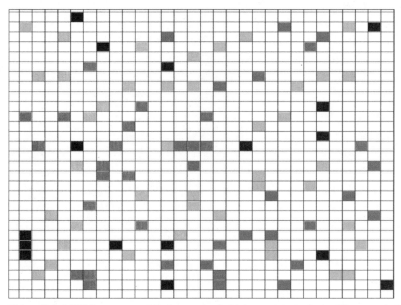

Figure 7-1 A CCD is an array of diodes, each of which can detect minute differences in the intensity of light.

You might be surprised to learn that this process is analog since light travels in a continuous wave. CCDs are extremely sensitive to light, and the different amounts of electricity they store are closely related to precise levels of light that strike them. In other words, CCDs record light levels very accurately. The camera senses the amount of electricity accumulated by each diode in the CCD and turns that into a number. This analog-to-digital conversion is a way to change the real world into a world the computer can manipulate and store.

That takes care of light levels, or *intensity*, which gives us an equivalent for black and white photography. But what about color? Digital cameras record color in one of two ways. You can call them the *expensive* way and the *inexpensive* way; that's pretty accurate. The expensive way of recording color requires that the camera has three different CCDs inside, one for each of the three primary colors. Light entering the camera is split and filtered so that one CCD responds to red light, one to green light, and one to blue light. The numbers from each diode of each CCD are combined into one value that records the intensity of light and the color of light that stimulated that triad of diodes. This method is actually called the *3-CCD* method. It's more expensive both because it costs more to put three CCDs and a prism inside a camera and because 3-CCD cameras generally take higher-quality pictures.

The inexpensive way of recording color requires only one CCD. However, in this configuration, the diodes are arranged into side-by-side groups of four, much like the triads of phosphors on the inside of your PC's monitor. (See Chapter 4.) A filter is placed in front of each diode. Because our eyes are especially sensitive to levels of green light, half of the diodes are filtered to respond to green, and the remainder respond to either red or blue light. We still end up with one value that reflects the color and intensity received by the groups of four diodes, but one CCD is cheaper than three. Here we encounter our old friend balanced integration again.

Think about how the 3-CCD scheme works. Let's imagine a camera with 3 CCDs, each of which is an array of 12 diodes vertically and 12 horizontally. That's 144 diodes per CCD, making 432 in total. When we take a picture, each of the 432 diodes records its level of red, green, or blue light. Each diode's response is converted to a digital number and combined with the other two. That combined value eventually determines the color of a single pixel in a 144-pixel digital image.

Now consider a 1-CCD camera with the same number of diodes. In this camera, a quarter of the diodes record the intensity of red light, half record green light, and a quarter record blue light. Put together, the result is not a 144-pixel digital image; it's a 36-pixel image—we lost three-quarters of the pixels to our need to keep track of red, green, and blue light! Some mathematical trickery is used to produce a final image that is made up of the full 144 pixels, but the result isn't as good as a true 144-pixel image. (This trickery is called *interpolation*, and it's an important consideration for digital cameras as well as scanners and printers.)

It also takes faster electronics throughout the camera to observe, manipulate, and store 144 pixels of light in a given amount of time than it does to do the same job with only 36 pixels. Every bit of the camera's circuitry has to be up to the job, or you don't get pictures. Because you're going to end up with an image that has higher true resolution, the camera's lens also needs to be of better quality, to keep the light focused sharply. This concept is one of the most important ones to understand in the world of digital cameras. With traditional photography, you can buy an average camera, put in really excellent film, add a good eye and some talent, and wind up with breathtaking photographs. With digital photography, once you select a camera, the best it can do is the best it can do, forever. Unfortunately, the marketing for digital cameras isn't always the clearest. It can be difficult to assess exactly what *is* a camera's best.

Some good techniques can help you clear the marketing air. You've already learned about the difference between 3- and 1-CCD cameras. That's easily the most fundamental difference, and if a camera has three CCDs, its manufacturer will make sure you know it. If you can't immediately tell how many CCDs are in a camera, it doesn't have three. Also, digital cameras are advertised by their resolution, but not in the terms you might expect. You won't likely read about a camera with, say, 2000 by 1800 diodes. What you'll see is a measurement of the camera's *megapixels*. The term simply means 1 million pixels. It is the latest generation of 6-and-higher-megapixel cameras that are turning professional photographers' heads. If you have 6 megapixels, it means that 6 million diodes work together to form each image. Until 2002, cameras of this quality weren't available at any price. Today, they're surprisingly affordable. One reason is because several of these newest high-pixel-count cameras use a different means of sensing light, called a *complementary metal oxide semiconductor (CMOS) chip*. CMOS chips work differently than CCDs, but a more important factor for our purposes is that CMOS chips are much less costly to manufacture than are CCDs.

Even if you know a camera's megapixels, judging a digital camera's resolution can be difficult because of interpolation. Interpolation is that math trickery I mentioned earlier that allows the light-reading of 4 diodes to be combined into a single value and then turned back into values for 4 pixels. It's complex, but interpolation is a matter of considering a single 4-diode value of intensity and color, and then examining the values for the 4-diode groups surrounding the first. Depending on what those surrounding values are, the camera makes an educated guess about what values would have been recorded if each diode functioned independently (like they do in a 3-CCD camera) rather than as part of a 4-diode group. It's not a precise science or perfect, but most argue that it's better than obtaining an image that is actually a quarter of the resolution. (Those who argue otherwise purchase 3-CCD cameras.)

If you're shopping for a digital camera, be on the watch for interpolation. It's used in every single-sensor camera, but it's marketed differently. Currently, a 3.5-megapixel camera is being marketed as a 7-megapixel camera because the manufacturer has added some math to its interpolation techniques. It claims this doubles the effective resolution of the camera. Reviewers have been unimpressed, so look out for the word *effective* when you read digital camera marketing. It means that the computer in the camera is trying to simulate something better than what the camera can actually provide.

If you read the very fine print in a digital camera's specifications, you will find resolution measurements. A 4-megapixel camera might reveal that it can produce images with a resolution of roughly 2200 × 1700 pixels. Do the math, and this is about right. It comes out to roughly 3.7 megapixels; some of the diodes are used for support purposes. When you consider images of this resolution, you think about storage. Fact is, they're big. If one picture requires about 3 megabytes (MB) of storage, you're not going to get many pictures into your camera's default 32 MB memory, are you? So let's consider how digital images are stored. It's a topic that leads us to look at compression, too.

How Digital Images Are Stored

Not surprisingly, digital images are stored digitally. That is, the numbers you get when the camera does its analog-to-digital conversion (ADC) trick are stored like any other binary data: in memory. Almost every digital camera uses either CompactFlash (CF) memory (a type of electrically erasable programmable read-only memory that we looked at briefly in Chapter 3) or Sony Corporation's proprietary Memory Stick technology (which is basically the same thing, packaged differently). Which camera you want to own might be determined by the type of memory it uses, because your PC might have built-in support for one or the other type of memory chip. Even if you don't have built-in hardware support (a socket on your PC that you can slide a memory chip into), you can purchase a small, portable reader for under $20 that plugs into a PC's USB port. Windows XP does the rest.

Two types of CF memory exist, called Type I and Type II. The primary difference is that a CF Type II card is thicker than a Type I card. This extra space has proved useful. IBM sells a product called the IBM MicroDrive that currently has a capacity of up to 1 GB. Believe it or not, it's an actual hard disk in the space of roughly two (thick) postage stamps. The MicroDrive works just like other CF cards or Sony Memory Sticks, as far as digital cameras are concerned. When you press the camera shutter, the imaging device (CCD or CMOS) does its job, and the results are written as a file to the device.

With a memory card reader, like the USB models I just mentioned, Windows XP will automatically recognize the memory and will treat it like a removable hard drive. This strategy is universally faster than downloading pictures from the camera to your PC, and it allows you to look at thumbnails of each picture you've taken just like Windows XP lets you see thumbnails of any pictures on your PC, as shown in Figure 7-2.

Figure 7-2 Windows XP will automatically create and display thumbnails of digital images on your PC or on any digital camera's memory card without needing any extra software.

You can drag images directly from the memory card "drive" to your My Pictures folder, or any other folder. You can also attach pictures to e-mail messages directly from the digital camera's memory chip, and they'll be copied to your PC and shared with whomever you choose.

Unfortunately, when you want to share digital images, you need to consider their size. As I said, high-quality digital pictures are big. If you're using a 56K modem connection, you're going to spend a long time online if you try to transfer any number of 3-MB family vacation photos to your folks. There are two solutions to this problem.

First, you can set your digital camera to reduce the resolution of the pictures it takes. The 2200-×-1700-pixel camera I mentioned previously can be reduced to take 640-×-480-pixel images if you want. But when you throw away all those pixels, you also throw away quality. Resolution is something like a digital audio sampling rate. You need to take enough samples of sound to get an accurate digital recording; you need to use enough pixels to accurately record the details of what life looks like.

The second solution is to use compression. Digital cameras have their own lossy compression techniques that are analogous to the Moving Pictures Experts Group (MPEG) and Windows Media Audio (WMA) compressions used for digital audio. By far, the most popular compression scheme for digital images is called *JPEG* (pronounced "jay-peg"), named after the Joint Photographic Experts

Group. The JPEG format is probably familiar to you because it's easily the most popular picture format used on the Internet. Image files with a .jpg extension are JPEG images. Most digital cameras use the JPEG format as their native image format, meaning that every picture they take is saved as a JPEG image.

The benefit of this solution is clear. Within the JPEG format, an image can be compressed anywhere along the spectrum of 100 percent (no compression) to 1 percent (so much compression, you'll be lucky if you can even recognize what you photographed). The JPEG method uses some clever math so a photograph's color and intensity values can be analyzed and reduced so that the final picture looks *virtually* like the original (at reasonable levels of compression—usually down to 70 percent, although it greatly depends on what the picture is). Information the viewer is not likely to see is thrown out, just as WMA throws away audio information unlikely to be missed.

The downside to JPEG compression is that every time you save a JPEG image, you risk losing quality. Here's why. If you shoot an image with the camera set to 90 percent—that is, 10 percent compression and you move that image to the PC and view it with photo-editing software, you'll want to access the software's advanced saving settings before you resave the image. If the software is set to default at 90 percent also, the image will be recompressed with another 10 percent of lossy compression. Do it again, and you'll lose more. Eventually, the picture is ruined, and if you use the same file name each time, you might unknowingly destroy it—there's no lossless "decompression" for JPEG. Unless you specifically want to recompress an image, you'll want to be certain to re-save it at the 100 percent setting every time. It's not a huge disadvantage, but it's a trap that many people don't learn about until it's too late to retrieve a ruined image.

Digital cameras use other compression tricks, too. Let's say you've got a digital photograph of a yellow flower. It's possible that within that picture, you'll have pixel after pixel in a row of exactly the same color and intensity. Compressing this sort of thing is easy, and it's actually a lossless compression. You don't have to record the color of each pixel. You just record the color, and indicate that the next 73 (or whatever) pixels use that color. When the image is displayed, this information is read, the process is reversed, and you get 73 dots of color.

Digital Video: A Special Case

Digital video is basically a special case of digital photography, just as motion-picture shooting is a special case of traditional still photography. Motion picture photography is just taking a huge number of still photos in rapid succession. Digital video relies on CCDs and analog-to-digital converters just as digital still cameras do—and the 3-CCD vs. 1-CCD phenomenon actually started in the camcorder world, so it's definitely a factor to consider with video as with still digital imagery. But digital video takes up so much storage space, you won't get too much of it on a CF memory card. For that reason, when we're talking about digital video cameras, we're talking about digital videotape.

Digital videotape is to sound and pictures what digital audio tape (DAT) has been to audio and PC data for years. (DAT is often used to back up huge amounts of computer data.) Digital videotape shares the same limitations of all tape: it's a sequential media. That means to jump to a particular scene, you have to fast forward or rewind sequentially through the tape until you arrive at the right spot. (Remember, random-access, as opposed to sequential access, means that you can say, "OK, bit number 1,820,394,285, what's your value? Zero? Great, thanks!" and be done with it.)

Digital videotape is also fragile, and shuttling the tape back and forth at high speeds (as you do when rewinding and fast forwarding) will eventually make the tape stretch. When that happens, the contents will probably be lost. Similarly, digital videotape's magnetic signals can fade like those of any magnetic tape—over a period of probably 30 years, compared to DVD's expected life of a century.

On the other hand, digital videotape gives you exactly what you need: lots and lots of storage in a small package. Some of this capacity is achieved by using really thin tape. (Sadly, really thin tape stretches really fast.) The remainder of the capacity we enjoy from digital videotape comes from lossy compression. In this case, it's not JPEG compression that's used. JPEG is great for still images, but no provision exists within the normal JPEG algorithm for situations that happen all the time in video, like, "Not only are the next 73 pixels the same color, but they are the same color in this image and in the next 3000 images."

Note   When we speak of moving video, we usually call the signals that make up a single full screen of video a *frame*. If you like, you can think of these frames the way you think of frames of motion-picture film. It's not all that different, for our purposes. We also usually speak of video resolution not as *x by y* pixels, but in terms of *horizontal lines* of resolution. This is because all standard televisions display the same number of illuminated spots, horizontally, but some models have their rows of phosphor set closer together. A regular TV image usually uses about 240 lines of horizontal resolution. The popular digital video formats support over 500 lines, providing better detail and sharper images.

To accommodate the many special circumstances that arise, different compression is necessary. Several schemes exist, some of which are used internally by the digital video cameras, or camcorders, and some of which can be applied later on a PC. One of these compression formats is called MPEG-2 (remember MPEG-3, from Chapter 6?) and is used in DVD movies. MPEG-2 can achieve a lot of compression at high quality, but it takes time, so it's not used by the smallest-format digital camcorders where the tape simply moves too fast for the camera to capture images, perform the compression, and write the result to tape. For these, other compression systems exist.

Compression makes a lot of difference because of something called *artifacts*. Artifacts exist in the still digital image world, too—they're the blockiness that you get if you use a JPEG compression setting that is too high. Digital video has the same problem, and more. Digital video compression can make the resulting image blocky, make movement jerky, reduce the number of colors in a scene so that everything looks harsh, and cause weird patterns to appear all over the screen, which can be quite distracting.

Unfortunately, you can't choose your compression type or your compression level once you've selected a digital camcorder. You get what you buy. The best plan is to set aside time to go to a store where they'll allow you to try models that interest you, and see the result on a television the same size as what you expect to use to watch most of your movies.

All digital video camcorders come with some form of PC interface. In most cases, this is an IEEE 1394, or *FireWire* connection. Naturally, your PC will need to have FireWire support too. There are FireWire CD recorders and digital music players, and so forth, but its most popular use has definitely been to facilitate getting digital video off of videotape and onto a PC's hard disk. What's the point of that? Digital editing.

Lingo   *FireWire* is a high-speed path over which data can move between devices.

Digital Editing with Windows Movie Maker Windows XP—and Windows Millennium Edition (Windows Me), for that matter—comes with a great piece of software called Windows Movie Maker. Many of the capabilities of expensive editing programs are part of Windows Movie Maker—and, so, are included with Windows XP. Once your digital video is stored on disk, you can edit it until you've got exactly what you want. Move scenes around, replace audio tracks, or underlie a musical soundtrack on live audio. You can create titles and other special effects, incorporating still images right into your videos. And you can do quite a lot more.

Movie Maker divides your video into a series of *key frames*, which it displays in the workspace at the bottom of the window, as shown in Figure 7-3.

Figure 7-3 The Windows Movie Maker provides an intuitive, easy environment in which you can do some amazing things with digital video.

You can then treat the frames of digital video like puzzle pieces and move them around into whatever order you want. This is key to any kind of video or motion-picture photography, because it's often impossible to film a movie in the order in which you intend to watch it. In addition, while the 30 minutes you shot of flamingoes walking in a pond might have seemed tranquil at the time, you might decide that 30 seconds of flamingoes is all you really need in a finished vacation video.

Some of the live audio you've recorded probably isn't what you want, either. You could rerecord it, or replace it entirely. (In either case, the process is called *dubbing*.) In Windows Movie Maker, you can drag digital audio files around on-screen in parallel to your video in the workspace. It's extremely easy to delete audio tracks or add additional tracks, and you can select the relative volume of each track you include. No use drowning out your great script with a soundtrack, you know?

Movie Maker brings all the pieces together. You can view it, make changes, and get it perfect. You can then export it back to digital videotape, make digital copies or play the video into a VCR to make copies for friends, family, or that grant-proposal committee you desperately need to "wow." You could also write the video to a video DVD and distribute it to family and colleagues that way.

Digital video is an amazing technology, and its usefulness in the workplace is only just starting to be appreciated. Another digital imaging technology, document scanning, has been around for a long time, and it's now an established part of many businesses. In the next sections, we'll examine scanners and their reverse-counterparts: printers. Understanding these bits of technology can really help you work faster and smarter.

Scanners

Scanners are to documents what digital still cameras are to the 3D world around us. Scanners take something that has been printed, such as a letter, a book, or a full-color photograph, and import it into the PC. All modern scanners support scanning all of these types of documents and more—quite a few scanners can scan photographic transparencies, too, like color slides.

Scanners work much the same way as do digital still cameras. In that sense, scanners are also a special case in the world of digital photography. Because that's what scanners do: they use CCDs or similar light-sensitive electronics to "photograph" whatever document they "see." Most consumer scanners are simple and consist of only a sheet of glass on which a document is placed, the scanning electronics, and a lid. Higher-end and commercial scanners commonly have sheet-feeders, like those that are part of nearly every fax machine.

If you've never used a scanner, just think of it as a photocopier attached to a PC, and you've got the general idea. A document is placed on the glass. Software running on the PC determines the resolution of the scan and its color depth, and provides the user with the equivalent of a Start button. In most cases, after an image is scanned, it is automatically stored in a file on the PC in a preselected location.

Unlike digital cameras, scanners provide their own light source. Digital cameras rely on the reflected light that we also use to see. But if you put a document face down on a scanner, there's not a whole lot of light there to reflect. Therefore, a light source is attached to the scanner head. It is usually a color-balanced fluorescent bulb that provides an intense white light. (The more light a scanner has to work with, the more accurately it will be able to reproduce whatever you're scanning, particularly if you're scanning a color photograph.)

The issue of scanner resolution, while related to digital camera resolution, actually has more in common with the world of printers than it does general-purpose digital photography. You will never see a scanner advertised as being Scapable of producing, say, 2000-×-1800-pixel scans. Scanner resolution is expressed in terms of the number of pixels per inch the scanner can image. Why the difference? In a digital camera, you've got a grid of CCDs or other imaging technology that captures an entire scene in a burst of light. When you push the shutter, all the CCDs do their job at once. Although some extremely expensive photocopiers work this way, too, that's not at all how digital scanners work. And that is a great thing for us, as it turns out.

Rather than having a grid of imagers (rows and columns), a scanner has only one row. These are mounted on a moving arm (the *head*), which also usually has the light source attached to it. (This scheme provides even lighting and reduces the appearance of shadows and uneven colors.) To scan an image, the scanner motor moves the scan head slowly across the face of the document. As the scan head moves, light is reflected off the document into the imagers, converted into digital data, and sent to the PC. Unlike a camera, then, scanners photograph their subjects one line at a time.

The key is that there's no fixed definition of how big a *line* is. The smallest line a scanner can image is simply the smallest amount of space over which its motor can precisely move the scan arm. Each line of movement translates into a horizontal row of pixels. Thus, we refer to this capability as a scanner's *vertical resolution*, and it's a measure of how many rows the scanner can capture in a single inch of space.

This measurement of resolution is the familiar *dots per inch (DPI)* by which scanners are differentiated on the sales floors. Thus, a scanner that has fine enough control to produce 2400 lines of pixels in a single vertical inch gets called a 2400-DPI scanner. Through software, it's possible to cause the scan arm to make larger movements down the page, which has the effect of reducing the resolution of the scanner. So a 2400-DPI scanner can also make a 72-DPI scan of a document, if you want it to.

Scanners have a horizontal resolution, too, naturally. Unlike their vertical resolution, *horizontal resolution* is technically fixed—set by the number of imaging sensors lined up in a row on the scan head. So if a scanner is called a 2400-DPI scanner, it should have a horizontal and vertical resolution of 2400 DPI. It doesn't always work that way, however. Indeed, even vertical resolution isn't always a clear issue. Welcome back to the world of interpolation!

Interpolated Scanner Resolution

In many cases, the resolution you see marketed for a scanner isn't actually its highest true resolution. *True resolution* means the number of pixels the scanner can put into an image based strictly on its ability to move the scan head. Sometimes, a scanner's resolution is only an interpolated value. Like digital camera interpolation, color and intensity values of a pixel are considered with respect to the same qualities of pixels surrounding it. Consider a scanner with a true horizontal and vertical resolution of 2400 DPI. This could create a 4800-DPI image, simply doubling the pixels it's already scanned. Yes, the resulting image will have 4800 pixels per inch, but the *effective resolution* of the image (in other words, the level of quality you actually get) is still 2400 DPI.

Interpolation actually does something useful in other cases, where a scanner's horizontal resolution isn't up to snuff with its vertical resolution. In this case, a scanner might have a 2400-DPI vertical resolution, but only 1200-DPI horizontal resolution. Here, roughly three rows of pixels will be analyzed at a time, and pixels will be added in the horizontal dimension based on the value of surrounding pixels. This interpolation can actually do some good, because you're adding pixels where none existed, not simply inserting duplicates of existing pixels, but you won't get the same quality you would from a higher true resolution. The interpolated image resolution is sometimes referred to as the image's *apparent resolution*, because the image will appear to have a somewhat higher resolution than it actually does.

As you've probably guessed, I'm not overly fond of interpolation. I don't consider it an inherently inferior process—it's not, when it's done well. Interpolation plays an important role in image compression. What I *do* object to, however, is product packaging that says "8 billion dots per inch resolution!" all over the front of the box, with the word *apparent* hidden in parentheses and tiny type somewhere at the back of the user's guide. If you're like me and like to get what you pay for, you might feel the same way.

Scanner Color Depth

Color depth is a scanner's second-most important quality. Sadly, there's misinformation here, too. Color depth, as I've said many times, is the number of bits used to store the color of a single pixel in an image. A scanner's color depth *should* be an indication of how many different colors a scanner can create, but this isn't always the case. Instead, scanner color depth is often a measurement of the number of bits used internally by the scanner. This might be more bits than the scanner can actually send to your PC—in other words, more bits than it can actually scan into an image. The argument goes that, by scanning with a 64-bit number (for example) to record each pixel's color and intensity, you get a larger sample, which allegedly gives you a more accurate 24-bit color number when the image is sent out to the PC. In other words, if you look at a document more carefully, you'll allegedly be able to reproduce it more accurately.

In my experience, this isn't real life. A scanner might indeed use a 64-bit number to store each pixel's color internally, but throwing bits away is throwing bits away. The likelihood of ending up with a pixel that is a more accurate copy of the original is basically zero. This is technomarketing at its worst. When you're looking at scanner specifications, be sure the scanner's only advertised color depth isn't labeled with the word *internal*. If it is, you should consider a different scanner manufacturer. Short of doing that, investigate to learn the maximum color depth that the scanner can actually send to your PC. It would be tragic to spend extra money for a 64-bit scanner that can produce images with only the same 24 or 32 bits used by all the other, far less costly models.

Color Balancing and Profiles

I just mentioned that the light sources used in most scanners are bright, balanced, fluorescent bulbs that provide neutral illumination for the original. What does all that mean? Consider a red-lit room. The red light is hitting every exposed surface and is bouncing off. Everything your eyes see is the result of that reflected light. Anything in the room that is what we call "red" will reflect most of the light it receives and will appear bright red, indeed. Objects that are "green" or "blue" will absorb much of the red light, and that will give them a black or gray appearance. The impact of a red lightbulb is that you can't really tell the natural color of anything in the room—not even the things that are red, because they'll appear unnaturally red. The only way to see the colors of things in the room accurately is to use a light source that is reflected and absorbed evenly by objects of all colors. Because it is made up of all colors—and therefore avoids prejudicing the results—the only logical light source is white light.

But what is white light? It's a mixture of light of all other colors, but it's never a perfectly even mixture. Some whites have a slight pink cast to them because there's just a little more red in their mix. The lingo is to say that these are *warm* whites, and that their photographic color temperature is hotter than others. Whites with a slightly blue cast are called *cool* whites. Depending on whether a scanner's light source is warmer or cooler, the images scanned might be prejudiced toward either the red or blue end of the spectrum. Fortunately, the PC can correct for variances in the scanner's light source. This process is known as *color balancing*. It's a matter of making whites their whitest, and adjusting every other color in an image accordingly. Color balancing gives us a level playing field. If you're working with digital photographs and are trying to put together a composite image (or a collage), things can look really awful if you don't balance each image's color properly with respect to all the others. This has the effect of changing the conditions under which the image was taken. An image taken under an incandescent lamp's yellow hue can be adjusted to look better and more natural next to one taken in daylight.

Color balancing isn't used just to adjust for poor scanning or to make images from different sources seem more alike. It's also an important tool for improving the appearance of an excellent scan of a poor-quality original. Paper tends to yellow as it ages, and photographs usually turn red. Some careful and sophisticated color balancing can remove the artifacts of age. Once you get the knack, you'll be amazed by how much more useful your scanner is, and how much more you can do with digital images, overall, regardless of their source.

Printing Your Vision, Producing Your Product

Almost nothing is as frustrating as putting hours into expressing your vision, only to have the final product seem something out of left field. Sometimes problems don't appear until the last minute, when you've started to allow yourself a sense of relief—phew! You're done! And then you click Print, get something to drink, wander casually over to the printer—and have to spend the next eight hours trying to figure out what went wrong. You know some common causes of such problems: overcompressing a digital image, over-reducing the color depth, using a resolution that's too low in the first place, disregarding color balance. In these cases, prevention definitely beats a cure. So the first principle for getting your product to look like your vision is this: understand the relationship between your sources and your destination, which is probably a printer.

Basic Printer Types

Printing can get pretty complicated, even when you're working only in black and white (or 256 shades of gray, more commonly). Add 16 million colors to the mix and…. So let's put complications aside and see how printers work. It might seem simplistic to break printers down into two basic types—black and white and color—but some issues relate to black and white (gray) printing and other issues relate only to color printing. (Of course, color printers print in black and white, too, so when I talk about a color printer, you should assume that I'm talking about using it to print in full color.) Within these two realms, three basic technologies make printing possible: laser printing, ink-jet printing, and "others," which includes a variety of special solid-ink printers and printers that use colored film, like the world's most expensive holiday cling-wrap. As it so happens, my favorite printer of all is one of the "others," but let's first take a look at the two printer families you're more likely to own.

Laser Printers

Laser printers come in black and white and full color varieties, but they all work the same way. Data is sent to the printer using a special computer language the printer understands. This language is tailored for telling a printer where on a page to put its black or colored spots. Inside the laser printer, a photosensitive metal drum develops a bad case of static cling after it turns in the path of a laser beam that "draws" or traces the image you want to print onto the drum. Dry colored dust called *toner* is attracted to the pattern of static cling on the drum and sticks where the laser has drawn. The drum then rotates against a moving piece of paper, and the toner is transferred from the drum to the page. Finally, the toner-covered paper passes between heated rollers at incredible pressure, which fuses the toner dust permanently to the paper fibers. Ka-chunk, ka-chunk, and out comes your report!

In a color laser printer, the process repeats four times, once for each of the printer's four primary toner colors (cyan, magenta, yellow, and black). These four toner colors are represented by the term *CMYK* (cyan-magenta-yellow-black), which is for printing what the primary colors *RGB* (red-green-blue) are for on-screen images. With each pass through the printer, the paper picks up another layer of color, until all four colors have been fused to the page. This is called an *additive color* process. In the RGB world, levels of red, green, and blue are combined with a brightness setting to describe every possible color that can be displayed. It's the same for CMYK, with black representing a measurement of brightness, and the three other colors doing the rest. Cyan, magenta, and yellow toners (or inks) provide the widest-possible range of printed colors because red, green, and blue inks, when mixed equally, don't actually create black like you'd expect they would; they create a nasty dark green. Mixing cyan, magenta, and yellow inks, on the other hand, provides a deep, true black, so these inks were chosen for color printing.

One of the great weaknesses of color laser printing is that it is necessary to image each of the four colors independently on the drum, and the paper must be moved past the drum four times. At the resolutions laser printers provide, even a minute error in the paper-handling or positioning of the laser can cause an image to be printed improperly. This is called a *registration error*, and it basically amounts to drawing outside the lines. Supplies for color laser printers are expensive, and the printers themselves are expensive to maintain, too—which is necessary to avoid registration errors and other problems.

Ink-Jet Printers

Ink-jet printers work nothing like laser printers, although they do share the CMYK model with color laser printing. As the name implies, ink-jet printers do what they do as a moving print head sprays microscopic bubbles of ink onto paper. The print head moves horizontally while the paper is slowly scrolled vertically past the head. As multiple drops of ink hit the same tiny spot on the page, colors blend and dry instantly. The process repeats until the illusion of a continuous image is formed by our brains combining all the dots together.

Ink-jet printing is popular because printers are inexpensive, but this technology has its unique problems, too. Registration errors aren't common because the nozzles don't move with respect to each other. Each dot on the page can be formed of all four primary inks, and has a precise location—or *should* have a precise location, anyway. The problem with spraying wet ink at dry paper is that, depending on the ink, the paper, and how much ink you spray, your printout might end up looking like a paper-towel demonstration. Liquid inks do spread when they touch paper. Dots that spread aren't precise dots, and the images formed aren't what they should be.

The best solution is a combination of printer settings and paper selection. The printer drivers allow you to indicate which type of image you're printing— text, a color photograph, and so forth. Most drivers also let you specify the type of paper you're using. If you spray photograph-quality amounts of ink at plain paper, you'll probably end up with a poor-quality image on a soaked page. Too much ink and too much spreading of the individual dots make for a mess. Also, paper isn't smooth on the microscopic level where the colored dots exist. The fibers from a sheet of office paper are as rough as an army blanket on that scale. You can't print on a hole, and if you're expecting the paper to be a precise distance away from the print head (so you spray the right amount of ink for the dot you want), your plans will be defeated by lumpy, rough paper. Enter the specialty paper market, where you can find papers that are coated with a variety of substances that absorb ink more precisely than the paper they're coating and that smooth out the bumps and pits on a page's surface.

Selecting a Printer

Choose your printer wisely because your choice will determine the quality of everything you produce. If you never print anything but black and white text and grayscale images, a traditional laser printer is your obvious choice. If you print in color, you'll need a color laser, an ink-jet, or my own favorite, a color wax printer from Xerox Tektronix. You must consider a variety of issues when making your choice, the first of which, naturally, is cost. If your budget is practically unlimited, congratulations! If you're a mere mortal like I am, however, it's worth knowing that the world of printers is a world of hidden costs. So here are some things to consider.

First, look at the cost of the printer itself. If you can't afford the initial outlay for a particular model or type, your decision is easier. Second, consider how much you print, and how many pages a toner or ink cartridge prints considering the type of printing you'll do. If you print 5000 pages a month and a toner cartridge will print roughly 10,000 pages of text, you know you'll probably be buying six toner cartridges a year. (Actually, you'll probably end up buying a new printer at that rate. They do wear out.)

If you're considering a color laser printer, remember that you must buy toner in each of four colors, along with other consumables, like the unique imaging drum that color laser printers require. At the time of this writing, a complete set of consumables for one popular model of laser printer costs about $700. That's for a printer that costs only about twice as much. That's a high consumable cost.

Keep a close eye on a printer's toner-capacity ratings, too. Usually, they say something like "4000 pages, at 7 percent coverage," meaning you can expect 4000 printed pages—*if* your average page is 7 percent covered with toner. That's about average for a full page of text. If you're buying a color printer, you probably want to print color graphics. A single, small, full-color image on a page can dramatically increase your coverage. If you regularly print full-page, full-color, photographic-quality images, you'll want to be on your printer manufacturer's bulk-buying plan. Consider, too, that certain printers might use ink or toner sold exclusively by their own manufacturer. That can have a supply-and-demand effect on the price of your consumables.

Tip   Color printers use colors at different rates. I *strongly* urge you not to buy a printer that requires that you replace all four colors together. Many like this are available, and they often have delightfully low price tags. But things start to get expensive if you have to replace all four colors of ink every time you run out of one color.

Consider a printer's maximum resolution, too. This is measured in DPI like scanners. I strongly suggest patronizing a store that will provide samples of actual output. Many will do this, and it's an important test. You might feel strongly that a 600-DPI laser printer has more than high enough resolution for your business; however, when you actually see 600-DPI output and compare it with 1200-DPI output, you might decide that the quality difference is obvious enough that your company's image is worth the investment in the more precise printer.

In addition, think about balanced integration again for a moment. If you're spending the money for a high-resolution scanner, you'll want to balance the quality of your scans with the quality at which you can print them. Don't break the bank on a true 4800-DPI scanner if you've just got an older, 300-DPI printer. Buy a more reasonable-quality scanner and spend the money you save on upgrading your printer.

Resolution is as important to black and white printers as to color printers. Millions of colors on a page can give an effect that seems better than the resolution used, but if you're printing in gray—and most printers support just 256 different gray tones—the accuracy and detail of higher-resolution output can make a tremendous difference. With color printers, the smaller each dot, and the more densely they're packed, the more your product will look like a traditional continuous-tone photograph (which, after all, is the standard against which everybody judges digital pictures). Remember that printing at high resolutions requires more consumables, and might require costly specialty papers to get the quality you require. Factor these considerations in before you buy.

Finally, if you require precise color to get your product to acceptably resemble your vision, consider selecting a printer that supports widely accepted color systems like Pantone. These proprietary systems are basically color profiles that bridge the gap between your PC screen and your clients. Their beauty is that, if you specify a certain color in software and your printer driver recognizes that specification, what you'll get on paper will be the closest your printer can come to what you saw in your mind's eye. These systems force you to choose from fewer colors—although fundamental colors can be mixed into others–but if you need *that* blue to look exactly like *this* blue, your success will compensate you for the trade.

Key Points

- The history of digital imaging has been the pursuit of photographic-quality perfection.

- A digital camera is both camera and film in one. You can't overcome a digital camera's limitations just by loading a higher quality of film. You must select a digital camera that meets your quality needs from the outset.

- Digital cameras can have one imaging element that filters the three primary colors of light, or it can have three imaging elements, each responsible for one primary color. The output from a multiple element camera will generally exceed that from a comparable single-element camera.

- Digital images at high resolution are large to store. The solution is compression. JPEG is the most common method used to reduce the size of a digital image. It is successful at shrinking file size without destroying an image's apparent quality.

- The resolution in pixels and the degree of compression used can both be set within any digital camera. This consideration is important because you won't obtain an image of higher quality than that which you originally shoot.

- Windows XP treats a digital camera's memory card like a hard disk. Windows XP provides both automatic thumbnails and basic photo-editing capabilities.

- The Windows Movie Maker allows you to take your digital video, digital still images, and digital audio and combine them easily.

- Printers use primarily laser technology or microscopic ink jets to put on paper what you envision and create inside the PC.

- You should consider a number of significant hidden costs in the world of printing before selecting the type and model of printer for your needs.

Chapter 8

Reaching Out

In most of today's computer systems, PC and otherwise, communication is what it's all about. One way or another, we need to get digital data in and out of the PC. We can accomplish that goal in basically three ways. This chapter talks about two of these, modem connections and ports; the third method, networking, is covered in Chapter 9.

Modems and Telephone Connections

Modems have been around for roughly 50 years, and they've been so insanely popular over the past decade that most computers in the United States have one. So you probably already know that a modem is that thing that's either part of your PC or else sits next to your PC that you plug into a telephone jack so you can connect to the world at large. Although modems have recently decreased in popularity, they're not likely to disappear for quite a long time. Too many of us have them, they're amazingly easy to use, and the world just isn't ready to throw modems out completely and adopt alternate means.

How Modems Work: And What's a Modem, Anyway?

We've been talking a lot about converting analog real-world information into digital data, and vice versa. That's what a *modem* does. But if every PC is digital, why can't you just run a cord from one PC to another and communicate that way? Well you can, but that's jumping ahead of my story. Not too long ago, a directly digital connection wasn't common at all for most PC users. You can't run a special wire from your home all over the world, just to send pictures to your parents. Fortunately, someone else already has: it's called a telephone wire.

Lingo   A *modem* is a device used to convert digital data into analog signals (sound) that can be transmitted over traditional telephone lines. A modem also converts the analog signals back into digital data your PC can use.

Telephone service is analog, so if you're going to use telephone lines for moving PC data, you're going to have to turn that data into an analog signal (that is, sound), and you need to be able to turn the sound back into data at the other end. Sound isn't the most precise thing in the world, but digital data is exceptionally precise. If you're transmitting a computer program you've written, even one wrong bit transmitted over that distance would make the program useless when it's received.

So modems do more than just turn digital ones and zeros into that annoying chirpy sound and back again. They're also responsible for making sure that the modem that they're connecting to hears the sounds properly. Modems have a built-in error-checking system that causes whichever modem is "speaking" (sending data) to back up and repeat the bit that wasn't communicated successfully. Historically, some basic error checking was provided through the use of *parity*, which I first introduced in Chapter 3.

Lingo   *Parity* is a way of providing error checking for digital data. It's like a secret code that identifies whether a byte of data was transmitted correctly. At the sending (transmitting) end of a connection, a calculation is made on a byte of data, and the one-or-zero values of a set of *parity bits* are determined based on that calculation. The parity bits are sent, generally, following the data byte. At the receiving end, the same calculation is performed on the data and the result is compared to the parity bits. Anything other than a perfect match means the data byte was not transmitted successfully, and the receiving modem sends instructions to the transmitting modem to repeat the "misheard" byte.

If you've ever seen the sort of instructions we used to have to manage to set up our modems, you've seen something like this:

1200, 8 bits, no parity, 1 stop bit

This code means, among other things, that this connection will use traditional 8-bit bytes of data, and no parity error checking. Parity is limited in what it can do, and many modems that supported parity didn't do it well. Modern modems have some sophisticated alternative methods of both checking for and even correcting errors. The original data can often now be reconstructed, rather than wasting time having it retransmit.

Nevertheless, a noisy telephone line is as troublesome for a modem as it is for you and me. When you start a connection, the modem picks up the telephone line, checks to make sure no one is already using it, and then dials. If a modem answers the call at the other end, the two modems do an electronic equivalent of "Hello, my name is…" Once the modems *handshake*, they then negotiate a speed at which they can talk to each other. They do this by trying to send a little chunk of data back and forth at their highest mutual speed. If it's not received successfully, they drop down to the next-fastest speed at which they can both work and try again. Modems are designed to work at specific preset speeds, but many of these are available between any modern modem's fastest and slowest speed.

Lingo   *Handshaking* is the process two modems go through to make sure they're connected successfully and are both planning on sending and receiving chunks of data of the same size, sometimes using error checking and other special features. It's a bit like how we answer the telephone and listen for the person calling us to say hello, introduce themselves, and, by so doing, show that we both speak the same language.

Modems also generally perform some degree of lossless compression so that they need to transmit as little data as possible. This compression is done by the modem hardware automatically and transparently. Whether compression is used depends on a few factors, the most important of which is determined during the modem's handshake: can the modem at the other end decompress compressed data? There's no sense stuffing all your holiday presents in a locked suitcase for travel if nobody at your destination has the key.

Modem speed is measured in two ways: *bit rate*, measured in bits per second (bps), and baud. Whereas baud is the more technical statement of a modem's performance, bit rate is more meaningful to us. The earliest popular modems for PCs communicated at 300 bits per second (bps). A 300 bps modem could move roughly about 30 bytes of data per second. I like to think of a modem's bit rate rather than its baud because bit rate is a lot closer to what I actually care about: moving my data.

Baud refers to how quickly a modem can send individual electronic signals across the telephone line—in essence, how fast it can "talk." But a modem encodes data before it sends it, adding error correction and compressing it, and so forth, so there's not a one-to-one relationship between baud and bits per second. After encoding, several bits of digital data can be transmitted in a single analog signal. This strategy is one way older modems achieved higher throughput. An old 2400 baud modem that could encode four bits of data for every analog signal it transmitted could be known as a 9600 bps modem (2400 × 4 = 9600).

Modems today use similar tricks, as well as even more sophisticated ones, to move data faster. For example, most of the modems known by some variant of the 56K name rely on compression, Error Checking and Correction (ECC), and a technical partnership between telephone companies and modem manufacturers that makes it possible to move data across traditional *Plain Old Telephone Service (POTS)* lines at speeds faster than previously thought possible. (This technology contrasts with special dedicated all-digital high-speed phone lines, which are the equivalent of paying the phone company to run a wire just for you between your office and anywhere in the world. It's expensive, and the cost keeps modems popular and drives the demand for alternatives.)

Lingo   *Plain Old Telephone Service (POTS)* is a term you'll probably encounter if you work with or around information technology (IT) folks responsible for moving your company's data from place to place. It simply means the phone lines that all of us have used for about a century.

POTS lines are limited in how fast data can move across them because of *limited bandwidth*: the amount of room a wire has for transmitting analog signals. To make the phone system manageable years ago, telephone companies limited the amount of room for sound to about 5 kilohertz (kHz). (As you may remember, this is the frequency below which most human speech occurs.) This same restriction limits the range of frequencies that modems can use, and so limits the speed at which data can be sent. This 5 kHz restriction isn't a limitation built into the actual telephone wires themselves; it's a restriction imposed on the design of telephone equipment, like switches, to make moving all of that sound manageable.

DSL and High-Speed Modems, Which Aren't Modems

Unfortunately, modems just aren't fast enough to carry us all into the Internet-enabled age. If it takes days to send video home to your grandparents, who's going to bother? So the success of the entire online industry started to stall because practically nobody could actually use the impressive online features the press so often touted. Yet research showed that thousands of people would love to have online ways of sending pictures, sounds, doing online banking, taking classes, and so on.

Try This! If your PC's modem is already configured and you belong to an online service, try this little exercise to get a feel for your modem performance. On your Microsoft Windows XP PC is a sample picture called Winter.jpg. It's about 100 kilobytes (KB) in size, and you'll find it here—C:\Documents and Settings\All Users\Documents\My Pictures\Sample Pictures—assuming that Windows XP is on your main hard disk, usually C, and that you haven't moved or deleted it.

Log on to your Internet service provider (ISP) and send a message to your e-mail address with the Winter.jpg file attached to it. Notice how long it takes to send the file from yourself to your electronic mailbox. Every file is different because some compress better than others. If you had a similar picture file that was 10 times the size, it would take about 10 times as long for your modem to send that picture to the online service. And a high-quality picture from your digital camera might easily be more like 70 times larger, not just 10 times. The uncompressed digital audio on a CD is about 7000 times larger.

Now, try opening the e-mail you just sent and download the attached file back to yourself. If you've got a 56K modem, you probably received the file a lot faster than you sent it. That's because 56K modems work asymmetrically—faster in one direction (download) than in the other (upload).

Although high-speed, dedicated digital phone lines have been available for some time, if you want to get one, the phone company has to come to you and run a wire from you back to its nearest switching station. You pay for this with high installation charges and *very* high service fees. It was never really in the telephone company's best interest to lower the service fees and make digital lines more popular, either—think of the work involved in basically rewiring the telephone systems of the world! It simply wasn't going to happen.

Instead, the phone companies replaced their switching equipment, rather than replacing the wires. This new equipment is able to transmit digital signals over POTS wires, alongside analog signals, by using the vast difference that exists between the bandwidth the wires can actually carry and the bandwidth they've carried up until the equipment change-out. Think of this as being like a change to your house's water pipes, which allows them to carry two different liquids at the same time, at different flow rates, in two different directions at the same time, without them mixing, and without reducing the amount of liquid the pipes can carry.

Those imaginary pipes are the real world of the *digital subscriber line (DSL)*. DSL establishes a completely digital connection between your PC and the telephone company's nearest switching station. This bit of magic allows you to send data at truly remarkable speeds relative to those available via modem.

When you select DSL service, you pay a different amount of money depending on the maximum transfer rate (highest bit rate) you want available to you. Your actual performance depends on a number of external factors, including how far you are from the telephone company's nearest switching station, to whom you're connecting, and so forth. At the time of this writing, 768 KB DSL is probably the most popular maximum speed selected, and it enables you to move data about 30 times faster than your modem probably provides.

To make DSL work, you need three pieces of hardware that you might not yet own. Most ISPs will sell you all three when you sign up for service because several different types of DSL service exist, and you must use hardware that's designed to work with your telephone company's DSL type. DSL requires a network card for your PC, a device incorrectly called a DSL modem, and a noise filter for each phone jack in your house (except the one the DSL modem plugs into). If you have a network card or connection in your PC already, you can use it to connect with DSL service. DSL will also connect to your small network by plugging into your network hub—more on that and network cards in Chapter 9.

The reason I say that a DSL modem isn't a modem is because—it isn't. A modem has its weird name because it *mo*dulates and *dem*odulates (converts) digital data into and from analog sound waves. The "DSL modem" is really just a special *transceiver* that can detect the digital signals running alongside your analog telephone sound signals, separate them, and send them on to your PC's network card in a manner the card will understand. (The same process happens in reverse, too, when you upload or transmit data.)

Lingo   A *transceiver* is a generic name for any device that can both transmit and receive signals of some variety. We don't usually think of a modem as a transceiver (although it technically is) because a modem's main purpose is seen as the converting of signals from digital to analog and back, rather than simply sending and receiving them.

The third piece of hardware you need to make a DSL connection work is a noise filter for each phone jack. Noise filters are necessary because the DSL signals sometimes cause what sounds like a hum or buzz on the analog line. The small filters eliminate that hum, so your telephone and fax systems work as they always have. Delightfully, you can even use your DSL connection and talk on the telephone or send and receive faxes at the same time.

A Permanent Connection

Although some telephone companies have tried to reduce their costs (a savings that is not generally passed on to their customers) by requiring DSL customers to log on and log off of their DSL connection, as though they were dialing up with a modem, this isn't necessary. DSL has the full potential to be a permanent connection that is always on, always ready for you to use. So there's no waiting for your connection to be established before you can get right to work. Just start Microsoft Internet Explorer, and you're instantly surfing the Web. Start Microsoft Outlook Express, and you're staring at new e-mail and newsgroup messages immediately. It's a delightful relief from experiences with traditional modems, in which getting knocked offline is familiar to us all.

The downside to a permanent connection, which we'll explore more in Chapter 9, is security. Your PC is vulnerable to outside attack only while it's connected to the outside. In your home or office, you often have absolute control over who has access to the physical machine and, thereby, eliminate most opportunities for anyone to endanger your data. When you're connected to the world permanently, however, your PC must be configured to address the sorts of attacks that might occur while you're asleep or away (assuming you leave your PC on 24/7, which I generally recommend).

A Permanent Connection: To Whom?

One thing can be quite confusing about DSL: from whom do you buy it? The actual DSL capability is something your local phone company provides. It's a feature that has to be added to your telephone line, and it usually requires a short visit from a telephone company technician to the connection block in your neighborhood, if not to your home. The local phone company can also function as your ISP, through whom you have your e-mail account and so forth. If you like, you can select any ISP that works with your telephone company's DSL to provide your online service.

Here's where it gets confusing, so bear with me. In my area, for example, at the time I'm writing this, the online ISP America Online works exclusively with the Pacific Bell telephone company. If you live in an area served by the Pacific Bell telephone company, you don't have to use America Online as your ISP to receive DSL service from Pacific Bell. But if you don't live in an area served by Pacific Bell, you can't get DSL service from America Online—however, you can still use America Online over your DSL connection.

OK, one step at a time. The phone company provides the physical support (wires, switches, and so on) you need for DSL. They are your DSL provider. This is not the complete picture, however. It's like having satellite TV service without subscribing to any channels—not particularly useful. You need an ISP to provide you with a connection to the Internet and other online features, like e-mail. The phone company could be your ISP, or you could select a different company to be your ISP, so long as that company and your phone company work together.

In the previous example, Pacific Bell could be your DSL provider, and America Online (or Pacific Bell, or any other company that works with Pacific Bell) could be your ISP. However, let's say you live across the street from me, in an area serviced by the Verizon telephone company. If you want DSL, Verizon will have to be your DSL provider because they're your phone company. You can select Verizon as your ISP, or you can select any ISP that works with Verizon. However, you can't select America Online as your ISP because they function as an ISP in this area only with Pacific Bell's DSL.

However, you can have an America Online account, and you can still connect to the America Online service via the same Internet connection you use to connect to everything else online—your DSL connection, working with your independent ISP. This configuration is possible because America Online has chosen to set itself up as a seamless (if enclosed) part of the greater Internet. By running the America Online software on your PC, you can connect to America Online as though your PC were permanently connected to America Online's network. America Online calls this "bringing your own access," and charges less for it than it would if you could subscribe to it as your ISP (which, as we've already established, you can't in this scenario).

> **Note**   Don't confuse this situation with the "always on" aspect of DSL. My DSL is always connected, but if I wanted to access America Online's special features, I would have to run America Online's software and log on to the service. To surf the Web, I just start Internet Explorer. I don't have to log on to America Online and then surf the Web because my ISP provides my Web-surfing capability.

Although DSL connects to your PC through a network connection, I've chosen to discuss it in this chapter rather than Chapter 9 because most people think of DSL as an alternative to traditional modems—which, of course, it is—rather than as a special network option (which it really isn't). Also, if you haven't subscribed to DSL, you're probably using a modem. Let's take a look at how modems integrate with your PC.

Windows XP and Modems

Windows XP supports almost any modem that's ever been available. Most modems require the installation of drivers to provide access to the modem's full features. Some modems even come with software that can turn your PC into a digital fax and answering machine. But whether your modem requires drivers or not, Windows XP needs to know it exists and how it's connected to your PC to communicate with it properly. When Windows detects that a modem has been installed inside your PC (as a card) or connected externally, it detects that modem's type and standard configuration, either installs its own drivers or prompts you to install drivers by inserting a CD provided by the modem maker, asks you a couple of questions about your phone service, and then you're set.

Windows performs all of these tasks through the Modem Setup Wizard. Although the wizard almost always runs automatically, you can access modem settings at any time, through Control Panel. Simply click Control Panel on the Start menu, select Printers And Other Hardware, and finally select Phone And Modem Options. You'll see the Phone And Modem Options dialog box shown in Figure 8-1.

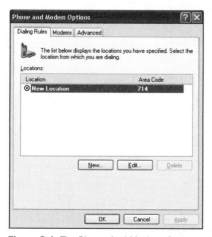

Figure 8-1 The Phone And Modem Options dialog box allows you to customize any of your dial-up settings.

Let's take a look at modem hardware options before we explore your phone settings. Click the Modems tab to access the window shown in Figure 8-2.

Figure 8-2 The Modems tab of the Phone And Modem Options dialog box displays your current modem hardware setup and provides access to settings.

In the extremely unlikely event that Windows XP doesn't detect that you've added a modem to your PC, you can run the Modem Setup Wizard simply by clicking Add. You'll see the special Modems version of the Windows XP Add Hardware Wizard, which we'll explore in depth in Chapter 16. You can step through the wizard, asking Windows XP to detect your modem automatically. If Windows XP can't do so, or if you want to tell Windows that you've installed a certain modem, you can disable the automatic detection and select the speed of your modem from a list, as shown in Figure 8-3.

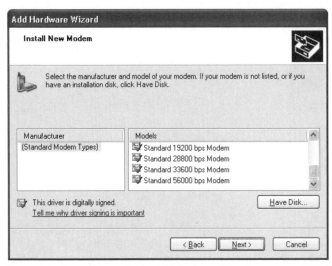

Figure 8-3   From this page in the Add Hardware Wizard, you can tell Windows which speed of modem you're installing.

If your modem manufacturer's documentation tells you that the modem is funky, well, frankly, go buy a different modem. But if necessary, you can click the Have Disk button and tell Windows XP where it can find customized drivers for the new hardware. Otherwise, just let Windows know what the maximum speed of your modem is, and click Next. If you're installing a custom driver, you might need to work your way through the manufacturer's own installation program before you find yourself at the next page of the wizard, shown in Figure 8-4. From here, you can select which *port* your modem will use to connect to your PC. We'll be looking at ports in the second half of this chapter.

Lingo   A *port* is a connection, usually a physical one, between the PC and some optional device. In the case of internal modems, a phantom or logical port is simulated by Windows so that your PC's physical port connections can still be used. Several ports can be in use at once, but only one device can use any one port at a time.

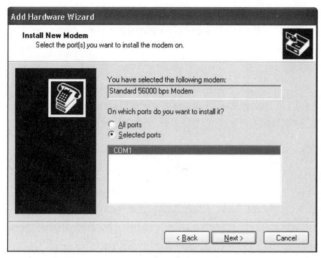

Figure 8-4 Here, you can select the port on which you want to install your modem.

Windows XP almost always displays the port to which your modem is already connected, whether that's an external port or a port that is being simulated by an internal modem. If the port shown isn't what you want used, you can click the All Ports option and see all of your PC's available connections. Choose the one you want, click Next, and wait for the wizard to finish. When it does, you'll see the modem you've added in the Modems tab, as previously shown in Figure 8-2.

Modifying Modem Settings

To modify a modem's settings, select it in the Modems tab of the Phone And Modem Options dialog box and click Properties. A Properties dialog box with a set of tabs will open, as shown in Figure 8-5.

Figure 8-5 From the Properties dialog box, you can modify the settings of many modem features.

Most modem properties will be set for their optimal values when
Windows XP initially detects the modem. You might change a few properties,
however, depending on your circumstances. Let's take a look at those. Three of
them are on the Modem tab.

Caution   If set incorrectly, some of the options here could cause your modem to function less
than optimally—or not at all. Unless you're following an expert's guidance, don't change any settings you don't understand.

First, you can manually set your modem's speaker volume. You might want
to hear your modem dial and try to connect if you're having trouble getting it to
work, as the sounds you hear (or don't hear) can help you diagnose the problem. For example, if you don't even hear it try to dial, you know the problem is
probably either a defective modem or one or more incorrect fundamental hardware installation settings. If it dials, tries to connect, and fails, you might have a
simpler problem based on feature settings. On the other hand, if your modem is
working just fine, why on earth would you want to listen to that squabble? Just
drag the slider to the left, which turns your modem sound off. You can always
turn it up again if you start to have problems.

Second, the Maximum Port Speed option allows you to connect a new
modem to an older one that can't work as fast. The older modem might be con-
fused by the faster modem's attempt to handshake and negotiate a speed. Rather
than negotiating a slower speed with your modem, it might just refuse to work
altogether. In that case, you can use the Maximum Port Speed option to reduce
the maximum speed of your modem so that it doesn't try faster speeds in the
first place.

This setting can also be useful if you're connecting over a phone line
that is often noisy. In that case, you can connect at a high speed but then get
knocked offline when the noise comes in too loud and fast for the modem
to negotiate a slower speed. Slow the modem down in the first place, and
you might solve your noise problem. (Of course, if you have a noisy phone line,
it's best to find out why and solve the problem at the source.)

Third, you can use the Maximum Port Speed option to resolve a type of
problem that can occur when you take a modem to a foreign country and try
to dial. Your "sold in America" modem might not want to work on the banks
of the Seine. Sometimes, this nuisance occurs because the dial tone in your

area is not detectable by the modem, even though it's there. You can turn off your modem's habit of waiting for the dial tone, and everything will work swimmingly. On the other hand, it's really annoying to be talking on the phone and have someone try to dial out on a modem using the same line. The modem's dialing tones are generally quite loud. By forcing the modem to listen for a dial tone before it starts dialing, you enable it to check whether the line is already in use before it interrupts.

In addition, the Power Management tab provides some rather nice features. It allows you to power off some modems when they're not in use, which is nice if you're using a notebook computer on battery power with a PC Card modem. PC Cards are generally kept powered all the time they're inserted in your computer, and they draw a lot of power. By turning the modem off when you're not online, you can extend battery life dramatically.

Note   The Power Management tab isn't supported by all modems.

On the other hand, if you're using your modem like a fax machine or an answering machine, you need it to be able to function whenever the phone rings. And although leaving your PC on all the time is a great idea, that presumes that you have your Power Management settings configured to put the PC to sleep when it's not being used. In any case, the Power Management tab lets you tell your PC to wake up from its power-saving slumber whenever the modem detects that the phone is ringing.

See Also   *The concept of power management is discussed in Chapter 14, where we'll take a look at the Windows XP Device Manager.*

Finally, getting a proper connection in a foreign country or to a customized online service or private bulletin board service (BBS) might require that you manually set your modem to work in certain ways. The Advanced tab allows you to enter customized initialization commands that Windows sends to your modem before it dials. In some cases, you won't be able to connect to a service at all if you don't first tell your modem how to behave.

The Modem Troubleshooter   If you're having trouble with your modem, you can try two possible solutions. First, if you want to check to see whether Windows can communicate with the modem at all, open the Properties dialog box for your modem and select the Diagnostics tab. Click Query Modem and wait. Windows XP will send out a command to the modem that says, basically, "Tell me what you are and what you can do." If the communication isn't successful, you can move on to the next step. If it is, you'll see a window like that in Figure 8-6.

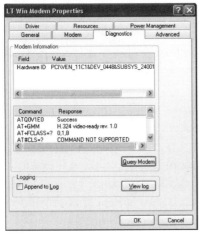

Figure 8-6 After successfully querying your modem, Windows XP displays its settings and the way it responds to certain standard commands.

If you scroll through the list that appears in the Command And Response section of the window and discover that your modem doesn't support—or registers failure in response to—a certain command that you're trying to use, perhaps with a customized initialization string, you've found your problem. Your modem's hardware can't do what you need it to do. You'll need a different modem or a workaround for the problem.

If everything in the Command And Response section looks fine, or if Windows can't communicate with the modem at all, you'll need to run the Modem Troubleshooter, which you can access from the General tab of the Properties dialog box by just clicking Troubleshoot. The Modem Troubleshooter is essentially a wizard that's part of the Windows XP Help And Support Center (covered in Chapter 15).

The Troubleshooter quickly steps you through basic questions about what you've observed, such as: "Does Windows not see your modem at all?" and "Does your modem connect to a private service, but not to the Internet?" As you answer the questions, Help And Support uses artificial intelligence to consider your answers and investigate your PC's hardware settings for potential causes.

The Troubleshooter then makes several suggestions for you to try. In most cases, it will discover that some setting is wrong, it will correct it for you, and you'll be ready to go. In a worst-case scenario, the Troubleshooter will direct you to online or personal (telephone) support, which will help you get your modem up and running smoothly.

Proper Settings for More than the Modem

To connect to an ISP successfully, you might need to change settings that don't strictly relate to the modem itself. You'll use the New Connection Wizard in Windows XP to make those settings initially, and you can modify many of them manually by using the Dialing Rules tab that's part of the Phone And Modem Options dialog box shown previously in Figure 8-1. Using the wizard is the easiest way to set up every aspect of a new online connection. Give it a try!

Try This!   Access the New Connection Wizard from the Start menu by selecting Programs, Accessories, Communications, and then New Connection Wizard. Because we'll see this wizard again in Chapter 9, we won't get into it in great detail here. But here are the steps to configure a new connection to your ISP using the New Connection Wizard:

1   Start the wizard and click Next. You want to set up a connection to an ISP, so make sure that Connect To The Internet is selected, and then click Next.

2   On the next page, you can either choose your ISP from a list of popular ones, or you can tell Windows you want to enter your settings manually. If you want to select your ISP from a list, the wizard will close and you'll be shown ISPs for which Windows XP has built-in support. In that case, just double-click your ISP, answer a few questions about where you're located, and you're on your way. To set up for an ISP not included in the Windows XP list, choose to enter your settings manually and click Next.

3   Tell the wizard that you're configuring a dial-up modem and click Next again.

4   Enter the name with which you want to identify this connection. Windows XP actually asks for the name of your ISP, but you can enter anything here. You can set up different settings for connecting with your ISP from different locations, so you could enter **ISP – Dialing from Home** or **ISP – Dialing from Paris** (where *ISP* would be the name of your ISP). Click Next.

5   Enter the phone number you want to dial. If you need to dial a number, often 9 or 8, before you can dial an external phone number, you'll need to enter that number here, followed by a comma, which tells the modem to wait a moment to allow the phone system to provide an external dial tone. After the comma, enter the number you need to dial, with no spaces or hyphens. For example, you might enter **9,5551212** to dial a local number, or **9,17145551212** to dial a number in the 714 area (presuming that's not your local area). Click Next.

6   You'll be prompted to enter your username and password. The password must be entered twice to make sure you type it correctly. You can also tell Windows whether this is your default Internet connection. If it is, whenever you start Internet Explorer or Outlook Express, this connection will be automatically dialed for you. (You also can turn the Windows XP Internet Connection Firewall on or off here, but we'll discuss that in Chapter 9.) Click Next to confirm your settings.

That's it. You're done. You're online!

Connecting to a Connection: Ports

To connect online, you've got to have a modem or a modem alternative. If you've got a modem, it has to be accessed through one of your PC's communication ports. As I said earlier in this chapter, ports are usually physical connections to the outside world—sockets on the front or back of your PC into which you plug cords that connect to peripherals.

In the case of an internal modem, which plugs into one of your PC's internal adapter slots (usually a PCI slot), Windows XP creates a logical port through which all of the modem's commands and data will flow. This way, all of your physical ports remain available for other devices. The connection on your PC that you plug your monitor into is a port, but it's dedicated to one purpose. It's not one of your PC's generic, multipurpose communications ports.

Parallel and Serial: But Mostly Parallel

Ports come in two different flavors, depending on how they move data into and out of your PC: serial ports and parallel ports. The term *parallel* refers to the fact that this port uses many wires, bundled together in a thick cable, to move data bits in parallel. Originally, parallel ports sent data only in one direction, but today, they are bi-directional—the wires can send data out, to a printer, for example, and they can receive data, too. The parallel port is sometimes called a printer port because it's rarely used for anything else.

Two different configurations exist for parallel ports, in addition to the standard parallel port. Most parallel ports can operate in accordance with either of these standards, to accommodate any type of hardware you might connect to them—Windows XP generally detects the device you're using and tells the parallel port how to behave depending on that device's needs.

The first configuration, called an Enhanced Parallel Port (EPP) is fast, and was created to make parallel ports work better with external storage devices, like tape backup drives. The second configuration, the Enhanced, or Extended, Capabilities Port (ECP) is faster still. If your PC doesn't properly respond to instructions from Windows XP, you might need to go into your hardware basic input/output system (BIOS) setup and manually configure your parallel port as being of one type or the other.

See Also   *We'll discuss the BIOS in Chapter 16.*

Today, the parallel port is something of an anachronism. Modern serial ports are faster, serial port cables are smaller, lighter, and cheaper, and serial port connectors are physically smaller than the monstrous connectors required to support the huge bundle of wires stuffed inside a parallel cable. Even most printers today connect to the PC through a network cable or through one of the high-speed serial ports. The parallel port remains to keep your PC compatible with older printers. After all, you might want to upgrade your PC every few years, but a good printer can last over a decade. If your printer happens to be approaching that age, it comes from a parallel-only world.

Serial Ports: A Little *Bit* at a Time

Serial ports used to be slower than parallel ports because, among other reasons, they moved only one bit of data at a time. The Serial Port (with capitals) has changed so much over time that we really think about three entirely different types of ports that move data in series (or serially): serial ports, universal serial bus (USB) ports, and FireWire (otherwise known as IEEE 1394) ports. The two ports that most people think of when they hear the phrase *serial port* are called COM1 and COM2 and are located at the back of the computer. These are the two traditional configurations. The only difference between them is the size of their connector, but they work in exactly the same way—moving one bit of data to or from the PC at a time. Serial connectors used to be 25-pin, but as technology improved, the size was reduced to the more common 9-pin variety.

Traditional serial ports were popular for connecting external modems and early models of mouse to PCs, but they were slow. (Perhaps I should say that they *are* slow, because, like their parallel cousin, every PC has at least one traditional serial port built directly into its motherboard.) When it came time to think about making connections between the PC and more advanced peripherals that would move lots of data quickly, it was obvious that traditional serial ports just wouldn't have the *throughput* necessary to do the job.

Lingo   A port's *throughput* is the amount of data it can actually process in some period of time. Throughput is usually measured in bits per second. Throughput might sound like a synonym for bandwidth, but it's best to think of bandwidth as relating to the room for signals of different analog frequencies, and throughput as measuring the capability to move bits of digital data.

Further enhancements to the parallel port were considered, but a better alternative was to come up with different types of serial ports that would meet the growing needs of an increasingly multimedia-oriented world. Along with providing higher throughput, research showed that consumers wanted a few specific features if they were to embrace a new type of connection:

- Much smaller connections
- Better connectors with no obnoxious tiny pins in them

- More ports on each PC, or some other way of connecting many more devices

- Plug and play support with hot-swappable capabilities (meaning that you could plug a device in or unplug it with the power on and everything would work just fine)

- Speed, speed, speed

From this and other research emerged two candidates for a replacement serial port: the USB port and the FireWire port. As it turns out, both candidates came out winners, and on many PCs, you'll find both, working in parallel—if you'll pardon the terrible pun. Let's take a look at each.

USB: The Universal Serial Bus

As you'll recall, a *bus* is a superhighway over which data can quickly move. Data on a bus is typically accompanied by control signals that indicate where it's coming from and where it needs to go. Consequently, the bus can allow a lot of data to move simultaneously, up to the maximum throughput of the bus. USB, which is now in its third major incarnation, called USB 2 (following versions 1 and 1.1), has all of the features necessary to make it a viable replacement for the antiquated serial port. Its throughput is fast—up to 480 megabits per second (Mbps). That's about 4000 times faster than the original serial port (115 kilobits per second, or Kbps).

Lingo   The terms *kilobits* and *megabits* refer to thousands and millions of bits, respectively. These terms are commonly used to discuss port, bus, and network speeds. To convert to kilobytes or megabytes, respectively, simply multiply by 8. You will usually see kilobits abbreviated Kb, kilobytes abbreviated KB, megabits abbreviated Mb, and megabytes abbreviated MB. But some product specifications use these abbreviations incorrectly (by accident, one hopes). Be certain you know a product's real capabilities; if it seems too good to be true for its price, it is.

USB allows up to 127 different products to be connected to your PC through the use of *hubs*: connection boxes that can turn a single USB port into many. Some hubs come with power adapters that plug into an electrical outlet, and these hubs also act as signal amplifiers and repeaters, extending the distance over which a USB connection can function reliably.

Although most PCs have two built-in USB ports, that doesn't mean you can connect 254 devices, total. Each USB controller can support the 127-device maximum. To support additional devices, you would have to install additional USB ports and additional bus controller hardware via an adapter card, many of which are available (although they are usually sold to provide USB capabilities to an older PC that has none).

Note USB signals normally travel about 16 feet before they start to degrade. Both powered hubs and nonpowered repeating extension cords that can extend this range significantly can be purchased.

If your PC is new, your keyboard and mouse probably plug in through a USB port. Many handheld devices, like Pocket PCs, connect to a full-size PC through USB. A variety of portable devices, including CD drives (both players and recorders), and even some hard disks use USB. It's also the connector of choice for digital cameras and for portable digital audio devices like MP3 players.

To simplify connections, USB uses two different plugs, depending on what's plugging where. The first type, known as Type A, is flat and rectangular, and is used to connect devices or hubs to the PC itself. The Type A connector is keyed so that it will fit into the socket only one way—the right way. The Type B connector is essentially a square with two rounded corners that prevent the connector from being plugged in wrong. It's used to connect the USB cable to devices, and its smaller size reflects the fact that old serial connectors were sometimes so large and heavy, they would drag the device they connected to right off the desk. USB connections are almost always hot-swappable, so you can add or remove devices whenever you like.

For example, I use a tiny USB CompactFlash card reader to move pictures I take with my digital camera onto my PC. When I need to use it, I just plug it in. Windows XP recognizes it immediately and treats it like a removable hard disk. I can see thumbnails of all my pictures instantly, as I can with all the pictures stored on my PC, and moving images to the PC is just a matter of drag-and-drop.

FireWire: IEEE 1394

If USB is so great, who needs a second option? Well, USB reached its current speed potential of 480 Mbps only in 2002, with the introduction of USB 2, and high-speed USB 2 devices are rare at the time of this writing. Before USB 2, the maximum throughput of USB was only 12 Mbps, with most devices operating at only 1.5 Mbps. FireWire was actually developed first, and had a throughput of 400 Mbps from the start. (I mentioned USB first because it is still more common than FireWire.)

FireWire has most of the same features as USB, but FireWire's far-faster throughput and complexity made it much more expensive to implement than USB. FireWire was better suited, technologically and economically, for use in high-end applications such as digital video, where cost was less important and data had to move really fast.

To move digital video data off of videotape and onto a PC in real time (that is, as the tape is playing—the only way to do it), you need to have what techies call "a really wide pipe." FireWire is really the only game in this particular town, and under a variety of names, including Sony's trademarked iLink, FireWire is found on every digital camcorder out there. A variety of high-performance CD and DVD burners and hard disks also support FireWire, where high throughput is necessary and where the cost of implementing FireWire doesn't make as much of a difference (because the products, like digital camcorders, are expensive already).

FireWire is undergoing its first major revision as I am writing this. The new technology, which was formerly called IEEE 1394b, uses a slightly different connector (which you can see contrasted with the original FireWire connector in Figure 8-7) and provides throughput up to 3.2 Gbps: eight times faster than current FireWire. (No new name has been selected for the revision.)

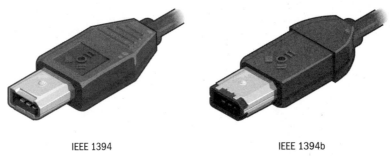

IEEE 1394   IEEE 1394b

Figure 8-7 The original FireWire connector (left) and its successor, the IEEE 1394b connector (right) look pretty similar, but there are some differences.

The new version of FireWire will continue to support today's slower FireWire devices without penalizing the performance of the high-speed, next-generation devices that might be connected to the PC. And it outshines even USB 2. Because FireWire devices can connect directly to each other, with no PC around for miles—a configuration known as *peer-to-peer*—you can connect two digital camcorders and make a perfect digital copy of your home video directly. FireWire's peer-to-peer configuration also means that FireWire devices can be daisy chained together, with up to 63 devices connecting to a single PC (or simply to each other).

You might suspect that if a FireWire device doesn't need a PC, then it must contain all of the circuitry necessary to control the movement of data. You'd be right. This is one of the reasons why FireWire is so much more expensive than USB. USB devices are, in a sense, *passive*, controlled by a single host controller. In contrast, FireWire devices are *active*, with the controller circuitry built into every FireWire product. They cost more money—but you get what you pay for.

Key Points

■ A modem is a device for converting digital data into analog signals that can be transmitted across Plain Old Telephone Service (POTS) lines.

■ Modern modems can move data up to a maximum speed of 56,000 bits per second (bps) when downloading and 28,000 bps when uploading, although maximum speeds of around 48,000 bps are more common.

■ Digital Subscriber Line (DSL) is a comparatively new technology that allows all-digital signals to be transmitted alongside traditional POTS analog signals (sound) using existing POTS wires. DSL performance begins at roughly 20 times that of modems, with 30-times modem performance being the most popular speed as this is being written. DSL performance currently tops out at over 300-times modem performance, and continues to increase.

■ The Add New Hardware Wizard automatically detects almost any modem you connect to your PC and sets it up for you effortlessly. The New Connection Wizard makes it easy to create custom setups that allow you to go online from different locations.

■ Ports are connections—usually physical ones—by which external peripherals plug into your PC.

■ Ports are either parallel ports, in which one bit of data is moved on each of several wires so that an entire byte is sent and received at once, or serial ports, in which single bits of data are moved in a continuous stream.

■ Parallel ports are usually used for connecting printers to PCs.

■ Serial ports come in three varieties. Traditional serial ports are used to connect external modems, mouse devices, and other small devices to a PC. Universal serial bus (USB) ports and FireWire ports are two newer, high-performance serial ports that allow many different devices to be connected to the PC at once.

■ Most USB and all FireWire devices are hot-swappable, and they can be plugged in or detached from a PC without any need to turn off or restart the computer.

Chapter 9

Works Well with Others

The idea of collaborative working on the PC has been around for some time. In theory, I could be in my home office, you could be on vacation in Florida, and a coworker could be in Tasmania, and we could all open the same file simultaneously and work together on it. Collaborative working has become extremely popular through the development of high-speed Internet connections like digital subscriber line (DSL), and, in a more general sense, the ability to connect a bunch of PCs, either locally or over great distances. Making those connections between computers is called *networking*. And fortunately, all the software you need to network is built right into Microsoft Windows XP, and all the hardware you need to network will cost you only about $25.

So why wait? If you're one of the millions of people interested in switching from modem use to DSL, you're going to want to know about networking even if you own only one PC. So let's start, as in every chapter in this part of the book, with a look at the necessary hardware.

Networking Hardware and Protocols

Why would you want to connect computers? To share data, to share programs, and to share resources like printers and huge storage devices like collections of hard disks working together in an array. Many of those hardware resources are expensive, and most businesses can't afford to put a color laser printer on the

desk of every employee who might ever need one. Instead, employees' computers are connected as part of a *network* (the word is a noun as well as a verb).
The expensive resource is also connected to the network, where it can be
shared by any employee who needs it.

> **Lingo**   When a device like a printer is part of a network, available to many different users, it's
> called a *shared resource*. Files and other software can also be shared, and *file sharing* is an
> important feature of Windows XP networking.

Before networking technology was practical, and in places where it hasn't
been implemented, people have to carry data from one computer to another
using what's been called the *Sneakernet*. Today, the majority of networking that
takes place in the world uses cables, connectors, and network adapter cards that
adhere to a standard called Fast Ethernet.

> **Lingo**   *Fast Ethernet* is a popular standard of network hardware that normally moves data at
> 100 megabits per second (Mbps), but can slow down to 10 Mbps to remain compatible with older
> Ethernet hardware.

Wired Fast Ethernet

The simplest Fast Ethernet network possible consists of two PCs, each with its
own network card, connected with an RJ-45, 10/100Base-T Cat5 crossover cable.
The *RJ-45* refers to the connector used at each end of the network cable. An RJ-45
connector looks like a large modular telephone connector. The *10/100Base-T* part
refers to the two speeds at which Fast Ethernet can move data, and the type of
cable being used. *Cat5* is a reference to an industry standard for shielding the
cable so that the traffic can move over the network reliably, without the signal
being lost or troubled with interference.

> **Lingo**   *Traffic* simply means all data that moves across a network. When we speak of the total
> amount of traffic a network can handle at one time, we refer to the network's *bandwidth*.

The lower the Cat (category) number, the slower traffic must move to maintain the integrity of the network and prevent signal drop-off. Finally, *crossover*
simply means that the wires responsible for sending and receiving reverse between
one end of the cable and another. This reversal is necessary to connect two Ethernet cards together without using a hub, and requires a special type of cable.

Lingo   A network *hub* is simply a box with sockets that provides a central connection point for many PCs on a network. A *switch* is an "intelligent" hub that learns the identity of computers connected to it, to better route network traffic.

In reality, even if you're connecting only two PCs, it's most common to connect them through a hub. Hubs are inexpensive (unlike crossover cables), and provide expandability in case you want to add PCs to the network down the road. A hub also makes it possible to add a device like a network-ready printer or scanner to the network so that it can be used from any connected PC. You can share a printer that is directly connected to a PC on the network, but that requires the involved PC to be turned on and working properly any time someone wants to print. It's far better to connect the printer to the hub so that it's always at your disposal, even if it's at the end of the hall and your PC is the only one in the office that isn't off.

Wireless Networks

All of that assumes that your network uses wires to connect PC to PC and to shared resources. There is another way: wireless. An industry standard called *802.11b* allows you to use radio waves to create a network that can stretch over distances with no physical connection between the devices. Each PC on this kind of network has one of several different types of wireless adapter connected to it. For a desktop PC, it's usually a standard adapter card with a small antenna that sticks out the back of the PC. Notebook computers connect with special PC Card devices.

At the center of this network is a *wireless access point (WAP),* which is like a wireless hub. It brings all of the radio signals together and routes the data traffic between them all. The WAP can also serve as a connection to a wired network. For example, at home, my DSL connection and my printer plug directly into a hub, and my desktop computers plug into that hub, so they can share my DSL. My WAP is also plugged into the hub, making it possible for me to work on a notebook computer anywhere in the house while still printing, using my DSL connection to the Internet, or sharing files with my desktop PCs. Some WAPs are also wired hubs.

If you're considering wireless networking, you'll want to make certain that any hardware you select is compliant with the 802.11b standard (802.11a exists, and is making a resurgence, but it's expensive) and that it uses Wireless Encryption Protocol (WEP) to keep your data and network secure. Windows XP fully supports all of the wireless security options you need.

Security Issues for Wireless Networks   Of course, security concerns abound with any kind of network, but wireless networks have unique problems. Because radio signals travel through the air, and because they spread out in all directions, it's possible for someone to sit outside your home or office and "sniff" the air, as it's called, with a radio receiver, capturing any data you send across your wireless network.

To eliminate the problem, encryption is used to scramble all data that is sent over a wireless network. Someone can still listen in and capture the data in the radio signals, but they won't be able to make any sense out of it. Encryption also prevents your next-door neighbor from using your Internet connection while leaving you with the joy of paying for it. Without the right password, no one will be able to connect to or make sense of anything happening on your wireless network.

Popular Protocols

The largest network in the world is the well-known Internet. In fact, the Internet is a huge collection of other networks that have all been, well, networked together. We'll talk more about the Internet, but the one point to remember about it for the moment is this: the Internet exists because many smaller networks are all connected, but far more important than all those networks using the same hardware—which they absolutely do not—is the fact that they all speak the same language.

Of course, PCs are machines, not people, and the concept of *computer languages* means something else—the code systems used to write applications for computers to run. So, naturally, it's necessary to open the lingo locker and introduce yet another term.

> **Lingo**   In a general sense, *protocol* means a structured, organized way of achieving some goal. In networking, a *network protocol* is the language the computers and network hardware all speak to work together harmoniously.

In the world of PC networking, many different protocols exist, each of which makes it possible for a networked computer to access different resources or retrieve different data in different ways. Probably the best-known protocol is called Hypertext Transfer Protocol (HTTP). In a nutshell, it's the networking language that makes the World Wide Web work. When you want to connect to a Web page, your request is typed as the Web protocol plus the address of the Web page you want, as in *http://www.microsoft.com*.

Your request to see that Web page is routed to the appropriate computer where the page is hosted, called a *Web server*. When the server receives your message, it interprets the *http://* before the Web address as "She is using *http://*; therefore, I know she wants to view the Web page she specified." The content on that Web page is sent back to your computer, is received by your Web browser, identified as Web content, and displayed properly.

Some networking protocols are called *secure* because any data that's transmitted in their language is encrypted before it moves across the network connections. Anyone who intercepts the data won't be able to read it unless they are the data's intended recipient. Secure protocols and encryption are exceedingly important, especially if any confidential data is going to be moved over the Internet. Why?

Remember that I said the Internet isn't a network, but is a huge collection of networks? Each of those individual networks is operated by different folks, some of whom might just be less honest than others. Because of how the Internet works, to get data from my home in California to my friend in North Carolina, the data might pass through any number of other networks, each of which is just part of the Internet.

Every time my data passes through someone's network, it's possible for that person to intercept it. Secure networking protocols help guarantee that my data won't make any sense to anyone who shouldn't possess it. The best-known of these is called the *Secure Sockets Layer (SSL)*, for reasons that don't matter to us at all. In brief, SSL is the secure version of HTTP and is used to send encrypted data to and from Web sites.

Other protocols might be familiar to you already. The File Transfer Protocol (FTP) is one of the oldest of the lot, and it's used strictly for what you'd think: to move files from one place to another over the network. It used to be necessary to run a dedicated FTP program to send or receive files in this manner, but not anymore. Windows XP and Microsoft Internet Explorer have built-in support for FTP.

Under Windows XP, you can open an FTP connection to another computer that looks and works just like a Windows XP folder. You can drag files freely in and out, using the mouse. Anyone who has your FTP address can access any of the files you drag into the folder, unless you protect your files by requiring anyone who wants to connect to enter a username and password.

Historically, FTP servers have allowed people to access public files without requiring usernames or passwords—a connection called *anonymous*. Windows XP supports anonymous FTP connections, too, but you might not want to give universal file access to anyone who happens to stumble across your FTP address.

TCP/IP

The protocol I haven't yet mentioned is the one everybody is talking about: the Transmission Control Protocol/Internet Protocol (TCP/IP). The thing is, TCP/IP isn't a protocol at all. It's actually a stack of protocols including those you've already read about: HTTP and FTP, and many others, among which are the Simple Mail Transfer Protocol (SMTP) and the Post Office Protocol (POP3), which make e-mail work. Together, all these protocols provide a majority of the functionality of the Internet and Windows XP–based home and business networks. All TCP/IP's various pieces function like a post office system for data.

Lingo   The TCP/IP *stack* is the collection of many protocols that work together to provide the Internet with all of its functionality.

You've probably heard of an *IP address*, which is a series of four numbers, separated by periods. For example, 192.168.0.17 is an IP address. Each IP address specifies a unique resource—a server, a printer—on the collection of networks we call the Internet. When you move data using TCP/IP—say, a file—it's broken into pieces and packaged into units called *packets*, which function a bit like envelopes. Each packet bears, among other information, the IP address of the destination resource, like a regular piece of mail is addressed with someone's name, apartment number, street, and so forth.

Each packet has a return address, as well, and this is used to send a message back to you that each packet of data has been received successfully. (You might recall this general idea from when we talked about error detection and modems back in Chapter 8.) Faulty packets are resent. At the destination, the packets are assembled in order, the extra data (addresses and so forth) are stripped out, and whatever you were sending is recreated as a file, an e-mail message, or streaming video.

Introducing Microsoft Networking for Windows XP

Networking has been part of Windows ever since the old Microsoft Windows 3.11 for Workgroups premiered more than a decade ago, but never has setting up a network been as easy as Windows XP makes it. And if you upgrade a networked PC to Windows XP, you likely won't have to do anything. If you're adding network hardware to a PC, you'll find that Windows XP makes installing Ethernet cards equally painless, thanks to the Network Setup Wizard.

The Network Setup Wizard

In some instances, you won't even see this wizard because Windows XP supports networking so well, there's just nothing for you to do. The wizard also allows you to customize your network setup later. As with all wizards, simply step through it, selecting the options that are best for you.

- Does your PC connect to the Internet directly, or do you share another computer's connection? If your Internet connection is provided through a hub to which each PC connects, you should choose the Direct Connection option. If you're using Windows XP's Internet Connection Sharing (ICS), you'll want to choose Sharing.

- What's your hardware connection to the network and the Internet? Windows XP automatically makes what it thinks is the best choice, but if you have several network adapters in your PC for some reason, you can choose the appropriate one from a list.

- What's the name of your PC? Windows XP asks you to name your PC when it's set up, but you can easily change the name here.

- What's the name of your workgroup? You'll usually want to use the default name here, but if you're adding a PC to an existing network, you should ask the network administrator for the name of your workgroup and enter it here. PCs on the network are organized into workgroups to make them and other resources like network printers easier to find.

   Delightfully, that's all there is to setting up a basic Windows XP network.

The New Connection Wizard

Most of the time, you won't need to set up any kind of Internet connection; Windows XP does the work for you. However, the New Connection Wizard, accessible from the Start menu by selecting All Programs, Accessories, and finally Communication, lets you create additional connections or customize your existing ones. If you don't yet have an Internet connection, you can use the wizard to select from a list of prominent Internet service providers (ISPs). If you have an existing connection and need to refine its settings, you can select whether you're using a dial-up modem (which we discussed in Chapter 8) or a broadband network connection like DSL.

Windows XP usually recognizes a broadband connection automatically, and you won't have to use this wizard at all. But in some cases, your ISP will require customized settings that aren't automatically detectable. The wizard allows you to access your network settings and make the changes your ISP requires. Make certain that you have the proper documentation from your ISP before you start manually changing settings. Microsoft Technical Support can't help you set up a specific ISP; you'll need to contact that company's support staff for assistance.

Sharing Resources

Once your network and Internet connections are established, you might want to make it possible for other people on your network to share the resources you have available to you. Sharing works differently depending on which of two types of resources you want to share. Windows XP lets you share a single Internet connection across many computers (as long as this is allowed by the user agreement you have with your ISP), and it lets you share files and devices like printers, too. We'll spend the remainder of this chapter looking at how you can share what you want to share without opening your PC up to security concerns or other vulnerabilities.

Internet Connection Sharing

Windows XP Internet Connection Sharing (ICS) allows you to pay for one household subscription to Internet access and then use it from any PC on your network. This configuration makes it possible for you to do things like work on a project while your children research answers to their homework and a friend plays an online game. With ICS configured properly, you'll each be able to connect to Internet resources, including Web sites and e-mail, as though your PC were connected directly.

ICS is set up for you automatically by the Network Setup Wizard, and unless your ISP has provided you with customized settings you need to make manually, you won't need to do anything to enjoy the benefits of ICS. What the Network Setup Wizard won't do automatically, however, is protect your PC from others on the Internet who might have malicious intent.

To get this protection—it's part of Windows XP, it's just not turned on automatically—you simply need to activate the Internet Connection Firewall (ICF).

Lingo   A *firewall* is a piece of software or hardware that carefully blocks access to your PC from outsiders so that your private files and other content can't be viewed, changed, or stolen over your network.

To turn this protection on, just follow these steps:

1   Click the Network Connections icon in Control Panel, and double-click your Internet connection. In most cases, this will be your Local Area Connection if you access the Internet through a broadband device.

2   Click Properties, and then select the Advanced tab.

3   Select the Protect My Computer option, and the Internet Connection Firewall will turn on immediately.

4   Click OK to close all of the network settings dialog boxes.

In a few cases, the Internet Connection Firewall might interfere with custom configurations that your ISP has required you set manually. If you have problems after turning on ICF, you should contact your ISP for advice. A firewall is one of two pieces of security protection—the other is antivirus software—that any PC that connects to the Internet or any other network should have enabled. If you have difficulty using your network with ICF turned on, something on your PC is probably set wrong, and your ISP can definitely set you right.

File and Device Sharing

The second type of resource you can share under Windows XP is local to you— files and other devices like printers that are on your networked PCs or are connected directly to the network. Two different types of file sharing are allowed in Windows XP: Windows 2000–style file sharing, in which each file on the entire PC has a permissions level set that determines who can access or modify it; and Simple File Sharing, the default file sharing system that allows universal access to all shared resources.

Simple File Sharing is disabled when Windows XP is first installed, but you can turn it on easily enough. The first folder you share—by right-clicking its icon and selecting Sharing And Security from the shortcut menu—displays a warning indicating that Sharing is off for security reasons. Simply click the underlined text (it's a hyperlink, just like underlined text on the Web), and sharing will be enabled.

Then, in the Network Sharing And Security part of the dialog box, you'll be able to select Share This Folder On The Network and assign a name to the folder you're sharing. You can use the folder's original name if you want, or you can select a new one by which everyone will see the shared content.

Caution   If you want to allow other users on the network to see—but not modify or delete—your shared files, make sure you don't select the Allow Network Users To Change My Files option. That way, your work will be protected from loss or changes.

Simple File Sharing also allows you to make your documents available—or not—to other people who use the same PC as you. For this aspect of Simple File Sharing to work, you must each have a different user name. It's best for each of you to have a password, too; otherwise, someone can simply log on as you and access your work.

Try This!   To create new usernames, open the User Accounts Control Panel and select Create A New Account. Give each user an account with a name they'll recognize. You'll also need to decide whether each account should have Administrator access—which basically means freedom to make major changes to all aspects of the PC, other than viewing private files.

Once your accounts are created, click each one in the User Accounts icon of Control Panel, and then click Create A Password. Enter the default password you want for each account. (You have to enter it twice, and then enter a hint to help the user remember it.) Each user can log on and change his or her password later.

Once you have separate user accounts active, every account will have access to all files on the PC except those that are private, so the next step in making this type of file sharing work is making your files private. From the Start menu, select My Computer. You'll see the Files Stored On This Computer window. Right-click the folder that bears your username and select Sharing And Security. In the dialog box that opens, select the Make This Folder Private option and click OK. Windows XP will assign privacy to your files so that only someone logged on as you will be able to access them (which is why you need password protection to control who can do that).

Now, to share your work, simply drag files into the Shared Documents folder at the top of the My Computer window. Any files, pictures, or music stored inside will be available to anyone using your local PC. If you drag a file out of Shared Documents back into your private documents folder, that file will become private again. Sharing a device is as easy as sharing files. Let's share a local printer as an example.

Tip   Keep in mind that sharing a local printer will put a burden on your PC when others print, so if you're doing intensive work, you might want to unshare the printer until you're done. Alternatively, you might want to connect the printer directly to your network hub (if the printer supports a network connection) so that anyone on the network can print without burdening anyone else.

To share a printer, from the Start menu, select the Printers And Other Hardware icon in Control Panel, and select View Installed Printers Or Fax Printers. Then right-click the printer you want to share and select Sharing. In the window that opens, select the Share This Printer option, and give the printer a simple name that will identify it. You might also want to install printer drivers so that people on your network using Microsoft Windows Millennium Edition (Windows Me) or Microsoft Windows 98 can easily connect to it. To do that, just click Additional Drivers and select the operating systems you want to support. You'll need your Windows XP setup CD to complete this process.

Once done, users on your network can simply open their Network Places folder, see the printer attached as a shared device to your PC, and select it as their own default printer. Keep in mind that your PC must be on whenever someone might want to use the shared printer—this is another benefit of using a printer directly connected to the network.

Key Points

- Connecting computers so that people using them can work together and communicate is called networking.

- Networking computers involves two components: a hardware component, consisting of a network adapter card or other network device, cables, and, often, a hub, and a software component, consisting of various software protocols, which are the different languages each computer on the network must speak to move different types of data around accurately.

- Most wired networking on PCs today adheres to a hardware standard called Fast Ethernet, which can move data at speeds up to 100 Mbps. Fast Ethernet has its own set of hardware protocols that work in conjunction with the many different software protocols to package data and move it around the network.

■   HTTP is the networking protocol that makes most of the World Wide
    Web function. SMTP and POP3 are protocols that support e-mail.

■   Protocols, and the connections they support, can be insecure or
    secure. Secure protocols use encryption to prevent anyone from inter-
    cepting and using your data.

■   TCP/IP isn't actually a protocol; it's a collection or stack of protocols
    that work together to provide the Internet and Windows XP network-
    ing with its functionality. TCP/IP organizes data into packets and
    moves them around the network (or the Internet) like letters in enve-
    lopes moving through the post office mail system (only much faster).

■   Setting up networking under Windows XP is almost entirely automatic.
    In the few cases when it's not, the Network Setup Wizard steps you
    through the entire process in a fraction of the time it used to take to set
    up a network.

■   Windows XP allows you to share your Internet connection and protect
    the files on your PC by using Internet Connection Sharing (ICS) and
    the Internet Connection Firewall (ICF), respectively.

■   You can share files with other people who use your PC or with people
    connected to your local area network.

Part III

Presenting Your OS: Windows XP

All the stuff you've read about in Part I and Part II—all the hardware and physical bits and pieces of a computer—is actually only half the story of what makes up a PC. The other half is *software*: the code that runs on your PC. All the applications, programs, applets, and utilities that you run on your computer are software. But the most integral software is the special collection of code that works full time behind the scenes to make everything you and your PC do together possible. This type of software is known as an *operating system (OS)*, and every computer of any modernity and complexity has one. The OS is so important, it's really what makes a PC a PC.

In our PC world—the hardware world you've spent the last nine chapters exploring— the OS happens to be named Microsoft Windows XP. Everything you've read so far has actually been about Windows XP—even though we were just trying to find out about the PC's hardware. In truth, Windows XP makes the PC.

Chapter 10

Between You and Your PC

Put all of the necessary hardware pieces of a PC together in a case. Assemble them perfectly and arrange them with the greatest of care. Check and double-check every connection. Buy each piece from the most reliable, reputable manufacturer you can find. Spend as much money as you like. Then turn it on, and what happens?

    `<BEEP!>`

And that's all you get. Just a beep and a few bits of text on the screen that say, rather sardonically, you might think, "OK, you put me together right. Bully for you." Then nothing. What did you forget? Why isn't the computer doing anything?

What the Operating System Is—And What It Does

What's missing is *everything*. The reason the computer isn't doing anything is because a computer can't do anything but check that its key parts are connected properly and apparently are in working order. That's all any PC does, without the help of an *operating system (OS)*. Your PC's processor is technically the hardware's brains, but it doesn't do much thinking without an OS. So what is it, what does it do, and why is it so important?

Imagine for a moment that you're hired to work in a big theater. There's a huge production going on, with great costumes, incredible music, a stellar cast. Sounds great, huh? I forgot to mention the wrinkle in my little nightmare: you are the only crew member in the entire building. And not just tonight; every performance.

You control the curtain, run the sound board, lights, move sets on and off stage, and assist with all costume changes. You operate the riggings, tune every instrument in the orchestra—and conduct as well; you sit in the prompter's box in case someone forgets a line, and you're the carpenter and welder who build all the sets. You're the lighting designer, the scenic artist, the usher; you even take the tickets and function as security. You're the director, you had to write most of the script, and you even have to mingle and entertain the patrons during the intermission.

Congratulations! You're an operating system.

Every job I mentioned—which, you'll notice, includes just about everyone except the actors—is a delightfully close analogy for one of the tasks that your PC's operating system performs. To explain, let's divide some of those theater jobs into two categories: "For the Production" and "For the Audience."

For the Production	For the Audience
Carpenter	Ticket taker
Sound engineer	Concierge
Electrician	Lounge singer
Set designer	Usher
Script writer and director	Sound board operator
Security	Security

Of course, everything that happens in a theater is ultimately for the audience, but in a more direct way, people like the electrician and set designers do their jobs to make the performance possible, whereas people like the sound board operator and concierge make the performance enjoyable. Of course, good security is important to everyone. The production depends on it to provide safety for famous actors and to make sure nobody gets in without paying. The audience depends on it to provide safety for themselves and to make sure nobody misbehaves and ruins the show. What you are for my theater of the mind, an operating system is for your PC.

Like your theater jobs, the operating system's jobs fit into one of two groups. We'll call all the "For the Production" duties *system tasks*, and we'll put all the "For the Audience" duties in a special category called the *user interface*. Every operating system performs these two types of tasks, either seeing to the needs of the PC itself, or seeing to the needs of the person operating the PC. As in theater, everything in the PC's world happens for the user's benefit, but a huge part of an operating system's time is spent minding those system tasks that make the "production" possible.

System Tasks

If you're putting on a show and you're responsible for everything except the acting, you're going to be busy long before opening night. The PC's operating system is also busy right from the start. Seconds after you apply power to your PC, the OS is working. During those seconds, your PC hardware is running a small set of self-tests to make sure it can find everything a PC needs, like memory, its video system, storage devices, and a keyboard.

Note   Remember that PCs were originally a text-oriented system in which you typed commands to make everything happen, rather than pointing and clicking. Historically, because a mouse was optional, searching for a mouse isn't part of most PC's *power-on self tests*, known collectively as the *POST*.

This process of starting itself up and making sure it's ready to work is traditionally called *booting*, and now often just called *starting up*.

Lingo   The term *booting* comes from the idea that, because the PC does everything necessary to bring itself to life, it's like being able to lift yourself up by pulling on your own bootstraps. Indeed, booting is just an abbreviation of *bootstrapping*, which is the correct—if antiquated—term.

As soon as your PC detects its storage devices, it knows how to do only one thing. It can move the device's read/write heads to a predefined location and read what's stored there. This predefined location is called the *boot sector*, and what's stored there is a tiny bit of code called the *bootstrap loader*.

The bootstrap loader is the first part of your PC's operating system. It's not built into the hard disk itself, but is written there like any other data when the operating system is installed and the hard disk is set up for that particular operating system to use (a process called *formatting*). The bootstrap loader code is read from disk, loaded into memory, and its instructions are performed by your PC's central processing unit (CPU). Those instructions simply tell your hard drive's read/write heads where to find the next piece of the operating system. That piece knows how to load the next pieces until finally, all of the underlying parts of the operating system are read from disk into memory and are running.

Those underlying system tasks never stop running until you turn your PC off again. What is the OS doing? Among many other things, it's detecting and configuring every bit of hardware that's part of your PC, from your memory to your sound card, to your USB ports. The entire time your PC is on, the OS manages all of that hardware, making sure that each piece operates in concert with every other piece, with no conflicts.

The OS is also always monitoring your storage devices, making sure that whenever data needs to be read or written, the job is done properly. The OS is also always managing any networking capabilities your PC has, checking for connections, and establishing which networking protocols will be used to actually do the job of networking. After all of these underlying jobs are up and running successfully, the OS begins to load and run the user interface.

See Also   *For detailed information about networking, see Chapter 9.*

User Interface

You see the results of the OS performing all of its system tasks, but you don't see those tasks directly. Everything you do see on your PC—except for the specific operation of each application and program—is the second half of the OS, the user interface.

A user interface can be simple, like the command-driven text-only world of the Microsoft Disk Operating System (MS-DOS). This world is all but gone, but its likeness remains in the Windows XP Command window, shown in Figure 10-1. This command-based environment was intimidating for new users, and it made writing applications hard, too.

Figure 10-1 The Windows XP Command window provides a text-only environment like the original MS-DOS.

Fortunately, the PC world changed when its primary user interface went from being command-driven to being graphical. A *graphical user interface* (GUI, pronounced "gooey") allows users to select objects using some type of pointing device and then manipulate those objects by clicking the pointer on them, or something similar. Windows XP is the latest OS generation that provides this interface for PCs. The Windows user interface, shown in Figure 10-2, might be the only one you've ever seen or used.

Figure 10-2 This is the desktop, the fundamental working environment provided by the graphical user interface of Windows XP.

Windows has changed a lot over the years, but its GUI still performs the same sorts of "For the Audience" tasks that it did originally. The GUI provides the windowing and menu-based environment to which we're all accustomed. It displays the mouse pointer (in conjunction with several system tasks that actually make the mouse operate), and it's responsible for the visual appearance of everything we see when we use Windows.

One of the most obvious and dramatic benefits of any GUI—and of Windows XP in particular—is that it makes sure all our applications look right. Whereas the Windows XP system tasks make sure that all our peripherals and hardware function properly, the GUI makes sure the applications look right, and they look *similar*. You don't need to know much about a GUI to work with it, and after you learn how one program operates, you'll find that you can work (at least fundamentally) with any well-behaved application.

All of the menus, windows, and icons that the Windows XP GUI provides are the sets for your PC's theater. The standardized look and feel is the product of the Windows operating system's careful set design, art direction, and costuming. Their regular appearance and operation are the products of the operating system's script writing and direction. In case you're wondering how the lounge singer fits into the picture, consider that everything the Windows Media Player does, along with your screen savers and other little digital distractions, are the entertainment that keeps you happy during intermission while the real actors (your productive applications) aren't busy.

Note   I don't include games in the list of entertainment for two reasons. First, many games are relics from the past, each working in its own way, sometimes even taking over the basic operation of many of your PC's functions. Second, while games benefit from Microsoft ActiveX 8, these capabilities are closer to system tasks than they are part of the user interface. ActiveX doesn't so much make sure that Adventure Works games look like Contoso's games as it makes the job of each manufacturer's game programmers easier by providing standard ways to achieve a certain quality of appearance and performance.

Windows XP Manages Devices

Many of the system tasks that the Windows XP operating system performs are far more technical and minute than we need to consider. Suffice it to say that, if you think it would be a lot of work to be the only person working in a theater, that's nothing compared to what Windows does behind the scenes. Windows system tasks that are closest and dearest to us users are the many jobs it does to keep all of our hardware working properly. Let's talk about a couple of the major points regarding how hardware works.

To work with Windows, each device needs to know something about Windows, and Windows needs to know something about each device. The devices need to know which hardware resources they're allowed to use, and Windows manages all of these very strictly. The devices need to get Windows' attention whenever they've got something to accomplish, and they need to know how to do that, how Windows will respond, and how to proceed. Windows, in turn, needs to know all the same things in reverse, as well as being able to detect each device's operating characteristics.

This last capability is provided not by Windows per se, but *to* Windows by a system called Plug and Play. Plug and Play is partly built into each modern peripheral's own circuitry, is partly built into each PC's motherboard, and is partly built into Windows. While Plug and Play tells Windows which hardware resources a device wants to use—and what it can use if those aren't available—the actual bridge between each device and the user interface is managed by the Windows system task side. Windows uses *drivers* to understand each peripheral's needs.

The Plug and Play system doesn't provide these drivers in the hardware because that would be too hard to change if changes needed to be made or if performance could be improved by making the device work differently than was originally conceived. Instead, Plug and Play simply identifies each device to Windows, and Windows loads the necessary device drivers into memory.

Device drivers come in two flavors: those built into Windows and those provided by each peripheral manufacturer. If a peripheral has been designed to work exactly in accordance with certain standards that Microsoft has developed for that type of peripheral, Windows uses one of its own *standard* drivers. If the manufacturer has provided a driver to Microsoft, that driver can be distributed on the Windows XP CD, and Windows will use it.

Note   Manufacturers also provide drivers on CD in the box with their products and make latest versions available for download over the Internet.

Windows manages the loading and operation of all the hardware drivers your system requires, and the drivers act as a bridge, or *translator*. Drivers know how their own hardware works, and they know how Windows works. If a manufacturer writes their driver code in accordance with the Windows Driver Model (WDM), perfect functioning is all but guaranteed. The Windows Driver Model sets forth standard ways of getting Windows to perform key peripheral tasks. The driver sends an instruction of this type to Windows, Windows responds, and the driver then knows how to convert the Windows response into whatever the peripheral needs.

Windows XP adheres to the WDM, which means that products that use a WDM driver were, in a sense, created for Windows XP. When you see the Microsoft logo on a product indicating that it is certified for Windows XP, that's part of what that means. It also means that the manufacturer has sent its drivers to Microsoft for rigorous testing and has passed Microsoft's standard tests of reliability. When a driver meets this standard, Microsoft signs it with a bit of code that identifies it uniquely. These *signed drivers* help Windows XP know that it is running the best possible version of a peripheral's driver, and that, once the right driver is selected, it isn't accidentally replaced by a less-acceptable version.

What Are Hardware Resources?

I mentioned that every piece of hardware requires *resources* to work with Windows, but what are they? In a broad sense, *hardware resources* are your PC's memory, your PC's processor, and the paths your hardware uses to work with that memory and processor. Every device, even your mouse, needs at least a little bit of memory to function. (That's what keeps the mouse pointer in one place; its position is stored in a tiny bit of memory set aside for that purpose.)

If some big application or some other device used the same bit of memory as the mouse, your mouse pointer would be all over the place. Similarly, if your word processor loaded into the same bits and bytes of memory that your video card was trying to use, your video display would be a mess, full of random spots of light meaning nothing (because the code that makes your word processor work doesn't follow the rules your video card requires to put an image on-screen).

Memory Allocation to the Rescue

For that reason, Windows sets aside areas of memory for each hardware device and for each application that runs. This process, called *memory allocation*, is part of what makes it possible for us to run multiple applications at once. Each application uses its own little bit of memory, and no other memory. If more memory is needed, it sends a polite request to Windows asking for more, which Windows will provide. If a program tries to use memory that doesn't belong to it, Windows shuts the offending application down to prevent it from ruining the functioning of other programs or causing your whole PC to crash.

The area of memory Windows gives each device is determined as part of the Plug and Play process while your PC is starting up. It's a compromise wherein a device asks Windows for a certain bit of memory. If that memory is available, great. If it's not, Windows says, "Sorry, you can't use that. What would be your second choice?" and the product responds. When Windows and the product agree on a piece of memory, Windows allocates the memory to the device and then moves on to see which resources are needed by other hardware.

The other two hardware resources—your PC's CPU and the paths to it—Windows manages collectively, working with the CPU. The CPU does its thing until it gets interrupted and asked to do something else. This interruption is a function of the CPU and the OS working together, and it's achieved by sending instructions to the CPU along one of several paths. The signals are called *interrupts*, and the paths are called *interrupt request lines (IRQs)*. An interrupt is basically a way of getting the CPU's attention and saying, "Ahem. I need something now." To keep things manageable, a CPU has a limited number of IRQs, although Plug and Play allows them to be shared in many instances.

You can see your PC's interrupt lines and the hardware assigned to each by opening the Windows Device Manager. From the Start menu, right-click My Computer and select Properties. Click the Hardware tab, and then click Device Manager. In the window that opens, go to the View menu and select Resources By Type, and then click the plus sign (+) next to Interrupt Request (IRQ). You'll see a screen similar to the one shown in Figure 10-3.

Figure 10-3 The Device Manager shows each IRQ and the hardware to which it's assigned.

When the CPU receives an interrupt request, it stops what it's doing when it's safe to do so, and then lets Windows know that it's ready to address the device's needs. The CPU then goes back to other tasks.

In addition to interrupt requests and a memory area, some devices, like the internal modems discussed in Chapter 8, communicate with Windows through a port. Although ports are usually part of hardware, as far as you and I are concerned, they're just reserved areas of memory, as far as Windows is concerned. These special areas, known as *I/O addresses* (for input/output) are allocated just like other memory is. Windows knows to look to them for messages from the device, and Windows knows that data and instructions that need to be sent *to* the device should be fed through those same memory locations.

For any given piece of hardware, you can see the system resources used by opening the Device Manager and looking at the peripheral's properties. Figure 10-4 shows a simple example. The memory addresses, I/O, and IRQ needed by my video system are all set forth here. I could customize them here, too, if I needed to.

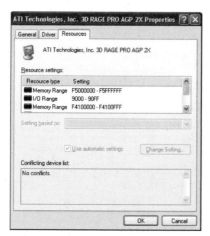

Figure 10-4   The Resources tab for a hardware component shows the system resources needed by that component.

Sometimes, if Windows encounters a piece of hardware that absolutely needs to use a certain area of memory, or a certain I/O address, or a certain IRQ, a *resource conflict* can occur. As I said, two devices can't use the same memory or I/O, and devices can share IRQs only in certain (although today, common) circumstances. Plug and Play, Peripheral Component Interconnect (PCI), and Windows can work together to get devices to share resources dynamically. If one peripheral requires an IRQ that's in use, the device using that resource might be more flexible, and be able to use any of several IRQs. When that's the case, Windows just shuffles IRQ assignments around until each piece of hardware is happy.

The Power of the Windows XP GUI

You know now that the look and feel that you experience when you use Windows XP is provided by the operating system's GUI, and that look and feel is pretty standard across any program you ever run. You'll also see in Chapter 11 that that same look and feel is highly customizable through a central set of tools—also part of Windows XP. If your PC is set up for multiple users, each person can make Windows look and operate exactly as she or he prefers. But what is a GUI, anyway?

A GUI is a collection of standardized ways of putting stuff on the PC screen and responding to user input. In Windows XP, those methods are defined as part of the Windows application programming interface (API). To make creating

Windows applications easy, the Windows API contains a huge collection of commands that any programmer can use to make applications function properly.

An *event* occurs whenever you move the mouse, click something, or type something, which makes Windows an *event-driven* operating system. (There are other events, too, like when a peripheral contacts Windows and the CPU by sending an interrupt request.) Windows applications basically use the API features to display their main window and menu on the screen and then just wait for an event to occur. When one does—when you select the File menu, for example—Windows runs the little bit of code necessary to respond to the event, and then it goes right back to waiting for the next event.

Benefits of the Windows API

Every programmer is supposed to follow and use the Windows API tools carefully. When that happens, the benefits are obvious. It's easier to operate Windows because the APIs guarantee that everything looks similar and works in similar ways. Once you learn to use any Windows program, you never need to learn to use the interface again—every Windows program works the same. The API is a tremendous benefit to programmers, too, because they can simply make use of the work that Microsoft has already put into designing the visual look and feel of Windows. No reinventing the wheel here.

The other benefit of the Windows GUI—powered as it is by the Windows APIs—is the special ability of Windows to make what you see on the PC screen look like what you'll see when your work is printed or produced. This characteristic, called *What You See Is What You Get* (*WYSIWYG*, pronounced "whizzee whig"), is one of the most important innovations of the Windows GUI over the text-only DOS environment. In DOS, all text looks more or less the same, and each program for displaying graphics works just a little differently. You never know exactly what you'll get when you issue a Print command.

Windows puts all that to rest. The Windows GUI and API include standardized ways of displaying graphic images. The GUI also includes a vast collection of different typefaces, or *fonts*, which you can use to create documents. Because Windows controls the printing process too, fonts displayed on the screen almost always look just like they do on paper. Combine this understanding with what you learned in Chapter 7 about turning your visions into a finished product, and you'll be working smarter and accomplishing your goals faster in no time.

Key Points

- Although an OS isn't hardware, it's a piece of software that works with hardware on such an intimate level that it is the two together—PC hardware and the OS—that really give us what we call the PC.

- An OS like Windows XP performs all of the fundamental and behind-the-scenes jobs needed to make a PC do anything. These are collectively called system tasks.

- An OS like Windows XP also performs tasks related to our human interaction with the hardware. These tasks are part of the user interface.

- Windows XP provides a graphical user interface (GUI), in which on-screen windows, menus, icons, and a visual pointer controlled by the mouse make running software and getting work done easier.

- Of all the many important system tasks performed by Windows, the nearest and dearest to users is its management of the different hardware devices and peripherals we connect to our PC. Windows works in conjunction with Plug and Play and software device drivers to guarantee that each device works cooperatively with all other devices.

- The Windows GUI is made possible through the use of standard procedures provided through the Windows application programming interface (API). Sending requests to Windows for it to execute these predefined functions guarantees that every Windows application will share a common look and feel.

- The ability of the Windows XP GUI to display on-screen exactly what it will also print on paper is called What You See Is What You Get (WYSIWYG).

Chapter 11

Your *Personal* Personal Computer

In a scathingly funny attack on the world of marketing, Douglas Adams once wrote that human beings almost failed to discover the wheel—the simplest tool in the universe—because prehistoric focus groups couldn't decide what color it should be. But people *do* need to be comfortable with even the simplest tools they use every day. Studies have shown that productivity can soar when you can customize tools to work in the way you prefer. The Microsoft Windows XP graphical user interface (GUI) gives you that power. Working faster and smarter starts with taking charge of your tools, and changing your personal computer into a *personal* computer.

Customizing Windows XP

As the bridge between you and your PC's hardware, Windows XP puts a lot of potential at your fingertips. There's probably never been another tool that you can customize and personalize as much as Windows. From colors on-screen to how fast the mouse moves, almost every aspect is maintained in a setting you can change. Some changes can be made without concern for performance; some changes might increase or decrease the speed at which you can get work done. Let's take a look at some of the basics first, such as access to the applications you use most, and the appearance of Windows.

The Start Menu: Access to Work

Before you can start using your tools, you've got to be able to get at them, whether they're hidden away at the back of the garage or hidden away on a hard disk. And although it's true that the Start menu automatically organizes different parts of programs together into folders, if your Start menu looks like the one in Figure 11-1, you've got trouble.

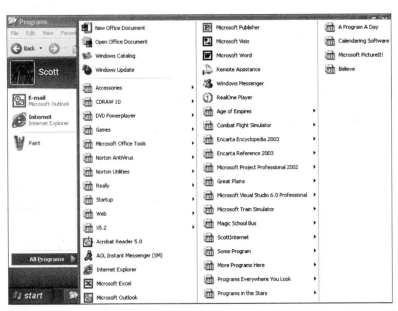

Figure 11-1 The Start menu keeps pieces of applications together, but it can grow to nightmarish size without a little attention, as you can see.

You can improve your productivity in just a few minutes by introducing some organization into your Start menu. It's easy and quick, and you'll find that it makes getting down to work far simpler than navigating through a huge menu of options. Even if your Start menu doesn't look like the one shown here, there's no better time to get organized than right now. All it takes to work faster is to think a little smarter. The Start menu can help you in two important ways: providing access to commonly used tools and organizing all programs.

Tip You can open your Start menu by pressing the Windows logo key or pressing Ctrl+Esc if your keyboard doesn't have a Windows key. (This means press and hold down the Ctrl key and then touch the Esc key. It's easy to press Ctrl with your left thumb and then just tap Esc with your left hand's third finger.) The Start menu pops up instantly. Because I'm usually typing, my hands are already on the keyboard, and I find opening the Start menu this way to be *much* faster than reaching for the mouse and clicking Start.

Commonly Used Tools

One of the best ways to improve your productivity is to have Windows XP keep at your fingertips the tools you use most often. If you do this, you can launch any application you use often with just a couple of keystrokes (or, naturally, the mouse). For example, all you'll need to do to start Microsoft Outlook and check your e-mail is press the Windows logo key (or Ctrl+Esc), press the Down Arrow key until Outlook is highlighted, and press Enter. You'll be able to do it in less than a second once you're used to it. Here's how to turn this feature on:

1 Click Start to open the Start menu, right-click in the blue space next to your username, and choose Properties.

2 When the Taskbar And Start Menu Properties dialog box opens, click the Start Menu tab, as shown in Figure 11-2.

Figure 11-2 The Taskbar And Start Menu Properties dialog box gives you control over which tools Windows XP puts at your fingertips.

3 Make sure the Start Menu option is selected, *not* Classic Start Menu, and click Customize.

4   At the bottom of the Customize dialog box, you'll see a section titled
Show On Start Menu. To give yourself that instant access to your
e-mail, select the E-mail option, and use the drop-down list to select
your e-mail program.

See Also   *Of course, you'll need to configure your e-mail account settings before
choosing this option, or Windows won't know whether you're using Microsoft Outlook
or another e-mail program instead of the default, Microsoft Outlook Express. We
talked about setting up your modem and network connections in Chapter 8 and
Chapter 9, respectively.*

---

5   Click OK twice, and you'll find your preferred e-mail tool available
right at the top of the Start menu. Press Ctrl+Esc, the Down Arrow key
until Outlook is highlighted, and Enter, and you're checking for mail!

You can access the other programs you use most often just as easily, with
only an extra Down Arrow key or three. When Windows XP was first loaded on
your PC, its program list (the tools you see on the left side of the Start menu)
was populated with commonly used Windows tools. Those default tools might
not be the ones *you* use most commonly—but they can be. To clear the defaults
and make room for your tools to immediately take their place, you'll want to
return to the Taskbar And Start Menu Properties dialog box you used a moment
ago. Perform the following steps:

1   Click Start to open the Start menu, right-click next to your username,
and select Properties.

2   Select the Start Menu tab, and click Customize.

3   The Programs area in the middle of the Customize dialog box lets you
choose how many of your favorite tools will be shown. You can select
zero, but we're trying to *un*hide your tools, not hide them. You can
increase the number of programs displayed to 30, but that's probably
far too many—you'll just end up searching for what you need. For me,
six is sufficient, but you can experiment and determine what works for
you.

4   After you select how many programs to show, click Clear List. This
won't delete your programs; it will simply remove those default tools
from the program list.

Your Start menu will look something like Figure 11-3 when you
open it after clicking OK twice.

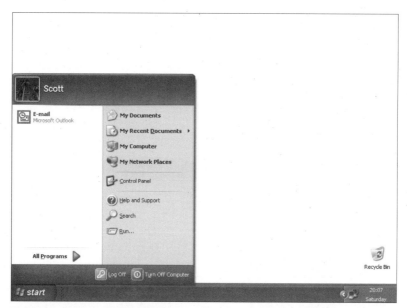

Figure 11-3 After you clear the program list, your Start menu will be ready to accept your preferences.

When you start applications, Windows XP will repopulate the Start menu's program list with the tools you use most often. If you ever stop using a particular tool, you can easily remove it from the list without clearing all your other favorites. Just right-click the program's name and choose Remove From This List. Similarly, if you want to guarantee that a tool remains in the Programs list regardless of how often you use it, just right-click its name and choose Pin To Start Menu. The program you select will join your e-mail tool at the top of the menu.

Programs aren't the only thing you can give a place of honor on your Start menu. Maybe there's a particular file or template that you open many times every day—letterhead, perhaps. You can give yourself instant access to it, too. To do so, perform the following steps:

1 Open the folder containing the file. This is probably your My Documents folder, or a folder you've created inside.

2 Find the file and click it.

3 Holding the mouse button down, drag the file until your mouse is pointing to the Start button on your desktop. You'll see a little bent-arrow icon appear, showing you that Windows is going to create a shortcut for you. (You're not actually moving the file to the Start menu, you're just creating a link to the file in a handy place.)

4   Release the mouse, and you're done. As you can see in Figure 11-4, this technique puts your favorite tools at your fingertips, whether those tools are programs or documents.

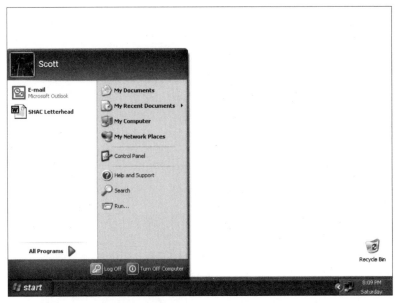

Figure 11-4 You can drag a document onto the Start menu for immediate access.

Tip   If you find that you can't drag a file to your Start menu, this option might be disabled. Turn it on by opening the Taskbar And Start Menu Properties dialog box, selecting the Start Menu tab, clicking Customize, and then selecting the Advanced tab. In the section of the dialog box called Start Menu Items, scroll down to make sure a check mark appears in the box next to Enable Dragging And Dropping, and click OK twice to close the dialog boxes. You should be successful now. If you're not, your user account might not have Administrator privileges.

Organizing All Programs

Although the programs I use most are given VIP treatment on my Start menu, I use many other programs occasionally. When I installed those programs, Windows put all of their pieces in one folder on the Start menu, but that still leaves me—and you, too, probably—with a full Start menu to search through to find what's wanted. Windows XP provides an easy solution to this situation, too. You can add organization to the All Programs list so that programs are where you want to find them—and you can delete links to all the little utilities you never use. This process is a little more complicated than the changes you made a moment ago, but it really requires only a steady mouse hand and some smarter thinking. I can't help you with your dexterity, so let's talk about thinking smarter.

The All Programs list shows a folder for almost every program you've installed on your PC. Inside each folder is usually a link to the program itself, along with several other links to Readme files and whatnot. I'm not a huge consumer of whatnot, myself, so I like to separate my programs from all that extra nonsense. This strategy dramatically cleans up my Start menu and gets me working faster every time I use my PC. But I don't want all my programs in an endless list, either. If I did—and if you do—I'd just set the Start menu to show my 30 most-used programs, and I'd probably be covered. The solution? I create some organizing folders inside my Start menu, and then move my programs into those. I finish up by placing all the whatnot into a whatnot folder—so those tools are still convenient if I ever need them.

To start this process, right-click Start and select Explore All Users. A window opens, showing you the contents of your Start menu. We're interested in the Programs folder, so click the small plus sign (+) next to its name in the left pane, and then click once on the word Programs. You'll see folders and links to programs, like those shown in Figure 11-5.

Figure 11-5 The Start menu's contents are made up of folders and links to applications.

Let's start by adding some quick organization. Think about how you think about working. I like having all my programs that do similar functions grouped together. For each category of program, I've created a folder. I've created Communications, Graphics, Games, and Page Layout, for example. To start creating the folders that are right for you, make sure you've clicked the word Programs in the left pane and then right-click in the white space on the right side and select New and then Folder. When the new folder appears, give it the name you want to use—Graphics, perhaps. You'll see that the new folder has also appeared in the left pane under the Programs heading.

Move shortcuts into the new folder by double-clicking to open a program's folder in the right pane. Click the shortcut you want to move and drag it into the left pane, onto the name of the folder you just created. When the folder name is highlighted in blue, release the mouse. To repeat the process, click Back at the upper left of the window so you can see all of your program folders again. Create whichever new folders are appropriate for you and move your program shortcuts into them. When you're finished, create one last folder, call it something like Miscellaneous, and drag the individual program folders (*not* the category folders you just created) into it.

When you next open your Start menu's All Programs list, you'll see something like Figure 11-6. Compare this with the Start menu shown in Figure 11-1. Now, when you want to use a tool (start a program), just click its category folder and then click the program name—short and sweet. If you keep your organization updated as you install new software, you'll be working faster for good.

Figure 11-6 This Start menu is organized into smart categories, like the Accessories category Windows creates for itself.

Caution Changes you make to the Start menu's All Programs list will change its appearance for every person who uses the PC. If you use a shared machine, you might want to gather your coworkers or family together and brainstorm how you'd like things organized. The list of most commonly used programs is specific for each user account on the PC.

Personalizing the Appearance of Windows

With your tools at your fingertips, you'll have a little time to indulge in a luxury or two—but I don't think of making Windows look like you want it to look as a luxury. Being graphical, the Windows XP user interface is in front of your eyes all the time. Recall from Chapter 4 that you can increase your monitor's refresh rate to eliminate flicker and reduce the likelihood that you'll get headaches; that's working smarter. Giving Windows an appearance that's easy for you to read and use will have you working faster, too.

The first aspect of Windows XP you might want to customize is your desktop. After all, you look at this whenever you're not looking at something else; you might as well look at something that appeals. Windows comes with a good selection of desktop pictures you can select—and, of course, you can select no picture at all (and you can select a desktop color if you go that route).

Personalizing the Gestalt

To modify the desktop's background picture, just right-click it. When the Display Properties dialog box opens, you've got several options. If you want to change the appearance of not only the desktop, but almost every audiovisual aspect of Windows, you can use the Themes tab and select a complete experience from the drop-down list. If you find one to which you're partial, just click OK, and wait a moment while Windows XP changes its skin and voice. You've seen the default theme throughout this book. In Figure 11-7, I've selected one of the themes from the Microsoft Plus! Pack.

If you want to change only the desktop background, select the Desktop tab and choose one of the pictures in the scrolling list. This list includes the defaults that come with Windows XP and every image in your My Pictures folder, inside My Documents. If you want to use a picture that's located elsewhere, clicking Browse will open a navigation dialog box that will let you choose from anywhere to which you have access.

Figure 11-7 By selecting a theme from the Display Properties dialog box, you can change most aspects of how Windows XP looks and sounds in one stroke.

Tip   If the desktop background you want to use is stored on a network drive, copy it to your local hard disk before you select it for your desktop. The desktop is displayed before some network connections will be established, and you'll have no desktop image at all if that happens.

You have three options for how images are displayed on your desktop. You just select the option you want from the Position drop-down list. First, you can *tile* an image so that a small image is repeated over and over until the desktop is full. This is how the desktop patterns like the one called Greenstone work.

Second, you can choose Center so that the picture is centered on the desktop. If the image is smaller than the desktop, you'll see the desktop's color like a frame around the picture. If the image is larger than your desktop's resolution, it'll be cropped, and only the part that fits will be shown.

Finally, you can choose Stretch, which will enlarge a small image or shrink a large one so that it perfectly fills the desktop with no frame. Be aware that this option will distort your image unless the picture you choose has the same horizontal and vertical proportions as your desktop's resolution. The results can be quite bizarre.

If you've chosen to center a picture that's smaller than the desktop, or if you want no desktop image at all (just choose None from the top of the scrolling list), you'll find the desktop's background color is visible. In this case, you'll want it to be something appealing to you. To change just the desktop color, click the Color drop-down list and select one of the default colors, or select Other. The Windows XP color picker will open, from which you can choose any color your video card's current color depth can show. Just click OK to complete the change and close the Display Properties Control Panel.

Personalizing the Details

You can personalize the details of how Windows XP appears, too. It's delightfully easy. Right-click the desktop and choose Properties to open the Display Properties dialog box again, and select the Appearance tab. Here, in the Windows And Buttons drop-down list, you can control the style used for every graphical element in Windows XP. You can also change the entire visual feel of Windows by selecting a new option from the Color Scheme drop-down list. And if your vision is less than perfect, you can increase the size of every font Windows shows on-screen; no more headaches from squinting and sitting 6 inches from the monitor!

You can make even more detailed changes by clicking Advanced. From the Advanced Appearance dialog box that opens, you can select individual elements of the Windows GUI—from message boxes to menus to inactive windows—and choose the color and, often, the font and style of text used for that element. You can make Windows XP look as individual as you are—keeping in mind that you also want Windows to be easy to use. You might be a purple, black, and lime kind of person, but you might find lime text on a black background isn't exactly an efficient read.

Still, there's no limiting what you can do. Any color your video card can display and any outline font that's installed on your system can be made part of the appearance of Windows XP. As you make changes, the small window at the top of the dialog box will show what Windows will look like if you click OK. Click Cancel to undo any changes you've made.

In addition to how the static Windows elements appear, you can personalize how they function. Close the Advanced Appearance dialog box if it's still open, and click Effects to gain access to the settings that control all that cool Windows animation and fading and sliding. Here you can choose transition effects or turn them off entirely. If your PC seems to be running slowly, turning effects off might improve your performance overall. Similarly, displaying shadows and the contents of a window while you're relocating it takes a good deal more power than not. If you want the fastest performance possible, turn these effects off, too.

Furthermore, you can select whether all the icons in Windows display as regular size or extra large, according to your tastes and vision, and you can make text on a notebook computer's screen easier to read by turning on screen font smoothing and selecting Microsoft ClearType from the drop-down list. (Font smooth also takes power, so you might need to choose between how fast your PC performs every task—because there are almost always fonts on the screen—and how well you can read text.)

The Display Properties dialog box also lets you select screen resolution and multiple monitors, as we explored in Chapter 4, and lets you choose which screen saver you use (if any) and how quickly it activates.

Windows Inside Windows: Personalizing Folders

You can personalize folders in Windows XP in so many ways, we can't possibly explore them all, so we'll focus on those ways that can really help your productivity. For the most part, these are accessible through Folder Options on the Tools menu of My Computer (or any other window that is displaying files, rather than a specific application). Depending on the power of your video card, it might take noticeable time to display certain folder options. Clearing these will show you your folder contents faster.

The General tab's Show Common Tasks In Folders option at the top of the Folder Options dialog box basically selects between Windows XP–style folders and those you might have seen under Microsoft Windows Millennium Edition (Windows Me) and earlier. The latter takes less power to display. Here you can choose whether you want Windows to draw a new window each time you open a folder, or whether you want to use the Forward and Back buttons and scroll through folders in a single window. You can also make Windows work so that a single mouse click will open folders or files, just like when you select a link on a Web page.

You can make other changes on a folder-by-folder basis through the View menu. You probably know that you can choose to see thumbnails of images when you open a folder that contains them, or you can see a table of details about the files in the folder. Did you know that you can choose which details you see and in what order they appear? You can.

From the View menu, select Choose Details, and the Choose Details dialog box shown in Figure 11-8 opens. Place a check mark in the box next to any file characteristic you want to see in the Details view, and use the Move Up and Move Down buttons to organize your choices. You might, for example, want to turn on the Owner detail if you're given the job of organizing files on a PC that is shared by many different people. (A far better choice would be to create a Windows XP user account for each person who uses the PC, as described in the next section, so that files are kept organized by default.)

Figure 11-8 The Choose Details dialog box makes it easy to see many different file characteristics at a glance.

Personalizing a PC for Several People

With the exception of the Start menu changes we worked through at the start of this chapter, your personalization of Windows XP needn't affect anyone else who uses your PC. We talked about user accounts briefly in Chapter 9, and user accounts are the key to keeping Windows personal. It's common for a PC to be shared by many different people—especially at home—but it's just as common for people to not take advantage of the ways that a PC can behave like it belongs to you and you alone while you're using it. All you need is your own user account.

When Windows XP is first set up, a single user account is created, and the option is given to create others. In my experience, few people do this, and it's a shame because they're missing a lot of features because of it.

Note   To create user accounts, you must have Administrator privileges on your PC. If only one user account is currently set up, it will be an Administrator account. As you create new accounts, you can choose whether to give each one the power of an Administrator. Administrators can make sweeping changes that affect every user of a PC, including changing the operating system itself. Windows XP provides protection (which is disabled for Administrator accounts because it restricts control) against certain types of rogue processes (Trojan horses). Administrators can also see files belonging to *every* user account, change user passwords, and modify other users' personal settings.

To work with user accounts, select Control Panel from the Start menu and choose User Accounts. The User Accounts dialog box opens. Select Create A New Account, and step through the wizard, assigning a username and account type—either Administrator or not. Once an account is created, you can modify it by double-clicking it in the User Accounts dialog box. You'll see the window in Figure 11-9.

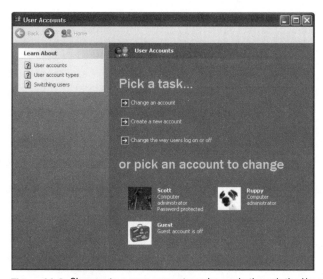

Figure 11-9 Changes to a user account can be made through the User Accounts window.

Here you can select a different picture to represent the account (pictures appear by the account name on the Windows XP logon screen) and activate password protection for the account. With password protection enabled, the user can prevent anyone but an Administrator from accessing his or her files or settings. We talked about this subject in Chapter 9 when we discussed shared folders. By making a folder private, access is limited.

All of a user's preferences and settings for appearance, sounds, and so forth are attached to that user's account, so every person who shares your PC can make it a truly personal computer.

Tailoring Windows to Your Personal Needs

For years, Windows has provided excellent support for individuals with different needs and abilities. Windows XP includes even more options for accessibility—and support for special hardware, like the unique keyboards we encountered in Chapter 2—than any previous version. The following sections describe how to customize Windows to suit your particular needs.

Personalizing Accessibility

Windows XP features several new options that allow you to customize the accessibility of your machine. These settings will follow a user account, too, so a PC can be shared by anyone.

We can't take an in-depth look at every one of the available options, but I do want you to know about several of the most significant features. Many of these options can be configured conveniently through the Accessibility Wizard, which is found in the Start menu's All Programs list by selecting Accessories and then Accessibility. The wizard asks you questions about a user's accessibility needs and steps you quickly through the settings that will best address those needs. Among the key accessibility features of Windows XP are the following:

- Sticky Keys make it possible for an individual with limited keyboarding ability to use standard Alt+, Ctrl+, and Windows logo key combinations.

- Sound Sentry provides visual indication whenever Windows produces a sound.

- MouseKeys allows the mouse pointer to be controlled through the keyboard.

- Narrator causes Windows to actually speak the contents of dialog boxes and message windows.

- Magnifier increases the size of graphical screen content.

- Speech Recognition supports voice recognition, making it possible for people who have difficulty using a keyboard to input text and control the PC.

This last option, Speech Recognition, isn't controlled through the normal Accessibility dialog box. Instead, the Speech dialog box, accessible by selecting Start, Control Panel, and then Sounds, Speech, and Audio Devices, allows each user of the PC to create and configure a speech profile, giving Windows the best ability to understand a single person's speech. This type of speech recognition requires time during which the recognition engine must be trained to recognize a user's speech patterns, but it is *far* more accurate and useful than any voice recognition that isn't first trained.

Personalizing Regional Options

If you use a notebook or other portable PC, you might want to establish a user account for when you're at home (or work) and a different user account for when you're abroad. If you do this, you can use the Date, Time, Language, And Regional Options dialog box to create a regional profile that you'll use when you're abroad. You might want to be able to use the spelling checker tool for French documents while you're in France, or automatically use the symbol for the euro while you're there.

In addition, Windows uses the Location setting to configure your preferences for receiving news as you travel. To make changes to these settings, simply create a user account and log in using that account. Then open the Date, Time, Language, And Regional Options dialog box and make your changes. When you click OK, your changes will be saved and automatically taken up whenever you log on through that account.

Key Points

- Windows XP makes it possible to configure a PC so that it looks and functions as you prefer.

- The Start menu can provide you nearly immediate access to the tools and files you use most often.

- Recently used programs will appear automatically in the Start menu's Programs list; programs and files can also be pinned to the Start menu so that they're always readily available.

- It's easy to personalize your Start menu's All Programs list so that your programs are organized by their type, rather than just by their name. Many users find this smart organization faster to use.

- User accounts make it possible for each user of a shared PC to control access to files and personalize the appearance of Windows.

■   Every aspect of the Windows GUI can be personalized, from the desktop background to the font used in a window's title bar, to the choice of a screen saver.

■   Several Windows XP visual effects can affect the performance of your PC. You can turn them off for each user account.

■   Windows XP can be used by people throughout the world—thanks to language and preferences support through the regional settings accessed through the icons in Control Panel—and by people with dramatically differing needs, through the use of the Accessibility Wizard and the accessibility and speech settings accessed through the icons in Control Panel. These settings follow a user account so that different user needs should never limit the ability of a PC to be shared.

Chapter 12

(Disk) Integrity Is Important

Here in Part III, we're taking a close look at the only computing relationship that's more important than the one between you and your PC. The relationship between the operating system and the PC is the most fundamental factor that determines how you get work done. By understanding that relationship, you're already working faster and smarter. In this chapter and in Chapter 13, we're going to look at how the operating system can make a difference in computing productivity.

Just about everything you do with the PC relies on its storage systems: disks. Your programs are stored there, as is your data. You know that your data is stored in many files. What you might not know is that all your programs are also stored in thousands of files. What's important is not what those many files are and why they exist, but just that they exist in the numbers they do. Why?

Windows XP File Systems

The files on our hard disks are a direct connection between the physical PC and the operating system. All of the bits have a physical existence as part of the magnetic media that coats the platters inside the drives.

See Also   *See Chapter 5 for a good look at how disks do what they do.*

The physical bits are organized into files by the operating system's design. If you like, think of a hard disk as being like a big apple or cherry pie. While it's whole, it can be cut into however many slices you like, up to some limit. After you cut the whole pie, you can serve only as many slices as you've cut (if we pretend that you can't cut a slice further). By cutting it into slices, you've given some structure to the whole pie. Originally, it was just a mass of goodness, but there was no way to say how many people could enjoy it. We might say that the organization or the *format* of the pie has been created by your knife work.

> **Lingo**   A hard disk must be *formatted* before it can be used. This means erasing any data that might already be stored on the drive, and then dividing up the drive into structures that allow the operating system to save and locate our files and programs later.

When the operating system formats a hard disk, it uses some of the magnetic material to set up structures on the disk that divide it into pieces, if you will. Actually, formatting gives a drive several different levels of organization, but the smallest level that your PC can work with is called a *cluster*. Like its name suggests, it's just a small collection of bits located next to each other on disk. When you save a file to disk, the operating system locates the first available unused cluster and tells the drive's read/write head to get to work.

As each cluster fills, the next one is used until the entire file is written. The operating system then writes information that associates the name of the file with the physical clusters it's using on the disk. When you access a file, the operating system looks up its location in the directory, or table, and puts the drive's hardware to work. But what if you delete a file? Do those clusters become useless? You already know that's a trick question, because you know that you can delete files from disk to get storage space back.

> **Lingo**   A disk has a directory that keeps track of which clusters are used by which files. Because this directory records how the disk space has been organized, it's known as the *file allocation table (FAT)*. When we talk about a particular method of using a FAT to organize a hard disk, we're talking about the disk's *file system*.

What happens, actually, is that the data itself isn't touched when you delete a file. Only the information in the cluster directory—the file allocation table (FAT)—is modified. The first little piece of directory information is changed so that it looks like that cluster isn't in use. Consequently, all the file's clusters seem available (because the clusters are organized into *chains*, one cluster's number after another). If you eliminate the first link of the chain, the other links become available to be part of a new chain. As you store new files on disk, the operating system tells the drive to reuse available clusters—whether they've been used before or not.

When a disk gets used a lot, with file saving and erasing happening over and over, you end up with available clusters here and there. You don't always have enough clusters free side by side (contiguous) to write all of the data in a file. So the operating system tells the read/write head to skip over the clusters already being used, and to continue writing in the next available cluster, wherever it might be. This jump is notated in the FAT so that the operating system can locate all the file pieces later.

We call this condition of files being saved here and there, all over the hard disk, *fragmentation*, because any given file might be split into several fragments. Each fragment can be as small as a single cluster. We'll talk more about fragmentation in a few moments.

Microsoft Windows XP creates a structure like I've described on any disk you format. Actually, you can choose from two different structures to use. Each has its strengths and limitations. For those of you who have been "playing along at home," here comes our friend balanced integration again.

FAT32

The first of the two disk organization methods, or *file systems*, you can use with Windows XP is called FAT32. This is a revamped version of an older system, called simply FAT, which Windows XP also supports (because older systems still use it). FAT32 provides support for features that were new to Windows when Microsoft Windows 95 was released, like long file names. (Before Windows 95, you couldn't use file names like Letter To Mom.June 2002, but were restricted to names like LTRMJ02.DOC. I don't think anybody misses those days.)

FAT32 also contains enhancements that provide support for the ever-increasing size of hard disks. You have to have an entry in the FAT for each cluster on disk. More clusters, more entries. The original "FAT" type of FAT couldn't support enough entries to manage the number of clusters on big disks, so it had to go.

Under Windows XP, FAT32 can manage formatted disks up to 2000 gigabytes (GB), although the largest disk you can actually format with FAT32 under Windows XP is 32 GB. If your hard disk's total capacity is larger than 32 GB, its space will need to be divided into separate sections, called *partitions*, and each partition will look like it's a separate physical hard disk. You might have just one 100-GB drive in the box, but you would have C, D, and E drives available inside Windows XP, each of which would give you roughly 36 GB of space.

You're not likely to encounter FAT32's other major limitation unless you work with really big database files or digital video. Under FAT32, a single file can't be any bigger than 4 GB.

NTFS

I mentioned FAT32 because it's popular, and many of us have upgraded to Windows XP from Microsoft Windows Millenium Edition (Windows Me) or earlier versions that support FAT32. FAT32 isn't the preferred file system for Windows XP, however. That honor goes to the *NT file system (NTFS)*, which is the latest generation of file systems available originally in Microsoft Windows NT and Microsoft Windows 2000.

NTFS scores over the older FAT32 in a number of important ways. First, NTFS can support a drive of almost any conceivable size. FAT32's 2000-GB (also known as 2 *terabytes*) limit isn't even close to the best that NTFS can manage. NTFS also doesn't impose any limits on how large an individual file can be. A file can grow to be as huge as the entire disk on which it's stored (assuming there's nothing else on the disk, naturally).

The benefits of NTFS only start there. In fact, although those numbers are often quoted, they don't really matter that much to 99 percent of us. How many people do you know with hard disks bigger than 2000 GB? Nobody. NTFS includes a number of features that are useful to almost everybody. Among these are automatic encryption of your files, through a variant of NTFS called encrypting file system (EFS), naturally enough. I've made a few comments about EFS later in this chapter, in the sidebar "EFS: The Encrypting File System."

NTFS also allows you to choose who has access to your files. It does this through a *permissions* system that allows you to say, for example, that all your files are available (indeed, *visible*) only when you're logged on to the PC. If a different user logs on, only that person's files will be visible. Actually, you can create many combinations of these possibilities, including one in which you're the main user of the PC and can see all files on disk, but everybody else who uses the computer sees only his or her own work.

User Accounts and Passwords: The Keys to Security You can use permissions only if you have Windows XP set up with more than one user, and you have the optional password system turned on. When Windows XP is first installed, it assumes you don't want to use passwords and that only you will use the PC. If you did the installation yourself, you can add more users at that time, but if you didn't, just open Control Panel and select User Accounts to change, add, remove, or configure settings for different people who will use your PC.

You can also click Create A Password and follow Windows XP's guidelines for creating a secure password. Once you do that, the password system will be turned on, and that user will have to enter a password to access the PC. Why would you want to do that? Well, if you're a parent, you might not want your children to have access to the software you use to manage your finances or taxes, or you might not want to risk that something important to you will get damaged or erased. You can also use the User Accounts system to manage settings that control things like Internet access to certain Web sites.

If your PC is in an office, passwords are a vital part of any company's security plan. Employees need to work with confidential data in files, and you don't want just anybody to step in and access your computer. If you combine Windows XP passwords with EFS, even if someone steals your PC, your data will remain secure (unless the thief has your passwords).

I mentioned that NTFS excels at working with large files and large disks, but there's a benefit to you, even if you don't have any 27 GB files hanging around. Windows XP's NTFS doesn't slow down as you ask it to manage bigger and bigger disks. FAT32 and FAT both do—a lot. So with disk sizes that are common today, you're almost guaranteed to get better performance from NTFS than you would with FAT32, all else being equal.

Our friend balanced integration enters the scheme when we start talking about compatibility. Versions before Windows NT 4 don't support NTFS at all. If you have your PC set up to let you use Windows XP and an old version, like Windows 98, when you're running Windows 98, you won't be able to see any data on the NTFS drive at all. This can be a significant concern if most of the programs you normally use—or most of your important data—is stored on the NTFS volume.

If you have a new PC and you haven't decided which file system to use, consider whether you'll need to run two different operating systems. If so, you might be forced to use FAT32 to keep your programs and data available.

Caution   If you're running under an earlier version of Windows, you might see a message indicating that the drive is empty or corrupted. You might be given the suggestion of formatting it. *Don't!* If you do, you'll destroy NTFS on the drive and all of the data and programs it contains.

EFS: The Encrypting File System EFS is a special feature of NTFS. *Encryption* is the process of modifying a file's contents so that any user who doesn't possess a secret key won't be able to make any sense of it. It's basically an egg scrambler for data, except that for once, you can unscramble the egg and put it back in the shell. With Windows XP passwords turned on, you can prevent anyone but yourself from accessing your data. (There is an expert-user technique for recovering your data even if you forget your password. The Help and Support Center can tell you exactly how to proceed.)

To tell Windows XP to encrypt a file, you have two choices. You can encrypt an individual file by right-clicking the file's icon, selecting Properties, clicking the Advanced button in the Attributes section of the General tab on the dialog box, and selecting the Encrypt Contents To Secure Data box.

You can also automatically encrypt all files in a selected folder. Perhaps you want to keep everything encrypted in your My Documents folder. No problem. Just right-click the My Documents folder on the desktop, select the General tab, click Advanced, and select the Encrypt option and click OK. When asked whether you want to apply encryption to just the folder or everything inside it, select Apply Changes To This Folder, Subfolders And Files, and click OK.

All files in the folder will be encrypted right away, and then files you add to the folder will be encrypted as you save or move them. When you need one of these files, Windows XP will decrypt (unscramble) it and open it for you, but no one else will be able to access the contents.

File System Maintenance: Best Practices

Before we started looking at the different Windows XP file systems, I was talking about the ways that files get fragmented. Why does it matter? Think about what your hard disk's read/write head has to do to read or write a fragmented file. It can't just find a blank space on disk, start writing, and stop when it's done. The head must move to the first available cluster, write data until it runs into a used cluster, stop writing, locate and move to the next available cluster, start writing again, and repeat the process every time it encounters a cluster that's not available. That takes time. Compared to how quickly your hard disk *can* work, it takes lots of time. A large number of fragmented files will diminish the performance of everything you do with your PC.

Fragmentation reduces the safety of your data, too. You remember the FAT that I mentioned earlier? If it gets corrupted, your files are probably toast. In some cases, data recovery software can restore the integrity of your disk and get your files back, but this strategy usually works only with nonfragmented files. If your files aren't fragmented, the recovery software can just search for the beginning of files, read the data until it encounters the special code that indicates the end of the file, and then write the data back into a new file.

If the file is fragmented, as soon as the software runs into the first cluster that doesn't belong to the file it's restoring, the party is over. Without the FAT, there's no way to know which cluster to read next, and the recovery will likely fail. Windows XP maintains an emergency backup of the FAT to prevent this kind of problem, but you can take steps to keep your data safer in the first place. You can keep your files defragmented, and you can check up on your drive integrity.

Disk Defragmenter

Windows XP includes a disk defragmenter that will analyze your drives, determine which files are fragmented, and then move all the files around so that most (or even all) of them can be stored with no fragmentation. As a result, performance will improve, and the chances of recovering your files in a worst-case scenario will increase. Running the defragmenter is as easy as selecting it from the Start menu and clicking a button, so let's try it. If you use your PC a lot, you should defragment the drive twice a month.

Try This! To defragment a disk drive, from the Start menu, select All Programs, then Accessories, System Tools, and Disk Defragmenter. When the program launches, you can select the drive you want to work with if there's more than one drive in your system, or you can just click Defragment.

Eliminating fragmentation (or *defragging*, as it's usually called) does take some time, however—hours, if you have lots of files, and many hours if you have lots of files and your drive is nearly full—so it's a great task to perform overnight. Just turn off the monitor and go to bed. Windows XP does the rest. When the process is done, you can view a report that tells you whether any files couldn't be moved or defragged. (Some system files can't be touched.) Close the program, and better performance is yours!

(Another way to start defragging a disk is to right-click the disk's icon in My Computer, select Properties, choose the Tools tab, and click Defragment Now.)

Check Disk

Another hardware-helper that's built into Windows XP is a program called Check Disk. Check Disk will check your drive's FAT, making sure that all of the information stored there is stored reliably. It makes sure that all the data that tracks your folders is intact, too. If you've selected NTFS, a thorough Check Disk scan won't run while you're doing anything else. (Fortunately, NTFS has some built-in systems that make using Check Disk less necessary, too.)

Let's try Check Disk, too, just so you're comfortable with it. I recommend using it once a month. (Incidentally, if you're a devout user of the Scandisk program, that's what Check Disk was called in earlier versions of Windows.)

Try This! Starting Check Disk is just as easy as using Disk Defragmenter. Right-click a drive's icon in My Computer, select the Tools tab, and click Check Now in the Error Checking area. If you want to perform a quick check of disk integrity, simply click Start. You should do this with no files open and no programs running to give Windows XP the best access to your drive. If Check Disk encounters problems, it will prompt you to fix them. Fix them, and you're good to go.

To perform a thorough check of your disk—the type of check you should do once a month—click to select the boxes for checking system files and scanning for bad sectors, and then click Start. Windows will let you know that the kind of scan you've selected can't be performed while you're using Windows, and it will let you schedule a scan for your next reboot.

This type of scan is quite thorough, and Windows will attempt to read every bit of data on your disk. If it finds that it can't properly read data the first time around, Windows will try to recover that data, store it in another location, update the FAT, and mark that space on the disk as "bad," so it's never used again for another file.

I expect I don't need to say that this process takes a good long time, too, and I recommend using Check Disk while you sleep, just as you should with Disk Defragmenter. Schedule a scan and then reboot and go to bed. When you get up, Windows XP will be waiting for you and your disk will be in great shape!

Key Points

- Hard disks (and floppies, for that matter) must be set up before they can be used. This setup is called formatting, and it organizes the space on the disk into structures that Windows will use to store and locate your files.

- The smallest accessible amount of space on a disk is called a cluster, and clusters are grouped into sectors, which are in turn parts of tracks.

- The different ways of formatting and organizing a disk's space are called file systems.

- Windows XP prefers to use NTFS because it generally provides the best performance. However, programs and data stored on an NTFS volume can't be accessed from earlier versions of Windows.

- Windows XP also supports the FAT32 and FAT file systems, which are leftovers from earlier versions of Windows. The FAT32 file system was developed to support large disks and long filenames.

- NTFS provides options for security, called permissions, and encryption that can guarantee that nobody but you can read the contents of your files.

- If you store and erase lots of files, your disk will get fragmented, meaning that all the parts of each file are not in contiguous space. Use the Disk Defragmenter tool to move your data around for better performance and data safety.

- Sometimes errors can creep onto hard disks. The wrong kinds of errors can make your data inaccessible. Use the Check Disk tool to periodically confirm that your disk is storing data reliably. If you encounter a lot of bad sectors on a disk, consider replacing the drive. You'll be glad you did sooner or later.

Chapter 13

Performance Perfection

A PC's performance is affected by bells, whistles, and visual effects—all of which can slow it down—but a number of other factors also determine how quickly you can get work done. If you've ever waited for a modem to move a large file from one place to another, you already know what I mean. There's nothing wrong with modems, of course. They're just not fast performers. This chapter will help you learn how to get the best performance and the most efficiency from your PC.

What Affects PC Performance?

The first factor that determines how quickly and efficiently your PC will perform is the hardware itself. We've talked about balanced integration many times— making sure that each piece of hardware in your PC is selected to complement the rest of the system's abilities. An aspect of balance that is often forgotten is the balance between what the hardware can do (however symbiotically its pieces relate) and what you expect of it. No matter what your choices, a CD-ROM can't store two hours of broadcast-quality digital video. An old PC with 64 megabytes (MB) of random access memory (RAM) and a 100-megahertz (MHz) central processing unit (CPU) can't run Microsoft Windows XP.

So if what you need from a PC is the distribution of digital video, or Windows XP, you must select hardware that's fit for the job: DVD+RW discs can easily move digital video around, and Windows XP will run beautifully on any modern PC. Let's look at a few examples of selecting hardware smarter:

If You Want to Do This...	Consider This
Work with digital audio	You'll want huge amounts of hard disk space, lots of memory, and a fast CPU.
Manage your business	You'll want a midrange system with a high-quality printer for a professional look and a backup device for data safety.
Play the latest 3D games	You'll want a high-powered video card with a lot of dedicated video memory, a good amount of system RAM, and a fast CPU.
Work with a large professional database	You'll want a large, fast hard disk, and a fast CPU if you query or sort often.
Work with graphic design or print layout	You'll want a large hard disk, as much memory as possible, and a fast CPU for moving and editing graphics.
Produce digital video	You'll want a huge hard disk, fast CPU, and a DVD+RW writer for distributing your work.
Write letters, simple reports, and papers	An entry-level PC will suffice, but your needs might grow quicker than you think. If you're sure they won't, spend the extra money on a high-quality printer so your writing looks professional.

Naturally, the flip side to choosing hardware well is choosing software well. There's always more than one way to complete any given task. You'll want to review the different software options carefully so that you purchase a product that does what you want it to do. For example, if you're going to do a lot of free-hand drawing, purchase an application made for the job. Although many wonderful niche products are available, before you buy one and pay for features you might never use (and possibly not get a full-featured version of what you *do* need), look for software that does exactly what you want.

Also, if you're trying to get the capabilities you need from running several products at once, you'll definitely find that running two or more memory-intensive and processor-intensive programs is less efficient than running one product that's fully featured. Consider the world of graphic design. An inexpensive product lets you work with text, another one lets you draw, and a third one lets you edit illustrations; each one uses a large amount of processor power and memory. When they're running all at once and you're cutting and pasting among them, your PC will almost surely run out of traditional RAM and will turn to virtual memory to pick up the slack.

You'll remember from Chapter 3 that virtual memory is dramatically slower than RAM. Even if you allow Windows XP to configure your virtual memory automatically—which you should do—you'll find yourself waiting for a long time while your hard disk chugs away. It could even freeze, making you lose work, and you'd have to start from scratch. Products from different manufacturers sometimes misbehave in each others' presence, and that can make you lose data, too. It's probably a much better decision—economically, too, because your time has a value—to buy a fully featured graphics package that won't crash your PC.

Running Processes

When you do run several products at once, you might think you're running three applications, but Windows might actually be running vastly more tasks than only three. When it seems to you that Windows is doing nothing but waiting for you, Windows is busy, indeed. On my notebook, when no applications are in use, Windows is running no fewer than 29 different tasks, called *processes*.

Lingo   A *process* is simply a computer program that accomplishes some specific task or tasks. A process, although an independent and complete entity, is usually part of a larger application. For example, a process called Explorer.exe is the program that supports the ability of the Windows XP graphical user interface (GUI) to display the contents of disks and folders. It's a program unto itself, but its purpose is to be part of Windows.

If you'd like to see just which processes are running on your PC, you can do it easily. And the tool we'll use to do it is also the tool we'll use to check on how busy your PC really is. Let's give it a try—on your keyboard, press and hold down the Ctrl and Alt keys, and press the Delete key once. This is the infamous Ctrl+Alt+Delete key combination people constantly used to restart the PC when it crashed. Now that our digital world is a more stable place, we just use it to grab the PC's attention when we want it so we can see what's really going on under the hood, as it were. When the Task Manager window opens, you can view running applications, active processes, CPU and network use, and other system statistics, as shown in Figure 13-1.

Figure 13-1 The Windows Task Manager is like a CAT scan into the heart of Windows XP.

With the Applications tab selected, you'll see a list of all the applications that are running on your PC. This is a living display; you can leave it open and start a program, and you'll see that name join those already in the list. The Status column indicates whether an application is running or not responding. If the latter, you can use this dialog box to force the application to quit so you can get on with other tasks. Simply select the application you want to stop and click End Task. In most cases, the application will quit immediately. Sometimes a brief delay might occur before Windows warns you that you might lose unsaved data. Click the warning's End Now button, and the program will be forced to quit.

Caution   Do *not* use the Task Manager and the End Task button to quit applications normally. Every application has a Quit command for that purpose, and you might well lose any unsaved work if you stop an application with End Task. Its purpose is to allow you to force a frozen program to quit so you can safely save your work in other applications and then restart Windows to restore system stability.

Tip   The Task Manager also lets you switch from any running application to any other; you select the program you want to switch to and click Switch To. But there's a better way. At any time, hold down the Alt key and then press the Tab key once. Windows shows you a small box indicating all the applications that are running. Keep the Alt key held down and press Tab repeatedly until the moving highlight is on the application to which you want to switch. Release the Alt key, and you'll instantly jump to that program. You can quickly move between two different applications with a single Alt+Tab key press. You'll find it a lot faster than taking your hand off the keyboard to click the program's name on the taskbar.

To view the many processes that are running, select the Processes tab. Here, shown in Figure 13-2, you'll see each process, which user is running it, and some other information. The CPU column, for example, shows which percentage of your CPU's time was just spent executing instructions from each process. A special process, called the System Idle Process, shows the percentage of your CPU's time that was just spent doing nothing at all. In the Image Name column, you'll see the Task Manager itself (called taskmgr.exe) and the various pieces of Windows and your applications that are running.

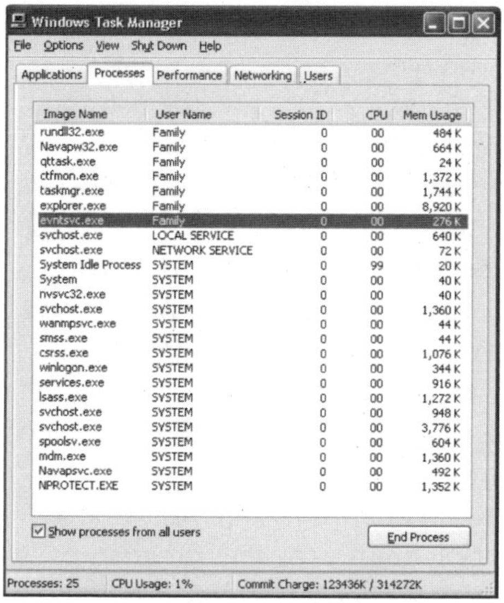

Windows Task Manager

File Options View Shut Down Help

| Applications | Processes | Performance | Networking | Users |

Image Name	User Name	Session ID	CPU	Mem Usage
rundll32.exe	Family	0	00	484 K
Navapw32.exe	Family	0	00	664 K
qttask.exe	Family	0	00	24 K
ctfmon.exe	Family	0	00	1,372 K
taskmgr.exe	Family	0	00	1,744 K
explorer.exe	Family	0	00	8,920 K
evntsvc.exe	Family	0	00	276 K
svchost.exe	LOCAL SERVICE	0	00	640 K
svchost.exe	NETWORK SERVICE	0	00	72 K
System Idle Process	SYSTEM	0	99	20 K
System	SYSTEM	0	00	40 K
nvsvc32.exe	SYSTEM	0	00	40 K
svchost.exe	SYSTEM	0	00	1,360 K
wanmpsvc.exe	SYSTEM	0	00	44 K
smss.exe	SYSTEM	0	00	44 K
csrss.exe	SYSTEM	0	00	1,076 K
winlogon.exe	SYSTEM	0	00	344 K
services.exe	SYSTEM	0	00	916 K
lsass.exe	SYSTEM	0	00	1,272 K
svchost.exe	SYSTEM	0	00	948 K
svchost.exe	SYSTEM	0	00	3,776 K
spoolsv.exe	SYSTEM	0	00	604 K
mdm.exe	SYSTEM	0	00	1,360 K
Navapsvc.exe	SYSTEM	0	00	492 K
NPROTECT.EXE	SYSTEM	0	00	1,352 K

☑ Show processes from all users   End Process

Processes: 25   CPU Usage: 1%   Commit Charge: 123436K / 314272K

Figure 13-2 The Processes tab shows the system and user processes running on your PC.

Note You might remember I spoke in Chapter 10 about the system tasks that Windows XP performs to keep everything running. For the most part, these are executed by the processes identified as belonging to the user named SYSTEM.

If you find that your PC seems to be locked up or functioning extremely slowly, you can learn a great deal from this tab of the Task Manager. Unless your system has become dangerously unstable, pressing Ctrl+Alt+Delete should open the Task Manager even if everything else seems to be frozen. That key combination is a bit like dangling chocolate in front of the boss; it's a way of grabbing the PC and shaking it until you have its full attention.

Once you get its attention, you can look to see which process is using so much CPU time. You'll know whether your 3D drafting application is simply rendering the scene you asked it to render, or whether some other process is monopolizing the PC. You don't want to force a process to stop unless you know exactly what it is—and, even then, you should rarely if ever stop a SYSTEM process. But if you find a process called something like Cpukill.exe (or Haha.exe, or some similarly obvious name) taking 92 percent of your processor time, you're the victim of a rogue process. Clicking End Now will force it to quit and should return control of your PC to you.

Rogue Processes

Two different types of rogue process could give your PC problems and cause you to suffer a loss of data or productivity. Poorly written software is the first type; Trojan horses and viruses are the second type.

The Windows application programming interface (API) and the Software Development Kit (SDK) provide programmers with an incredible amount of power. All that's asked in return is that programmers use these tools properly. But some programmers don't, won't, or simply aren't good enough coders, and can't. Windows XP is excellent at weeding out the products of these underclass developers, refusing to let software run when it demonstrates unruly behavior.

Every once in a while, unfortunately, you'll find yourself running two different programs whose creators cheated in ways that don't complement each other, and one or both programs will freeze. Open the Task Manager and select the Applications tab to see whether either application is marked as Not Responding. If it is, click End Now to force it to quit. Hopefully, you'll be able to rescue any unsaved data within the other program. If neither program is marked as Not Responding, however, you'll need to look at the Processes tab to find out what's going on.

What you're looking for is a process—other than System Idle, of course—that either obviously doesn't belong (like the Haha.exe I mentioned a moment ago) or that's using most of your CPU's time (like 80 percent or more). Now, before you simply kill the process, consider whether it's possibly doing exactly what it's supposed to do. Because Windows hasn't identified its owner as a non-responding application, it could be that the graphic you're trying to redraw or the database file you're trying to query is taking everything your PC's got to give.

If not, you can select the process from the list and click End Now. Windows warns you that ending a process manually can make your system unstable; that's true. If you ever need to force a process to quit, save your work in any other applications and then restart Windows immediately. (Don't simply log off and back on; restart the PC.)

A runaway program is an annoyance, but the second type of rogue process—one of malicious intent—is quite dangerous. Windows XP can automatically protect you from certain catastrophes, like a malicious program that wants to format your hard disk, as long as you don't regularly log on as Administrator. Malicious programmers can do a lot if they get a foothold inside your PC.

Rather than be sorry, be smarter—use an antivirus product that's actively supported by its maker (so you have updates against each new threat as it's detected) and that has some form of automatic protection. This automatic protection means that you're safe not just when you think to scan your files for problems, but at all times. The antivirus software watches data as it comes across your modem or network connection, weeding out viruses and other malicious code before it's even written to your hard disk.

Try This! If you want to see the protective power of Windows XP in action, give yourself this little demonstration. Log on to your PC through a user account that doesn't have Administrator privileges. (If you're the Administrator of your PC, just use Control Panel to create a limited account that you can delete in a moment.) Then open My Computer, right-click your C hard drive, and select Format. When the Format dialog box opens, click Start.

See? Windows won't allow you to format any hard drive in the system unless you have Administrator access. Microsoft recommends that even a single user avoid using the Administrator account for normal use so that this sort of protection remains active. (By the way, I've cheated here a little. Even if you do have Administrator access, Windows won't format the drive on which it's stored, so your C drive would still have its integrity even if you tried this exercise as an Administrator. However, because many of us have only one hard drive in our PC, it's the best I could do.)

Rogue processes are hard to identify, naturally, but if you've got no applications running, and no system tray processes, take a close look at any process that's running and says it belongs to your user name. You might have a bit of malicious code in your machine. Restart Windows XP after running a complete virus check on your system, just to be safe.

Memory Issues

When you buy a new PC or buy memory for your existing PC, purchase as much RAM as your system will support and you can afford. If you purchase less RAM than the maximum your system can handle, endeavor to purchase higher-capacity memory modules so that you can still expand your system when economy allows. It's that simple.

Disk Issues

In addition to processes running on your PC, system performance can be affected by a variety of disk issues. The choices you make and the good habits you develop can actually improve the speed with which you can get to any data on your drives. For the remainder of this chapter, we'll explore these issues. The payback to you for spending a little time reading a few pages could be better performance every time your PC accesses its hard drive.

Pairing Hardware with Your Needs

First, consider the drive itself. Every hard drive manufacturer measures the best-possible performance of each of their products under ideal conditions. Your mileage might vary. The average hard drive has about 13 performance specifications, which are all but useless to almost everyone. Nevertheless, three are worth considering. How fast a drive spins, its *rotational speed*, can make a noticeable difference in the performance of the entire drive. The faster the platters spin, the less time is wasted waiting for your data (or the appropriate unused space) to line up with the read/write head and start flowing to or from the PC.

Lingo   The dead time spent waiting for a hard drive's platters to spin to the appropriate location under the read/write heads is called *latency*.

Naturally, CPU power should complement drive speed; there's no reason to buy a high-end 10,000-revolution-per-minute (RPM) drive and put it into a 100 MHz system. Such a slow PC won't be able to process the data as quickly as it flows off the drive, so the read/write heads will actually have to back up and reread data over and over. A fast disk in a slow machine is a sure recipe for disaster. (Did somebody say "balanced integration"?) Similarly, yesterday's 5400 RPM drives (and their generally lower *buffer-to-disk rates*) can fall behind today's fastest CPUs and their high-performance motherboards.

Lingo   A hard drive's *buffer-to-disk rate* is the maximum speed at which it can move data to or from the drive. CPU performance, physical RAM, and even the size of the file being accessed can dramatically reduce the actual average transfer speed from this theoretical maximum. A drive's *seek time* is how long it takes the drive's read/write head to move from anyplace along the drive's radius to any other place, averaged out across the span of the disk.

The two other factors of value are the drive's buffer-to-disk rate and seek time. For the most part, no drive ever performs well enough in real life to live up to its advertised buffer rate. Too many variables can slow down the flow of data, one of which is fragmentation, which we'll talk about in the next section. Seek time is a far more reliable statistic because the drive's internal *read/write actuator* (the mechanism that moves the heads back and forth) works at a fixed speed regardless of external factors. So should you focus on seek time and ignore buffer rate? No. As it turns out, the type of work you do will sway which of these two factors you should most consider.

If you spend most of your working time researching online, writing documents, working with spreadsheets or managing projects, you're almost surely opening and closing, creating and erasing, small files all day long. That's because the sorts of things you do create an endless stream of temporary files that get written all over your drive or drives. You'll want to devote a little more attention to a drive's seek time simply because your drive will be doing a lot of seeking, the head moving back and forth, grabbing and stashing data for file after file. Buffer rate doesn't matter much to you because you rarely work with a file that's big enough for the speed of a continuous stream of data to matter. Put another way, why buy a Ferrari if you never drive more than a mile from home?

On the other hand, if "there and back again" is your kind of holiday, you might just love riding that Italian stallion. And if you work with large database files or digital multimedia, seek time means almost nothing to you, because you'll be working with just a few huge files, so you'll have tremendous amounts of data to get into and out of the PC as quickly as possible. Transfer rate will be closer to your heart.

Because all modern hard disks come with a RAM buffer (to prevent the necessity of rereading data if the PC can't keep up), transfer rate is actually the maximum speed at which the drive's buffer can perform. On top of this, any professional who does this sort of work will make certain that every hard disk within 50 miles stays defragmented, just to be safe.

If you work with graphic design and illustration, you're in hard drive limbo, caught between the huge files that you create and the hundreds of small, frequently opened, modified, and closed temporary files that your work requires. You could certainly just buy the highest-performing disk drive around, but that road is definitely the path to overspending. For you, and for most of us, a mid-performing drive of the highest-affordable capacity is the best choice.

What's mid-performing mean? At the time of this writing, it means a 7200 RPM drive (5400 RPM drives are not sufficiently less expensive to merit the loss of performance), a buffer rate of anything between 400 and 600 megabits per second, and a seek time between 8 and 9.5 milliseconds. Today's high-performance drives have buffer rates closer to 100 megabytes (800 megabits) per second, and seek times in the neighborhood of 5.3 milliseconds.

Whatever Happened to Transfer Rate? We used to talk about a drive's *transfer rate*, but the presence of a RAM buffer in today's drives confounds such simple and useful concepts—all to the greater glory of marketing. A drive's transfer rate today is simply advertised as the theoretical maximum performance of the different bus speeds the drive supports. No drive, and precious few buses, will perform up to this ideal.

File System Best Practices: NTFS

Once you've chosen a drive, you need to choose a file system, as we talked about in Chapter 12. By far, the NT file system (NTFS) is your best choice for a Windows XP file system. It has features that can protect your data from prying eyes and loss of integrity. It gives you the flexibility to work with considerably larger disks than does your only other reasonable choice—FAT32. And the power of NTFS scales up so much better than anything else out there under Windows, you won't run into a problem that has plagued FAT and FAT32 from the beginning.

As you work with ever-larger disks, FAT and FAT32 perform worse and worse, until they're crawling along, trying to keep up with the amount of data they have to sort through to find and care for your files. NTFS has the world of the big-disk better in hand; it performs as well with 200 GB drives as it does with a 1 GB disk (if such a thing still exists). FAT32 performs generally better than NTFS with disks smaller than 1 GB, but unless you're using the antiquated capacity of 100 MB Zip disks, you'll never miss the difference.

Once you've chosen the right file system, maintaining it is the key to performance perfection. You should check disks for errors on a weekly basis, especially if you use your PC eight hours a day, five days a week. Doing this task is as easy as opening My Computer and right-clicking the drive. Select Properties, and then choose the Tools menu. Click Check Now to either run the error check (if you're using a FAT32 file system) or to schedule the error check for the next time you restart Windows (if you're running NTFS).

The next best practice to keep in mind is to keep your disk uncluttered. And *uncluttered* means two different things. Its first meaning is the simplest, and its one my father told me far more often than I've ever had to remind him how to use Windows: throw away your junk. You should use Disk Cleanup twice a month to discourage file fragmentation and reduce the number of file and folder entries Windows must search through to find your data. If you've ever used the Windows Explorer Move To Folder command with a particularly full drive, you've probably sat and had a cup of coffee while Windows was reading the structure of your destination disk. Fewer files and fewer folders means fewer sips of that awful office coffee.

See Also   *See Chapter 5 for ways to get the most out of Disk Cleanup.*

The second meaning of *uncluttered* is also something my father told me regularly: put your stuff away. That is, after you throw out the junk, organize the junk that remains. Windows will do the job for you—all you have to do is run the Disk Defragmenter, which I discussed in Chapter 12.

Alternatively, you can gain even more performance benefits by running one of several third-party defragmenting utilities that will speed up the disk. These tools make it possible to move files that are rarely or never modified first on the disk. Files with this quality include the many program (*.EXE) and library (*.DLL) files on your system disk, and programs and Windows itself might run noticeably faster with them stored upfront.

If you're defragmenting a FAT32 disk with one of these external utilities, you might also be able to locate all of your folders at the start of the disk, where they, too, will load fastest. Of course, Microsoft won't be able to assist you with any concerns you have using another manufacturer's software; if you have questions, you'll need to contact the third-party software companies directly.

Key Points

- Performance is the direct beneficiary of balanced integration. Choose software that performs exactly the tasks you require and hardware that's well-suited to running the software you select.

- A process is either a program or a part of a program that performs a specific task.

- The Task Manager allows you to see running processes and applications. You can force nonresponsive applications to quit and can shut down rogue or misbehaving processes.

- For maximum performance, endow your PC with as much RAM as possible.

■ Performance statistics to consider when selecting a hard disk include its seek time and rotation speed. If you commonly work with extremely large files, look to the drive's buffer-to-disk rate as well.

■ Keep your drives error-free and defragmented. For the best possible performance, use Disk Cleanup.

■ Unless you have an extremely small hard disk, always use NTFS as your file system in Windows XP. NTFS provides better performance, better security, and better reliability than the FAT32 file system it replaces.

Chapter 14

Watching Your PC with the Device Manager

As we've looked at the hardware inside your PC, I've talked a lot about different hardware settings. From resources like interrupt request lines (IRQs) and ports to your local area code, Microsoft Windows XP makes all of these hardware settings accessible through the various icons in Control Panel. Behind the scenes, every peripheral, every system device is integrated into your PC by the *Windows Registry*—a kind of encyclopedia of hardware and software settings. From the user's perspective, these settings and their respective devices are managed through the *Device Manager*—an incredibly useful tool for detecting and diagnosing hardware difficulties in your PC.

The Device Manager Manages...Devices

It's difficult to appreciate *just* how useful the Device Manager is if you haven't worked with PCs in the pre-Windows world. Indulge me in an analogy, and you'll understand what I mean. If I challenged you to put together a jigsaw puzzle with about 75 pieces, you'd probably scoff. It's not much of a challenge. So, to make things more interesting, I tell you that my puzzle has special rules. Think how you'd feel as I tell you this:

1   It's a magic puzzle. You can see the picture on the puzzle only as each piece is fit together correctly. Randomly, some pieces might appear to be correct until you place the final piece, at which time, the entire picture will disappear if any piece is wrong.

2   I'm going to keep all the pieces in a closed box, and you can withdraw only one piece at a time, look at it, try to remember its shape, and then you must put it back in the box if you're not ready to snap it into its final place in the puzzle.

3   Most of the pieces have the exact same shape.

4   If you put a piece in the wrong place, the piece you *should* have used might change its shape, so it won't fit anywhere in the puzzle until you figure out where it *should* have gone and remove the incorrect piece.

5   The picture is lovely, but fickle. It might seem right for a while, but if you look too long at an improperly placed piece, the whole picture will vanish. If you know a piece is wrong, you can either start over completely or switch only two pieces at a time until you have it right.

If the challenge seems to have gone from childlike to impossible, I assure you that it's not. Many of us survived this challenge daily. You've simply entered the world of hardware configuration before Microsoft Windows. Here's how the analogy plays out, following each rule in order:

1   In many cases, assembling and configuring hardware in an early PC prevented it from working at all until everything was perfect. Sometimes, the PC worked fine until the last device was installed, and then it failed.

2   Most hardware settings were configured with *jumpers*—physical connectors on each device. You'd have to check each device's documentation, learn which settings might work, and then install the device and see. If you were unsuccessful, you needed to pull the device out, change a jumper, and try again. Installing multiple devices at once meant you had to remember the valid settings for each device, as well as those already installed. Some devices had settings configured by software, and couldn't be changed until everything else was working well enough to start the PC successfully.

3 Most settings could be used by only one device, and many devices could use any of the settings, so endless combinations were available, only some of which would work.

4 Some devices could use only certain resource settings, bringing the term *conflict* into PC lingo. It was entirely possible to buy a new device that simply *couldn't* be made to work at all with your existing devices.

5 Sometimes, all seemed well until you tried to use a certain device feature, at which point, the whole PC might fail. Problems (such as a *conflict* between two devices or a device set invalidly) could sometimes be weeded out by trying to adjust two devices at a time, but any given third device might require a setting you previously used to make the first two happy with each other—so you have to start from scratch.

Lingo   A device or resource *conflict* occurs when two or more devices attempt to use the same hardware resources, such as IRQs or memory addresses.

I'll tell you more about some of these nightmares in Chapter 16, when we take a good look at hardware management today. Unfortunately, the PC can still be quite a puzzle for many users, even experienced ones. The Device Manager is for hardware what seeing the pieces together on the table and the picture on the puzzle box could have been for my magic puzzle. In fact, the Device Manager is even better than that, because it not only allows you to see what each device needs to work, but it will also do the following:

■ Show you which devices aren't working

■ Identify the other device or devices with which a conflict exists

■ Allow you to resolve conflicts by disabling devices when they won't be used

■ Allow you to work as normally as possible by automatically disabling devices that are configured incorrectly or behave poorly

The Device Manager isn't the electronic magic that makes all of this possible—that honor goes to Plug and Play, which you'll learn more about in Chapter 16. It is the magician's wand, the tool that gives us control over a PC's devices and the resources they use.

Much of what this tool is good for is high-level stuff. But it's good to at least be aware of what's going on. In my estimation, it's preferable to say, "My PC won't work, and the symptoms suggest a conflict, so I need to get assistance from my coworker who knows how to use the Device Manager," than it is to learn you've paid a technician $80 an hour to diagnose a problem that a PC-savvy friend—or even you—could have fixed for free, had you known there was such a thing as a device conflict and a Device Manager available to seek out and solve such problems.

Caution   The settings you'll see in the Device Manager are the lifeblood of your PC and its peripherals. Any change you make will affect how your PC works, even if you can't detect any difference. Some changes wouldn't matter; some could crash your PC. There's nothing in the Device Manager that could burn up your central processing unit (CPU) or directly erase your hard disk, but you could make a device stop working or make it impossible to restart your PC. On the tour I'm about to give you, you can learn a lot; you have the luxury of not having anything really pressing to *do*, but you don't want to touch the wrong button, either.

Managing the Manager

It's often recognized as good business advice for a CEO to hire or promote excellent, talented people to be managers, and to let them do what they're paid to do. It's also good advice for a CEO to stay on top of things and step in when management needs a little managing. These two pieces of advice apply well to your relationship with your PC. The Device Manager does an excellent job, but it's still good to know what's going on inside the PC. So let's take a ride in the executive elevator down to where real work is happening and take a look.

Discovering the Device Manager

The Device Manager is accessible through the Hardware tab of your System Properties dialog box. Right-click My Computer, choose Properties, select the Hardware tab, and click Device Manager. Windows takes a moment to gather information about your PC and its devices. In fact, Windows is actually performing a quick hardware scan to see whether anything it thinks it knows about your hardware configuration has changed. You'll see a window like the one shown in Figure 14-1.

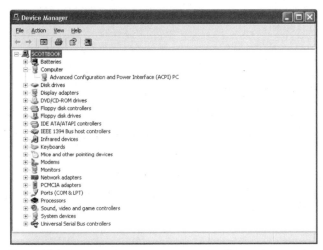

Figure 14-1 The Windows Device Manager classifies each piece of hardware or system in your PC into recognizable categories.

Try This! You can make Windows repeat this scan at any time by clicking the small computer-and-magnifying-glass icon on the Device Manager toolbar. This useful little trick can help identify whether you're having troubles with a removable device. Recall from Chapter 8 that universal serial bus (USB) and FireWire peripherals should be hot-swappable: if you plug one in while the PC is on, the PC is supposed to detect it and set it to work automatically.

If your PC is behaving erratically and you suspect the problem is with some device that's removable, open the Device Manager and plug the device in. The Device Manager should detect the new hardware and add it to the list. (You might need to double-click the appropriate category name to check.)

If your device isn't there, click to scan manually for hardware changes. If your device is still absent, either the hardware is defective or some other device—one that's already installed in your PC—is misbehaving. I'll talk about why this sort of thing still happens and what you can do about it in Chapter 16.

Let's take a look at what's inside this particular PC. Because you're seeing my notebook computer, there's a category for the intelligent batteries it uses. The Computer category is the home of my notebook's Advanced Configuration and Power Interface (ACPI), which is the system that turns off my monitor and eventually puts my notebook to sleep when I leave it idle. ACPI also does a lot to help me save battery life by intelligently powering off devices while I'm not using them.

Note   If you've got an older mobile device like a PC Card modem that isn't fully ACPI-compliant, you lose in two ways. First, a single non-ACPI device will disable the entire ACPI system. That means your notebook will be forced to use the older Advanced Power Management (APM), which is a lot less efficient. Second, PC Cards, also called PCMCIA, or CardBus cards, draw a tremendous amount of power. Some of them even get too hot to touch! (Remember in Chapter 2, I talked about the heat PC components can generate.)

Without ACPI, even an unused PC Card will remain on, and your battery life will plummet. If you open the Power Options dialog box and see an APM tab, you have a non-ACPI device installed. Check to see whether it's one that's removable and, if it is, always unplug it when you aren't using it. You'll be a lot more productive on that coast-to-coast flight if your battery isn't dead.

You'll probably recognize the other hardware categories you see: disk drives, display adapters (that's your video card or video support on the motherboard), floppy disk drives, and so forth. Some categories might have been entirely foreign to you—IDE controllers, for example—if you hadn't already read the first two parts of this book. The IDE controller is responsible for the operation of your hard disks.

A conflict of a device in this category usually prevents your PC from starting properly, but sometimes it might just make your hard disks behave erratically. If you suddenly encounter error messages when you try to read or write to the hard disk, check here for a conflict. If all looks well, your drive might be heading toward failure. And so it goes, down the list.

What do you do if you want to recommend your model of DVD drive to someone, but you've no idea where the box went or what's inside? You could open the PC, take out the drive and read the label on it, or you could just click the plus sign (+) next to DVD/CD-ROM drives and find your answer. Select information about your PC is available immediately when you open System Properties—stuff like the speed of your CPU and how much memory you have installed. That information and everything else about your hardware is also found in the Device Manager.

Understanding the Device Manager Icons

The Device Manager's purpose isn't to help you market someone's DVD drive, however. It's there to let you know when something's wrong. It does this by displaying one of three different icons—either a bright yellow question mark with a black exclamation point superimposed, a red *X*, or a white *i* in a blue circle.

■ The black exclamation point means that you have hardware installed but Windows can't find a driver for it. This hardware might function, but don't expect it to function reliably. You can use the Device Manager to instruct Windows to search for and install a proper driver.

> **See Also** In Chapter 16, the section called "Almost Everything You Need to Know About Drivers" will give you some tips on how to proceed.

■ A red *X* means that a device is disabled. This might happen because you or someone else has manually disabled it, or because Windows XP has detected a serious conflict and has disabled the device automatically.

> **Note** I'm using the rather awkward term *disabled* rather than just saying that the device has been turned off to avoid confusion with a device that has no power—one that is off in the traditional sense. A device that is disabled might still be drawing power; its functionality is simply unavailable. Similarly, a device that ACPI has turned off is by no means disabled. It would be working perfectly, presumably, if it were powered on, and ACPI will turn it on automatically if you attempt to use it.

■ A white *i* in a blue circle means that someone has manually configured a device rather than let Windows XP do the job automatically. This device might be working perfectly, but any time you manually configure something, you limit Windows' options. More on this in Chapter 16, too.

Fortunately for me, you don't see any of these symbols in Figure 14-1 because my system and its devices are working amicably.

Unless you intentionally disable a device—more about this in a moment— the presence of any red *X* symbols indicates a problem. When Windows XP starts, it thoroughly scans your PC's hardware and doles out resources as needed. If two pieces of hardware want the same resource, Windows simply tries to assign an alternative resource to one device.

If that fails, it tries again before starting over and trying to assign an alternate resource to the other of the conflicting pair. If that fails, too, Windows XP disables whichever of the two devices it considers less imperative—for example, a modem over a sound card; a hard disk controller over a modem—and continues starting up.

Only in the most catastrophic of situations will Windows fail to start entirely, forcing you to boot from an NT file system (NTFS) boot disk or seek professional assistance. Indeed, Windows disables multiple devices if necessary to start successfully. Only when a device critical to your PC's normal functioning fails—or when a device fails in some bizarre way, catching Windows off guard—will Windows itself not start.

Reviewing Device Settings

Once the Device Manager is running, you can review any hardware settings that interest you. If you're surprised by finding a device disabled, opening that device's properties will usually tell you why.

To review a device's properties, click the plus sign (+) to expand its category, right-click the device, and select Properties. A window the likes of which you saw back in Chapter 8 opens—there's one in Figure 14-2—with this piece of hardware's settings. As you can see in the figure, the device I selected is working properly. More to the point, Windows XP *knows* it's working properly. If there were a problem with this device, the status area would tell me to check on the device's Resources tab for a conflict.

Note   A device that has no Resource tab of its own is usually being controlled by another device that does use resources; for example, a DVD drive (with no Resource tab) is controlled by the IDE ATA/ATAPI controller, which has a Resource tab in its properties.

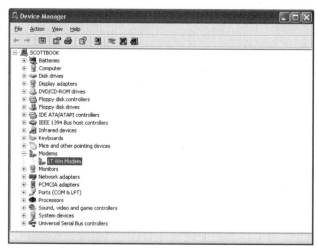

Figure 14-2 Clicking a plus sign in the Device Manager reveals the specific devices belonging to a category of hardware.

Even if Windows thinks everything is perfect, you might still think there's a problem, so the Troubleshooter button takes you directly to an online, interactive troubleshooting tool. We'll talk about these more in Chapter 15, but they're a great addition to the Windows XP Help And Support Center. In brief, they're wizards that ask you questions about the performance of your hardware to help you diagnose difficulties.

Certain devices, like the modem you see in Figure 14-2, have their own Diagnostics tab. Here you'll usually find buttons that'll launch the device's own diagnostic software or run brief routines that check the device and return errors if anything is amiss. (We used this tab in Chapter 8 when we ran modem diagnostics to make sure all was working properly.)

Disabling or Enabling a Device

Most of the time, if a device needs to be disabled, Windows will have already done it for you. In fact, about the only time users would ever need to disable a device manually is when they are diagnosing a problem with some *other* device and suspect a hidden conflict. If disabling one device suddenly makes another device work properly, you've found your culprit.

Of course, you'll still need to determine which of the two is behaving most poorly and which action is appropriate. Any modern device should allow itself to share resources with other devices and allow its resource settings to be modified freely by Windows. That makes the kind of conflict we're talking about pretty rare. Antiquated, or what's politely termed *legacy* hardware, is most often the culprit because it's from a time when resource flexibility was still just an engineer's dream.

In any case, you should know how to disable a device and enable it again, just in case you do have a problem or someone else was playing around with your PC. From inside the Device Manger, just right-click any working device and select Disable to disable it. Windows offers you one word of warning, after which the device is disabled. Windows XP won't generally allow you to disable any device that it knows is critical, but I'd like to repeat my earlier caution anyway. Don't change any settings unless you know what you're doing. Recovering from an innocent experiment might not be a simple matter.

To enable the device again, right-click and select Enable from the shortcut menu. Windows starts the device up and loads its necessary drivers into memory. Enabling the device could fail for a couple of reasons, the most likely and obvious of which is an irresolvable conflict with some other, already-enabled hardware. Windows won't fail in this situation; it simply returns the device to its disabled state. Open the device's properties for whatever information Windows can give you about the problem and to launch the hardware troubleshooter.

See Also　　We'll talk a lot more about hardware drivers in Chapter 16.

Manual Configuration: The Headache in Wait　Because Windows XP supports vast selections of hardware, and thanks to Plug and Play, resource conflicts are as rare today as they once were common. Devices can, as I mentioned, now share some of the same resources, and can usually use any available resources, not just one or two as was once the case. Consequently, if you find a device disabled, the likelihood that someone has forced another device into a manual configuration is high. Even a single device configured manually can make the job of Windows and Plug and Play immensely more difficult—even impossible.

Without getting mired in technical details, we can understand the problem just based on the numbers. Removing a resource from your list of available resources—which is what happens when you manually configure an IRQ or some other setting—dramatically reduces the number of possible resource combinations. Because not all devices can work with just *any* resource, say any IRQ, taking even a single IRQ or memory address out of the mix can leave a device unable to use any of the remaining resources. That device will be disabled by Windows and made unavailable.

Sometimes, manual configuration is necessary, but it's to be avoided if at all possible. In general, a device that's so old it must be manually configured to work under Windows XP is best replaced with a newer device. Doing that might sound like throwing good money after bad, but manual configurations can lead to system instability and a loss of productivity and data. Be safe; let Windows manage hardware resources automatically.

Hardware Profiles

Part of every device's properties, and close to the heart of the Device Manager, is the idea of hardware profiles. A *hardware profile* tells Windows which hardware to enable during startup. They're particularly useful for people who use notebook computers; you can set up one configuration for when you're at home and one for when you're on the road. In the first profile, you might have network support enabled to make use of your DSL connection to the Internet. Your PC Card modem could be disabled entirely unless you use it for faxing. In the second configuration, you could apply the opposite rules: your network connection might be disabled and your modem up and running.

Lingo   A *hardware profile* is a collection of specific hardware configured using specific settings.

During startup, Windows lets you choose which profile to use. Hardware profiles are also useful if you have a piece of hardware that you use only occasionally, but which conflicts with some other piece of hardware. Creating two profiles, with the devices taking turns at being enabled in one and disabled in the other, eliminates the need to uninstall or unplug one of the devices to maintain system stability. On a system connected to a Windows server, hardware profiles can also restrict access to specific devices.

To look at your current hardware profile, just open the Device Manager. What you see is what you get. By default, the first time Windows XP runs on a PC, every peripheral attached is enabled in the initial hardware profile. If you want to disable one of these devices, it's best to create a new hardware profile and disable the device in that profile, leaving your default profile intact. To disable a device permanently, just open its category in the Device Manager, right-click the device, select Uninstall, and remove the device after shutting the PC off. The device's driver files will be removed so you can disconnect the device from your system before you start up again.

Note   Be aware that Windows attempts to start up any device it finds connected to your PC unless that device is disabled in the hardware profile. Uninstalling a device without actually disconnecting it only adds to your startup time because Windows attempts to locate and reinstall drivers for any "uninstalled" device that's still present.

To create a new hardware profile, open the System Properties dialog box (right-click My Computer and select Properties) and select the Hardware tab. Click Hardware Profiles, and you'll see a dialog box like the one shown in Figure 14-3.

Figure 14-3 On this notebook computer, the undocked profile is the default Windows created the first time it ran on this hardware.

Creating a new hardware profile involves copying an existing profile and then making changes to device settings as necessary. In the example shown in Figure 14-3, my Undocked Profile is already selected. If I click Copy, Windows asks me to give the new profile a name, and then creates it. The new profile will have the same settings as my current one. To start personalizing it, select the Wait Until I Select A Hardware Profile option, and then click OK twice and restart Windows. When asked which profile you want to use, select the new one you want to customize.

When the desktop appears, reopen the Device Manager and expand the category for the device you want to modify. Right-click the device and choose Disable or Enable, if that's what you want to modify. Windows makes the change for you and saves it to the profile. If you want to make changes to other resource settings, right-click the device and select Properties. Make your resource changes—keeping in mind that, as I mentioned earlier, manual configuration isn't usually your best move—and click OK to close all the dialog boxes and save your changes. Each time you start Windows, you'll be asked which profile you want to use, and that hardware will start.

If you normally use one profile and don't want Windows to wait for you to choose it each time you start up, return to the Hardware Profiles dialog box and select the Select The First Profile Listed option. Decide how many seconds you want Windows to wait for you to choose a different profile before it automatically starts up with the first profile in the Available list. Changing the default profile is easy, too. Click the profile you want to use by default, and then click the up-arrow button until that profile's name is at the top of the list. Click OK to save your changes.

Key Points

- PC hardware configuration used to be a real nightmare. Modern Plug and Play devices work in conjunction with Windows XP and the ACPI now to make it completely automatic in all but a few situations.

- The Device Manager is the Windows XP tool for showing device conflicts and setting configurations for hardware profiles.

- Windows XP automatically disables any noncritical device that it can't successfully configure. A variety of troubleshooters are available to help step you through diagnosing and solving resource conflicts.

- The Device Manager displays a red X next to any disabled device. The functionality of a disabled device is entirely unavailable, even though the device can still be connected to the PC.

- The Device Manager displays a yellow question mark with a superimposed black exclamation point next to any device for which a driver can't be found. Such devices can still work, but they shouldn't be trusted to work reliably.

- To review any device's configuration, expand its hardware category in the Device Manager, right-click the device name, and select Properties.

- Changes made to hardware settings in the Device Manager or in the hardware properties of a specific device might cause the device or Windows itself to stop working properly. Windows can't tell the difference between a device whose settings were changed accidentally and one whose settings were manually configured intentionally. In either case, settings that don't work cause the device to be disabled. The disabling of a critical device can prevent the PC from starting. If you're not certain what you're doing, seek assistance before you make changes to any hardware configuration.

- Hardware profiles make it easy to enable or disable hardware at startup.

Part IV

No Time for Troubles

Working faster and smarter is simply a matter of knowing enough to develop good habits and to avoid problems. The first three parts of this book focused on good habits; this final part takes a good, hard look at the dark side. If you're like me, you've got no time for troubles.

Although I can't anticipate every concern you'll ever encounter with your PC, I can empower you with good ideas and tools to conquer what will most likely hinder you. Fortunately, Microsoft Windows XP prepares you for the challenges, as you'll discover in Chapter 15. In Chapter 16, you'll learn about Plug and Play, how it keeps hardware problems at bay, and why it doesn't work sometimes. Finally, Chapter 17 addresses the issue of personal data security, which has become an issue of national security. Protecting your PC means more today than just protecting your finances, papers, proposals, and pictures. Luckily, despite what you might hear, making your PC secure is so straightforward, you'll be amazed.

Chapter 15

Everybody Needs a Little Help...and Support

If I had to select the one part of Windows that's improved the most over the years, I'd pick the online help system. In Windows XP, it's called Help And Support, and it can take an intelligent look at what you're trying to accomplish and make suggestions about how best to proceed. It also includes a variety of interactive troubleshooters that ask you a few easy-to-understand questions about problems you're having and then step you through to a cure.

For those of you who run into the occasional really difficult problem, Help And Support links directly to Microsoft's Internet-based Knowledge Base of technical solutions. This saves you from having to launch Microsoft Internet Explorer and start over, running a new search. For those times when you're really stuck, Windows XP provides another tool—Remote Assistance—which gives help a personal touch like you've probably never before seen.

Get Help: It's Simple When You Know How

If you're working with some Windows XP feature and you're not certain what to do or how to get the result you need, help is at your fingertips—quite literally, assuming your hands are on the keyboard or mouse. And if you're just trying to get answers to Windows-related questions, help is there, too. In this section, we'll take a look at the different ways to get help from Windows XP and the different types of help you'll get depending on what's happening on your PC at the time.

Getting Help

First, Help And Support is available from the Start menu. Simply click Start and then click Help And Support. You'll see the Welcome screen shown in Figure 15-1. One of the most frustrating, confounding aspects of online help has always been knowing that the information you need is available but not knowing how to get at it. Now, if you have at least a general idea of the type of problem you're having, Help And Support can step you through to finding the solution. You don't have to know what some arcane feature or module is called; knowing what it's supposed to help you do should be enough.

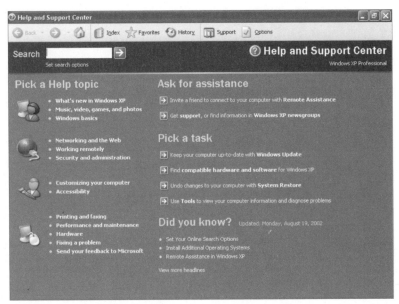

Figure 15-1 Help And Support opens with categories you can browse and a search engine for finding quick answers to specific questions.

Try This! If your Start menu doesn't contain Help And Support, don't despair. You can add it to the menu easily. Simply right-click the Start button and select Properties. When Taskbar And Start Menu in Control Panel opens, make certain that the option for Start Menu (not Classic Start Menu) is selected, and click Customize. When the dialog box opens, select the Advanced tab and scroll through the Start Menu Items list until you find Help And Support. Click to place a check mark in the box, and then click OK twice to save the change. The next time you open the Start menu, you'll find the help you want.

You can also open Help And Support from My Computer by selecting Help And Support Center from the Help menu. Context-sensitive help is always available; just press the F1 key and Windows does the rest. (If you're running an application, that application, and not Windows XP, is responsible for providing you with whatever help is available.)

Some of the categories available to you are designed to assist you with specific hardware configurations, like Networking And The Web and Printing And Faxing. Just click the category name to open it, as in Figure 15-2, and you'll see that Help and Support begins breaking the large category down into smaller ones, like Printing On A Network and Faxing.

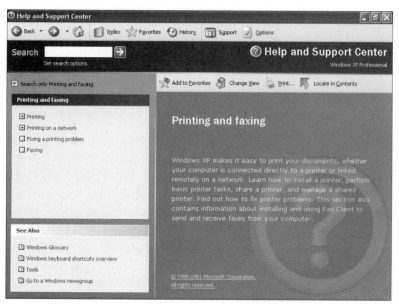

Figure 15-2 After selecting a general category, Help And Support shows more detailed options; continue to browse until you find your answers.

If there's a small plus sign (+) next to a category, you can click it to refine your options further—stepping down to the next level of categories. Eventually, you'll find entries with no plus sign, indicating that you've explored as far as you can into that general category. You're sitting at the border between general topics and specific answers. Click the entry text, and Windows presents you with a list of tasks you might want to accomplish and interactive tutorials that demonstrate how to get yourself back to work quickly—as in Figure 15-3, where you see that you're well on the way to learning about printer sharing.

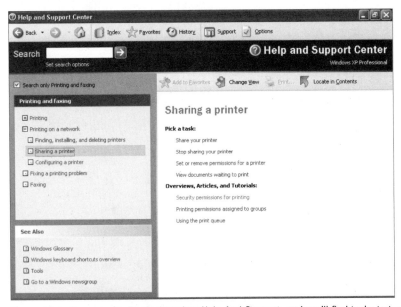

Figure 15-3 Browse a few levels down into Help And Support, and you'll find tasks to try and tutorials to expand your understanding.

Thanks to the way these options are organized, you can see that it's possible to set security permissions for printers. Perhaps your actual problem is that you have a color printer that most of your coworkers aren't supposed to use. You might not have used printer sharing—someone else enabled the feature for you, let's say—so you assume you'll just need to stop sharing the printer entirely. That's certainly not the ideal solution, but what else to do? By digging down to this level in Help, you've discovered the tutorial on security permissions for printers. In a few seconds, you've worked through this entire process:

- You have a problem you can't yet solve.

- You realize you don't know enough about the subject to know to how to quickly search for an answer, so you step through categories instead.

■ On the way to finding what you think is the best solution, you learn that better solutions exist that you didn't know about.

■ You learn how to solve the real problem and avoid the ongoing annoyance and unhappy compromise of cutting off your printer from authorized and unauthorized users alike.

■ You solve the problem.

In the past, this same scenario might have led you to seek personal assistance over the phone, costing money, time, and brain cells wasted by easy listening versions of "Stairway to Heaven" on hold. Depending on who you get on the phone, you might have been told about different sharing permissions, or you might have just been quickly guided through turning sharing off and "have a nice day." Help And Support might not always give you better answers than a person could, but it's a lot easier to see your options on the PC.

Allow me to introduce you to some of Help And Support's other interactive features. Take a look at Figure 15-4. The small arrow icon next to Add Or Remove Programs means that Help will open the tool you need to accomplish the steps that follow. It's a great way to avoid accidentally closing the Help window you're trying to use. Help also tells you the way to open each tool manually, so you don't have to search through Help again the next time you want to work with it.

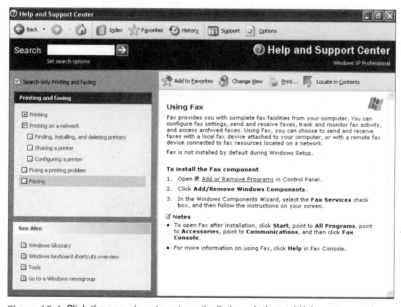

Figure 15-4 Click the arrow icon to automatically launch the tool Help recommends.

Finally, if you navigate through Help and click Related Topics, Help searches through the Help index and displays a list of considerations that might be relevant as you solve your current problem. If you happen to encounter any new jargon while you're using Help, just click in the lower left of the window to open the Windows Glossary. Of course, you can neatly print anything you find in Help And Support; just click the Print icon.

Searching Help

If you've got a more specific idea of the help you need, the search engine might find you answers faster than browsing through categories. Just type a few key words related to your problem and press Enter. Windows searches through Help And Support and, if you're online, through the Microsoft Knowledge Base, finds the most relevant entries.

In Figure 15-5, I've searched for help on printer sharing, and you can see that I've discovered the same solution you just encountered, but I've found it in one step. I've also found additional tutorials and tasks you might want to accomplish related to the original problem I posed previously. From here, you can learn about the entire permissions system—you might want to limit access to certain files as well as to the printer.

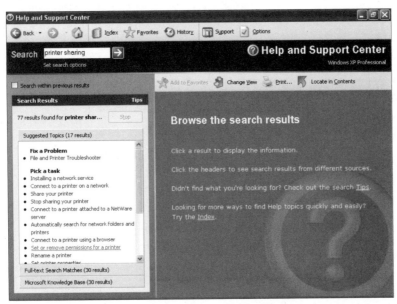

Figure 15-5 Searching for specific keywords can lead you directly to a solution, but you might need to select from more options.

In the left panel here, you can also see that there are 30 full-text search matches and 30 Knowledge Base articles relating to my search. If none of the featured tasks or overviews is what you want, you can click the Full-Text Search Matches header to open those and browse through them. These will be most useful when you're looking for a specific piece of information, not when you're trying to accomplish some specific task. It's the "think" to complement the Suggested Topics "do" entries.

Clicking the Knowledge Base header opens those results, too, and if you're online, you can jump directly to any of the thousands of technical articles available. If your search finds too many entries, or entries that are still too general, you can search again after selecting the Search Within Previous Results check box near the upper left corner of the window. This allows you to refine your findings so you don't spend a lot of time searching through your search. You can also click Set Search Options and increase or decrease the number of full-text and Knowledge Base results you see after searching. (You can also turn these options off entirely.)

If you plan on refining your search, make sure you think from the general to the specific. For example, if you're looking for information on configuring Remote Assistance to work with your firewall, search first for Remote Assistance, and then click the Search Within These Results check box and search for *firewall*. At the same time, don't think in terms that are too general, and try searching for nouns, rather than verbs or gerunds. You'll get what you want much faster if you search for Remote Assistance, instead of *configure* or *configuring*. Otherwise, you'll unearth a ridiculous number of entries, 99 percent of which would be off topic.

Notice back in Figure 15-5 that you can start the File And Printer Troubleshooter from here, too. *Troubleshooters* are interactive wizards that step you quickly toward a solution that's customized for your specific situation. Let's take a look.

Using Troubleshooters

Take a quick look at Figure 15-6. It shows the File And Printer Sharing Troubleshooter's opening screen. It's fairly indicative of other troubleshooters, and it should remind you of every wizard you've ever seen. Clicking selects options and steps you to the next screen. Each answer you give determines which question the troubleshooter asks next, until it understands what you're facing and suggests likely solutions.

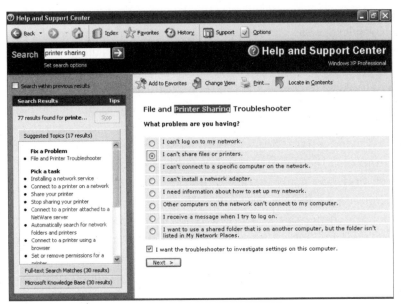

Figure 15-6 The File And Printer Sharing Troubleshooter, like all troubleshooters, steps you through questions about your hardware performance and configuration toward a solution.

You can give the troubleshooter an additional edge by allowing it to examine your Windows XP configuration files. If you like, this is a little like allowing the doctor to examine you after the nurse completes triage. However, because some people are wary of privacy concerns, you have the option of denying the troubleshooter this access. Be assured, the troubleshooter doesn't send the information anywhere; it simply adds it to the picture it's trying to form of your PC's "illness," so a better diagnosis and prognosis result.

If you're faced with a problem that just can't be solved by Help, it's time to seek out support. If you've worked all the way through a troubleshooter and reached an impasse, you might be guided to seek out telephone or online assistance. As unfond as I am of music-on-hold, I'm partial to online assistance. You might have a bias if you've ever tried some company's Web-based live help chat service and found it wanting. No fear; Remote Assistance is here. And if you want *really* personal help, Remote Assistance lets you get help from someone you know!

Remote Assistance

Before you can use Remote Assistance to obtain help either from Microsoft or a friend you know through Microsoft Windows Messenger, you'll need to set up a Microsoft .NET Passport. It's easy to do; a quick wizard runs automatically, asking you to provide a little information about yourself and also to select a password. If you've already got a .NET Passport, you're good to go.

A Little Help from Your Friends

To launch Remote Assistance and get help from a friend who's also using Windows XP, just click Support at the top of the Help And Support window, and click Ask A Friend To Help when Support opens. After you click Invite Someone To Help You, you'll see the screen in Figure 15-7. Here you can sign in to Windows Messenger, or you can send e-mail to someone, seeking assistance. If you select the e-mail option, you don't need a .NET Passport, but you'll have to wait for that person to receive your invitation.

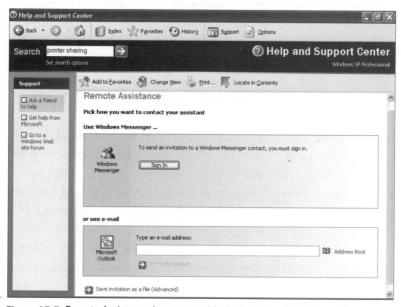

Figure 15-7 Remote Assistance lets you send invitations through Windows Messenger or e-mail.

Using Windows Messenger is instant. If you send an e-mail, you'll be given the opportunity to include a personal message, as well as select a password that your friend will need to know to connect to your PC. You'll need to tell your friend the password in person—it's not included in your message, in case the e-mail is intercepted—but that's a small price to pay to keep an unauthorized user out of your PC.

You can also select a time after which the invitation to connect will expire. This is a secondary security measure that prevents someone from connecting to your PC after the time you specify. If your friend is waiting online to receive your invitation, the default expiration of one hour should suffice. Once your e-mail invitation is sent, you'll be returned to the Remote Assistance screen where you can click to check the status of your invitation and wait for your friend.

Note   The time you select for invitation expiration does not limit how long you can be connected with your friend once the connection is established. It restricts only the invitation itself. It's like a theater ticket that says "No latecomers will be seated."

If you use Windows Messenger, you'll be shown a list of Messenger friends who are online. Select the friend's e-mail address or username, and click Invite This Friend. In seconds, you're up and running. Your friend will see a window open in which your entire desktop is displayed. The two of you can chat together online and even use Microsoft NetMeeting to speak with each other, and your friend can see everything you do on your PC.

If you're having problems you just can't solve, a knowledgeable friend can ask for permission to take over control of your PC so that she or he can explore your system, check your configuration, and solve the problem for you. No more late-night drives across town to help out a friend in an emergency! The two of you can simply connect using Remote Assistance, and you can do anything from your PC that you could do at your friend's PC (except share a cup of Earl Grey, naturally).

At any time, you can click to disconnect your friend and sever his or her control over your PC. If you don't like the idea of someone else controlling your PC, even with you watching, your friend can just talk (or chat) you through the necessary steps toward solution and can watch you do the work yourself.

Microsoft Assisted Support

If your friends don't have the answer, Microsoft probably does. Simply click Get Help From Microsoft and you'll be asked to sign in using your .NET Passport.

Once your identity is authenticated, you can select the product you need help with, and then choose the support option that fits your needs. (If you don't have a .NET Passport, you can set one up, or you can choose from several Web-based support options.) If you're trying to install Windows XP on a new PC, you can get unlimited free support.

In other situations, you might be entitled to free or for-charge support. The Microsoft support engineer will work with you, and might ask for permission to control your PC remotely. This is often—by far—the quickest route to an answer, because she or he will know exactly where to find settings and configuration options that you might otherwise need to search for. You can cut off remote control of your PC at any time, of course, just by clicking Stop in the chat window or by hitting the Escape key.

Once your problem is solved, you can close the connection and get right back to work. Basic assistance is available during selected hours; you'll find the current hours available online by clicking the Get More Information About Support Options link you'll see after connecting to Remote Assistance. Professional assistance with advanced aspects of Windows XP is available 24/7.

Calling a Complete Stranger

If you need assistance but don't need it immediately, you can use the excellent Windows Newsgroups. Newsgroups are almost as old as the Internet itself. They're like bulletin boards where anyone can post a message and anyone can post a reply. The Windows Newsgroups are focused on different aspects of Windows, so you can select the newsgroup that's best suited to your question. Many industry experts and professionals participate in the different Windows newsgroups, so it's actually possible to get free assistance on a tremendous range of topics, however basic or advanced.

Caution   Naturally, there's always the possibility that no one will know the answer you need, or that someone will provide you with an incorrect answer, so always endeavor to wait for two or more responses before you try *anything* that requires deleting files or changing system settings that seem buried behind endless technical safeguards. Some settings are hidden for good reason. Nevertheless, the Windows Newsgroups are a great way to get answers and stay in touch with what's happening in the Windows world. You might even make a friend or make someone else's day—you never know when someone else's question will be one *you* can answer.

Remote Assistance and Security Concerns Always consider the implications when you give someone access to your PC. At the most superficial level, you're letting somebody mess with your stuff. Anyone you allow to control your PC could accidentally or intentionally open files you would rather keep private. Your personal finances or correspondence really isn't anyone's business but your own.

Sometimes even a file's name contains content you wouldn't want made public. If your boss also happens to be the friend you're asking to help you with your PC, a file named Resume Sent To Competitor is going to be hard to explain regardless of its actual contents. Remote Assistance lets you sever the remote control immediately if you need to, but my first security-related recommendations are as follows:

- Connect only to a friend you trust.
- Don't wander off leaving someone else in control of your PC if your privacy is a concern.

Naturally, no Microsoft Remote Assistance professional will *ever* open your personal files or folders. But if someone you scarcely know offers to "show you something really cool" in Windows XP if you'll only relinquish control of your PC, discretion is the better part of valor.

On a more general level, the Remote Assistance feature could allow someone to exploit your PC if you leave invitations outstanding for unduly long. Always set your invitations to expire in as short a time as possible.

> **Tip**   Remember that a different feature—Remote Desktop—is designed to let you control your own PC remotely, say your home PC from your office. Use Remote Desktop if you want to manipulate your own system.

Because it works through your normal online connection, you might discover that your firewall prevents the use of Remote Assistance. You might need to arrange for your firewall settings to be modified to allow Remote Assistance data to pass through. A setting known to experts as Port 3389 needs to be configured properly.

At the other end of the spectrum, if you want to absolutely guarantee that no one can control your PC remotely, open the Control Panel, select Performance and Maintenance, and open the System dialog box. Click the Remote tab, click Advanced, and clear the Allow This Computer To Be Controlled Remotely check box. Remote Assistance will be disabled until you change the setting back.

Key Points

- The Windows XP Help And Support system provides a sophisticated, context-sensitive solution to questions and concerns you have about Windows.

- Help And Support can detect what you're doing when you invoke it and provide an answer tailored to your circumstances.

- Press F1 at any time to activate context-sensitive Help.

- The troubleshooters step you through a variety of questions that ask you about your hardware and recommend solutions that exactly fit your needs.

- You can browse through Help categories or search for specific answers.

- Online Help and Support is integrated with the Microsoft Knowledge Base so that your Internet connection gives you access to every Help resource available from Microsoft.

- Remote Assistance allows you to ask a friend or a Microsoft support engineer to help you with PC problems. You can also give an expert control over your PC so that he or she can solve your problem quickly.

- Windows Newsgroups are an online resource that puts you in contact with people in the PC industry all over the world. You can seek advice, get answers to technical questions, and find more ways to increase your productivity.

Chapter 16

The Good and Bad of Adding Peripherals

With all this talk of help and support, isn't there some way to just avoid the whole mess? Can't you just enjoy your PC in peace? You bet! If you buy a new PC with Microsoft Windows XP pre-installed and you don't ever change anything, I can almost guarantee you'll never have any problems—until a piece of hardware fails, which, eventually, a piece will. And problems will likely stay at bay until you decide you need to install more memory, more storage, more processor power, or some kind of new capability.

Working faster and smarter mostly means looking at old tools in new ways—but sometimes you've just got to buy a new tool. Naturally, if you don't have any sound support, you'll need to add it if you find yourself tasked with editing digital video for the company annual awards dinner. Fortunately, adding hardware isn't what it once was—thank goodness! There's virtually nothing you can do with your PC today that wasn't harder to do and more expensive yesterday. Times were when just about every PC owner would wonder why PCs couldn't just be a "plug and play" experience.

Understanding Plug and Play

Today, plug and play isn't just a dream and a wish; it's a specific technical reality. Hardware devices that are designed in accordance with industry Plug and Play specifications has some special and useful properties, including the following:

- They can use a variety of resources, maximizing their flexibility with other installed hardware.

- They can accept and release resources assigned by Windows XP, allowing other devices to be installed or removed at will.

- They can be dynamically enabled or disabled, without restarting Windows.

- They can, if designed to be removable, be plugged in or unplugged without risk of data loss and without restarting Windows.

As you've probably guessed, these capabilities don't simply rely on the hardware. In fact, Windows has the hard job. The devices themselves need only identify themselves when asked, passively accept what resources are given them, and "give up their toys" when told to share. Windows, on the other hand, must know how to inquire about the type and needs of every conceivable component and peripheral, manage all the resources available, and dole them out as necessary. When a new piece of hardware appears—or when a piece suddenly disappears—it's the job of Windows to make sure your work isn't lost and your PC doesn't crash.

In addition to managing hardware connections, resources, and data safety when devices are added or removed, Windows must manage the functionality of the devices while they're present in the system. Many thousands of devices can be supported by the power of Windows alone. Others are sufficiently unique in some aspect that they require software of their own, in addition to what Windows can do. This software is collectively called the family of *device drivers*.

Lingo   A *device driver* is a piece of software that "understands" how some given hardware works and understands how Windows works. It bridges this gap, making it possible for Windows (and us) to use the hardware.

Handle with Care Although Windows XP does most of the work of Plug and Play, getting the devices in and out of your PC case or connecting them to its various ports is entirely your turf. When it comes to plugging stuff in, nothing beats a careful hand. But be mindful of a few points before you ever start to work on a computer. I know of no better to way let you know about these than to simply list them. Every single one of these could be highlighted with a "Caution" heading.

- Never open your PC case without making certain that its power is off. Most PCs today turn off with a Shut Down command selected from the Start menu. In addition to using that command, if your PC has an actual power switch on the back, near where the power cable plugs in, turn it off, too.

- Keep your PC plugged in to the wall when you're going to work on it after checking that it's connected to a three-prong properly grounded outlet. Any stray electricity is more likely to flow safely away through the ground than dangerously through your body.

- Your PC can be seriously damaged by stray static electricity—the sort of thing that gives you a shock when you reach out to touch a doorknob or a light switch on a cold, dry day. Always touch the steel of the case to discharge any static that might be built up on your body. If possible, use one of the disposable static wrist straps that drains static electricity away from your body if used properly.

- *Never* ever attempt to open your PC power supply. High voltage charges can remain built up inside long after the PC has been turned off. These could easily hurt you or even kill you. Nothing lives inside a power supply that you can fix or upgrade. If one fails, replace it.

- *Never* ever attempt to open your PC monitor. Extremely high voltage charges can remain built up inside the monitor even if it has been unplugged for weeks. You could die. Nothing lives inside a monitor that you can fix or upgrade. If your monitor fails, you could have it serviced, but you might find that a new monitor doesn't cost much more than a repair.

When you disconnect any device, consciously notice where it was plugged in so that you can plug it back in again correctly. Most PC connections are keyed so you can't plug things in backwards, so never force a connection. If you press and encounter hard resistance, you've probably got something the wrong way around. Be certain that you follow any instructions that accompany new hardware you purchase. No one knows a product better than its manufacturer; heed their guidance and recommendations carefully.

The name *driver* is particularly apt. Your car is your car whether it's parked in the garage or whether you're driving from Omaha to Oahu. You're your car's brains; you provide the key to the usefulness and abilities of your car when you sit behind the wheel and drive. A device driver, too, is the brains of hardware; what the hardware can actually do and how well it works is defined by the software. A poorly crafted driver can dramatically restrict what perfectly good hardware can do. And when such a thing happens, drivers are updated by the hardware manufacturer. More on this shortly.

In a nutshell, Plug and Play is part of the all-encompassing power and resource management system of your PC. Part of this is built into each bit of hardware, part of it is built into your PC motherboard, and part of it is built into Windows. To remove or add hardware conveniently and safely, all three parts must work together with one more part—you.

Almost Everything You Need to Know About Drivers

Device drivers bridge the gap between Windows and the various bits of hardware that make up your PC. Many of these are now part of Windows XP. Indeed, these drivers provide the highly regarded support of Windows XP for so many different devices. If you plug a new bit of hardware into your PC for the first time, Windows might ask you to insert the Windows XP CD so that files can be installed, but once that's done, your hardware will probably work immediately. It's no longer necessary to install huge applications for tasks like moving pictures from a digital camera to a hard disk, producing sound, or burning a CD-RW. Windows XP does the work.

Of course, you can still use the software that a device manufacturer provides, but you've got choices. In some cases, this software provides access to advanced features that Windows XP doesn't natively support. In other cases, a manufacturer's software might actually make using the device less efficient and slower than simply using Windows. Device drivers are normally installed into a folder called System32, which is inside your Windows folder. Opening this folder isn't recommended because accidentally moving or deleting even one of the files you'll find inside might cause you to lose important functionality. But many of these 1500-plus files are the various device drivers that Windows needs to make your PC work.

Device drivers usually remain on your hard disk even when a piece of hardware is no longer present, but that's a good thing. The files themselves take precious little room, and if you ever reinstall their requisite hardware, Windows can load the driver software into memory dynamically, without asking for any CD and without requiring that you select any settings. At the same time, a driver that's installed on your hard disk doesn't use up any system resources or memory when its device is absent or powered off. There's certainly no reason to waste vital system memory on your digital camera's driver if the camera is away on a shelf.

You might have heard about or seen the Add Hardware Wizard in your Windows Control Panel. In some cases, like when you install a modem, Windows runs the wizard the first time it detects new hardware. But you shouldn't expect to see it. Windows uses it to ask you about settings it can't possibly detect, like your area code and whether you need your modem to dial 9 to reach an outside line.

But Windows won't bother you with the wizard if it can install all of the software it needs automatically. In that case, you'll simply see a small balloon pop up in the system tray that says Found New Hardware, and names what has been detected, as shown in Figure 16-1.

Figure 16-1 Once Windows XP detects that new hardware is present, it notifies you as soon as the device's drivers are installed, loaded, and the device is up and running.

If you connect a new piece of hardware and Windows gives no indication that it has noticed, you might have an older device that's not fully compliant with Plug and Play, or your system might be in an unstable state. In such a case, shut down Windows, remove the hardware, and restart. After successfully reaching the desktop, shut down again, reconnect the hardware, and start up again. If Windows still doesn't detect new hardware—Windows should detect the presence of new hardware even if it doesn't have the drivers necessary to make the hardware function—you'll need to start the Add Hardware Wizard manually and go through it step by step.

Tip   If you purchase hardware that's supposed to be safe to plug in or unplug while your PC is powered on, that hardware should be fully Plug and Play compliant, so Windows should detect it. You have three possibilities to consider if Windows doesn't. First, the device could be defective or damaged. Second, you could have insufficient resources available to install the device, so make sure you save your work and quit any open applications. Third, the device manufacturer could have "cheated." Creating software and hardware for Windows XP does involve following a few rules. Sometimes rules are bent or broken to save development time or costs, and that can cause problems sooner or later.

On the "sooner" side of things, broken rules might prevent Windows from detecting the hardware until device drivers have been installed. This is backwards from how the process is supposed to work today (although it's how things always worked before Plug and Play). If your device comes with a CD and instructions telling you to run some program on the CD before you plug the hardware in for the first time, Windows might not automatically detect the hardware if you don't.

When in doubt, read the manual and follow the directions carefully. And to be as safe as possible, purchase hardware that bears the "Designed for Microsoft Windows XP" logo. That means the company has sent the product and its drivers to Microsoft for testing to make certain all the rules were followed and the device will work properly.

When you run the Add Hardware Wizard, Windows performs a little basic triage on your PC and redetects every connected piece of hardware—whether you've installed drivers yet or not. Windows might be able to identify that the hardware needs files from a manufacturer's CD—in which case, it will ask you to install the CD so it can load drivers and let you get back to work. If Windows doesn't see the new hardware, it asks you to confirm whether you've actually plugged it in or not, as in Figure 16-2.

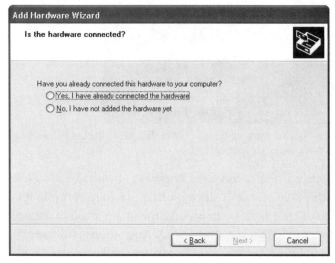

Figure 16-2 The Add Hardware Wizard rescans all hardware in your PC to detect new devices; if it finds none, it asks you to confirm that you've already installed the new hardware.

Sign In, Please   One of the services Microsoft provides to hardware developers is the "Designed for Microsoft Windows XP" logo program. To display the logo on product packaging, manufacturers must submit their hardware and its drivers to Microsoft for testing. After determining that the product works reliably with Windows XP, Microsoft issues a special code that gets incorporated into the device driver files.

This code is called a *digital signature*, and it identifies a verified device driver to Windows XP. If you try to install device drivers that aren't digitally signed, Windows asks you to verify that you want to continue. In some cases, you'll be prevented from installing any driver that isn't signed, unless you're the system administrator for your PC. Bear this in mind if you don't normally log in under an Administrator account. You'll need to log in as Administrator to install most hardware.

Windows also protects signed drivers and other system files against being inappropriately removed or replaced. This is helpful because some unscrupulous individuals have found ways to hide dangerous virus code in device drivers, which could get inadvertently installed. Sometimes, too, a manufacturer includes a system file with a piece of software that might simply be older than the file you already have installed on your PC. Windows checks the digital signature of any system file that's installed and doesn't allow an older or invalid file to be installed.

You can configure this behavior to meet your preferences by clicking the Driver Signing button on the Hardware tab of System Properties. As in Figure 16-3, you can instruct Windows to refuse to install unsigned drivers, to always install them, or to ask whether the person doing the installation is certain of what he or she wants. This last option is the default, and it's probably your best choice. People who don't have Administrator privileges can't install most hardware anyway, so a gentle reminder is usually sufficient to remind valid administrators of the dangers of installing unsigned software.

Figure 16-3 The driver signing control in Windows is entirely configurable.

If you haven't plugged it in, you'll be instructed to quit the wizard, plug in the hardware, and let Windows try to detect it automatically again. If you have, Windows asks you to identify the product so it can load its own drivers or to locate product drivers either on a disk or online. If the new hardware isn't in the Windows list, select Add A New Hardware Device and let Windows search again for drivers. You might be prompted for a manufacturer's CD at this time, or to locate on your hard disk a driver file that you've downloaded from the manufacturer's Web site.

Once the driver is detected and loaded, Windows assigns system resources like memory and interrupt request lines (IRQs) to the device, if it needs them. A device that needs certain resources prompts Windows to automatically shuffle things around until each device is content and functioning. If all of your devices are Plug and Play compliant, you should never encounter a situation in which all of your selected devices won't work together.

If a device isn't Plug and Play compliant, I strongly suggest you contact its manufacturer before installing it to determine whether the device can work with Windows XP at all. Most product Web sites have an archive or a "Windows XP Compatibility" section where you can verify that your older hardware will or won't work. You might find updated drivers there, too, which can make an incompatible product compatible.

When New Hardware Doesn't Work

If you install a piece of hardware that isn't fully Plug and Play compliant, all bets could be off with respect to all the devices in your system. Even one older device that demands a specific interrupt channel or a limited bit of memory can make it impossible for Windows to successfully shuffle resources around to keep all devices happy. Similarly, an older device might be perfectly happy to work with a selection of different resources, but might not accept Windows' instructions to change those resources on the fly.

Hardware problems can be tricky to diagnose and solve. You might install an older network card that isn't Plug and Play friendly, but it might be your sound card that stops working. The failure of your entire PC to start after you plug in new hardware might sound like the worst possible outcome, but it is, at least, a definitive answer. You know the hardware you just installed is the culprit. Now you need only determine why.

A Living Legacy Literally thousands of older hardware devices out there will work perfectly with Windows XP. Whether you use one of them or upgrade to a newer device is entirely your decision, naturally, but it's one you should make advisedly. If you do choose to use an old piece of hardware, don't forget that you made that decision. Someday, you might install something brand new and it or the older hardware will suddenly fail to work.

If you keep in mind that you've got an older, or *legacy*, bit of hardware installed, you can try removing that older hardware first if you encounter hardware troubles. If everything works properly once the legacy device is removed, your legacy device can no longer be thought to work perfectly anymore. You can either replace it or return the new hardware.

Your third option is to try—or to pay an expert to try—to diagnose the problem and manually assign resources to make everything work. Unfortunately, manually assigning resources just solidifies the problem of legacy hardware. You might inadvertently cause some other piece of hardware to fail, and you will almost surely reduce the likelihood that some other new product will work. When in doubt, look for Windows XP–certified hardware; it will be fully Plug and Play compliant.

If your PC does start and appears to work properly, you're in much worse shape if a problem exists. It might manifest itself at the worst possible time— say, when you stand to lose an hour of work you've simply forgotten to save. Believe me, it can happen to the most experienced of users, particularly if you find yourself pulling an all-nighter. So let's take a quick look at the best practices for installing a new device.

Tip Much software, including the Microsoft Office suite, includes an automatic recovery feature. This saves your work even when you fail to—not that it's an acceptable alternative to good saving habits. You'll find AutoRecover in the Office suite on the Tools menu, under Options. On the Save tab, select the Save AutoRecovery check box and decide how often you want data saved. Unless you have an exceptionally old PC, I strongly urge you to set AutoRecovery to one minute, unless you're working with an exceptionally large file or a particularly slow PC. I can get a lot done in one minute—a lot that I don't want to have to redo, most of the time. You'll never even notice that AutoRecovery is enabled until it saves your work—maybe even your job!

Diagnosing Simple Hardware Problems

When you've first installed a new piece of hardware, never simply assume that it's working properly. To be as safe as possible, don't just instantly try using it to see whether it works, either. Resources are tricky; some of the device's functionality might work fine, and some of it might not. Your first stop should be to the Device Manager, which I first introduced back in Chapter 14. Recall that you can open it by right-clicking My Computer, selecting Properties, and then choosing the Hardware tab and clicking Device Manager.

Any device that isn't working properly—whether it seems fine or not—will be identified in the Device Manager with one of the warning icons we talked about in Chapter 14. Most often, if there's a problem, you'll see the red *X* icon, which indicates that Windows knows there's a problem and has deactivated the device to keep the system working and stable. (The device shouldn't work at all in this case, because it's turned off.) You can try a few different techniques in this case, but the most reliable solution is to use the Device Manager to try to update the device driver files.

From the Device Manager's Action menu, select Update Driver. (You won't find this option available if you haven't first selected the hardware you want to update.) You'll start a wizard, shown in Figure 16-4, which prompts you to insert any manufacturer CD that you've received and then choose whether Windows or you will figure out how to install the necessary software. Always try letting Windows figure things out on its own first. Only if that fails should you normally opt to search for a driver manually and tell Windows what to install. Windows installs the drivers and either activates the hardware or instructs you to restart to make the hardware active.

Figure 16-4 Through the Device Manager, you can quickly search for a newer driver than the one you're using and update automatically.

If installing an updated driver isn't successful or if no updated driver exists, you might want to reconsider using the device at all. If you do need to use the device, you'll need to try to force Windows to try some resource alternatives. Before making that rather advanced step, let Windows run its hardware trouble-shooter on the device. To do this, right-click the troublesome device in the Device Manager and choose Properties. On the General tab, click Troubleshoot to run the troubleshooter and step through a few questions that will help diagnose your difficulty. Chances are excellent that the troubleshooter will get you up and running, but if that doesn't work either, it's time to get a little digital dirt under your fingernails.

Manually Working with Resources

When you open a device's properties in the Device Manager, you might see a tab labeled Resources, as shown in Figure 16-5.

Note   If the Resources tab isn't present, Windows hasn't assigned any variable resources like IRQs or memory to the device. If that's the case and your device isn't working—and you've given the troubleshooter a try—it's time to contact the device manufacturer's customer support. Something outside the norm is happening, and the solution might require some specific changes. (Or, of course, the device might be so old, it won't work with Windows XP at all.)

Figure 16-5 A device's Resource tab shows the hardware resources Windows has assigned to a device and allows for manual changes to the configuration.

If the Resource tab is available, you can select it to see which resources Windows has assigned. Here you can also see whether those resource selections conflict with any other device. (The only time that will happen is if a non–Plug and Play device has demanded a specific resource.) You can manually change individual resources, but that task is really advanced. One step short is manually selecting one of several different combinations of resources that Windows has predefined.

Note   You might wonder why, if Windows has predefined combinations of resources, it hasn't already tried them to get things working. In fact, it has, and it has chosen what it determined to be the best combination available. If things aren't working, however, you might be able to find a different combination that allows the device to work.

Normally, the Use Automatic Settings check box will be selected. This option gives Windows the largest possible flexibility to configure resources. If you want to select a configuration manually, clear the check box so that the Setting Based On drop-down list becomes available. By scrolling through the list, you select from among the different configurations, as in Figure 16-6. Watch the Conflicting Device List space at the bottom of the dialog box to see whether the listed conflict disappears. If it does, great! Click OK to complete the change, and then restart Windows.

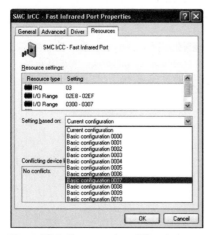

Figure 16-6 You can select different resource combinations if the choices presented by Windows aren't what you want.

When the desktop appears, reopen the Device Manager and check to see whether all conflicts are resolved. In some cases, when you're lucky, you'll find that they are. In other cases, you might find that solving one conflict causes a new conflict once Windows restarts. If that happens, you can again work through manually selecting a configuration, or you can choose to contact the device-maker's customer support.

Device Driver Rollback

Occasionally, you might install a new device driver only to find that you've obtained a new family of difficulties. This situation can occur because of conflicts between two different drivers, or it can occur because you've accidentally allowed Windows to install an unsigned driver that doesn't behave well. It can also occur because an unsigned driver isn't subject to the protection against deletion that signed drivers enjoy, so it might simply be that you've installed an old driver over a new one.

To go back to where you used to be was once simply impossible. You might have to completely uninstall the device and start over. Not so now. You can roll back a device driver so that the previously used driver is reactivated. To do so, open the Device Manager and select the troubled device. Right-click to open the device's properties and select the Driver tab.

From here, you can completely uninstall a device's drivers if you want to, but in the situation we're currently considering, you'll instead click Roll Back Driver and let Windows restore your previous configuration, as in Figure 16-7. Click OK to close the device properties, and then close the Device Manager and restart Windows. You'll find yourself as well off as you were before you installed the replacement driver.

Figure 16-7 If a driver for a piece of hardware causes system problems, clicking Roll Back Driver can simply restore the previous driver.

Your BIOS

Near the beginning of this chapter, I mentioned that one of the three components of a successful Plug and Play system is the *basic input/output system (BIOS)*. The BIOS is a small bit of program code that's normally stored in an *erasable programmable read-only memory (EPROM)* on the motherboard. This program knows how to perform a basic set of startup tests to see that things are connected properly and functioning. It also tells the startup disk drive—be it a CD-ROM drive, a hard drive, or a floppy disk drive—to search for and begin reading the disk's *Master Boot Record (MBR)*. This is a second tiny bit of program code that tells the drive how to read the next bit of code, and so on, until Windows loads and takes over.

To get Plug and Play to work properly, the peripheral devices and the BIOS of the PC must all be designed to understand it. Traditionally, the BIOS assigned system resources. Windows has taken over all of this job, but the BIOS must be designed to, frankly, get out of the operating system's way. These days, the BIOS has a setting that confirms that the PC is running a Plug and Play operating system by default.

That setting basically tells the BIOS to run its startup tests, start the drive working, and then have a coffee; the operating system—Windows XP, in our case—takes care of the rest. That's necessary because part of the original job of the BIOS was to guarantee that resource settings didn't get changed or tramped upon while the PC is running. That protection would keep Windows from doing its Plug and Play job, so it needs to be disabled before Windows starts to load.

Key Points

- Plug and Play is an industry standard that allows hardware devices and a compatible operating system to work together to apportion and control available resources.

- A PC has a limited set of resources, but Plug and Play devices can share these resources dynamically so that conflicts don't impede functionality.

- When one Plug and Play device wants to use resources assigned to another device, Windows simply shuffles resources around until all devices have resources that they can use.

- You must consider a few important safety tips when you're going to work inside your PC to prevent damage to your PC or injury to yourself.

- A device driver is a piece of software that communicates with both Windows and hardware, making the hardware's capabilities available to users.

- If a device driver has been certified as reliable for use with Windows XP, it has a digital signature that Windows can identify and use to prevent rogue or antiquated files from replacing those that are newer and reliable.

- Windows XP lets you roll back a newly installed driver if that driver inadvertently reduces functionality or system stability.

Chapter 17

Safe at Home and Abroad

It seems best to bring *this* collection of knowledge about your PC to a close with some words about PC safety and security. It's not just for professionals; PC security is a concern for each of us. Indeed, PC security has recently been called a cornerstone of national security.

In this chapter, you'll learn the realities of hardware security. I hope that you'll close this book with a useful grasp of PC hardware and the knowledge you need to keep your property and data safe. Throughout this book, one of my goals has been to help you think smarter about your needs; in the PC world, that means not spending money on junk you'll never use. This final chapter has the same goal.

Basic Hardware Security

A lot of the basics of hardware security come down to common sense—treat your computer like you would any other valuable, fragile object. That means keeping the case closed so that air circulation draws heat away from your components; it means locking the case if your PC case has a lock and you have a little one around who might otherwise open it to explore. It means using precautions to keep static electricity from damaging the innards when you upgrade components; it means putting your PC to the side or under your desk where you won't spill coffee into it.

Folks get surprised by maliciousness because they haven't anticipated and guarded against it. You should always limit access to hardware that contains sensitive data and keep a backup copy of vital information at some secure, offsite location. If someone really wants to destroy a piece of data, stealing the entire computer might seem an easy way. With your data backed up, you can restore that data and everything else onto a replacement PC. The more irreplaceable data is, the more certain you should be about maintaining a current backup of it.

Tip   Microsoft Windows XP comes with a data backup program that's compatible with most of the backup hardware available. To back up, just open My Computer, right-click the drive where the data is stored, select Properties, select the Tools tab, and click Backup Now. Windows asks you to select what you want backed up and where you want it stored, then completes the job. How heavily you use your PC should determine how often you perform a backup, but consider twice a month as an absolute minimum. Also, always choose the Verify Data After Backup option to make certain your backup is valid. In some ways, you're worse off with a backup you think is good—but isn't—than you are if you simply never back up. You might behave in less safe ways, feeling it's OK because you've backed up. Finally, third-party software can produce password-protected and encrypted backups of extremely sensitive data.

Data that's both irreplaceable and sensitive should be kept encrypted and password-protected on disk. In Chapter 12, we looked at the encrypting file system (EFS) that's part of the Microsoft Windows XP NT file system (NTFS). If your data is sensitive, use EFS along with a good login password. We'll look at passwords in a moment, and I'll show you how to turn off Simple File Sharing to increase the security of your local data. With files or folders encrypted and password-protected, even if your computer is stolen, your secrets will remain your own.

Finally, because portable hardware is (by nature) easier to relocate, if your PC is portable, you might want to consider special notebook-locking hardware. This will prevent your notebook from disappearing off a desk or table. Almost every notebook case now supports a locking hasp. Run a steel cable through this, and your notebook won't go anywhere.

Tip   Even the most experienced of us can make a silly mistake. Don't be like the well-known PC columnist who secured his notebook to a table leg. A thief simply lifted the corner of the table, slipped the cable off the leg, and took the PC. Make sure you run a security cable through something that can't easily be removed, dislodged, or just raised out of the way.

Cables are available for desktop PCs, too, but a desktop unit is harder to steal than a notebook. It's easier to take just the desktop's data if it's the data thieves are after. To hinder someone from opening your desktop case and stealing a hard drive, keep the case locked if it has that option, and replace the normal case screws with security screws that need a special tool for removal. In personal offices containing sensitive data, consider leaving waste paper outside the door for cleaning staff so that the office itself can be locked overnight.

The Three P's: Profiles, Passwords, and Permissions

Just as the "three R's" are considered the fundamentals of an education, the "three P's" set forth the basics of PC security. Understanding these three ideas will set you up for success no matter how advanced your PC security needs become or how simple they stay.

Caution Please take my advice and don't think that the people in your company's information technology (IT) department are the only ones who need to consider security. That's just not true. Your work with a company PC will run much more smoothly if you understand what's going on when you run into access restrictions, when you try to get intraoffice videoconferencing to work and it *just won't*, or when you share a file with a coworker who can't open it—in some cases, can't even see it.

If you're ignorant of security concerns, it's exceptionally easy to spend an hour trying to solve the unsolvable when you could have changed the rules of the game and been back to productive work in a few seconds. You'll also make the jobs of your coworkers in IT a lot easier and keep them a lot happier. They'll then be better disposed to helping you when you *do* have trouble.

The three P's are profiles, passwords, and permissions. Although dedicated hardware does exist to provide security control at a sophisticated level, that hardware has to be programmed, and the three P's are what it's all about.

Profiles

Profiles, or user accounts, which you've already encountered, establish who can even use a PC. In a secure system, each authorized user has her or his own profile, and there's no availability of a Guest account through which infrequent users can gain some access. Unless your need is overwhelming, don't allow multiple users access through one user account, like the Guest account. It takes only moments to establish an account for each user, and you'll be better able to track what's happening on your PC. In addition, separate user accounts make it easy to do the following:

- Suspend or delete a person's access or restrict his or her use of resources or files without forcing you to distribute a new password to everyone else who shares the account.

- Increase a person's access to resources and files without compromising those resources by globally giving access to everyone who shares the account.

■   Keep passwords secure by eliminating the need to distribute them, making an individual accountable for his or her password.

Other benefits exist as well. If you need to grant the same access to collections of people, that's no problem. Windows XP lets you gather user accounts into *groups*, and you can assign group permissions.

Try This!   If you're going to establish a secure environment, a guest account can undermine all your efforts. Windows XP provides a Guest account, but it's disabled by default. If your PC's Guest account has been turned on and you want to disable it, try this: After logging in as Administrator, from the Start menu, select Control Panel. Select the User Accounts icon, and then click Guest in the Accounts list. In the window that opens, click Turn Off The Guest Account and then verify that the colored suitcase icon has gone gray—this indicates that the account is disabled. Close Control Panel and you're done. Naturally, if someone has been using the Guest account for access, you'll need to create a user account for that person or else explain that he or she will no longer be able to use your PC.

If you are trying this at work and your computer is connected to a network, your User Accounts dialog box will look considerably different. Security on a corporate network is a much broader issue and is outside the scope of this book.

Under Windows XP, a profile also keeps track of personalized settings so that each authorized user can have the visual and interactive computing experience that suits him or her best.

See Also   *For more about user profiles and how to create, modify, and delete them, see Chapter 11, where we explored making your personal computer more personal.*

Passwords

For each profile, exactly one *password* grants access. A *password* is just a secret code known only to its owner. Under Windows XP, passwords are optional— user accounts can be used solely to keep files organized and to provide a personal touch. But passwords are *not* optional in any system you want to keep secure. There's no other way to manage access to your PC and attached resources. Yes, you can have user accounts with no password—that's the Windows XP default, in fact, which assumes that you're running Windows XP Professional on a PC in your home in a locked room to which no other people ever have access.

But security is a multicourse meal, not an à la carte buffet. It makes no sense to restrict certain user accounts from certain kinds of access if you don't use passwords to prevent someone from just logging in through a less restricted account! In addition, if you don't use passwords consistently, each nonpass-worded account is basically a Guest account. Anyone who gains physical access to your PC can, unless you've changed other defaults, open, modify, or delete any file on it.

What qualifies as a good password? I hope it's no surprise to you that *password* is a rather wretched password because it's so easy to guess. A surprising number of people use it. But if you're thinking of being one of them, don't. *Password* is often the first password criminals try when they want to break into a system. Windows XP can enforce good password selection, and it applies good rules. A password complying with enforcement rules must contain three of the following four types of characters:

- UPPERCASE LETTERS
- lowercase letters
- numerics (1234567890)
- symbols (! @ # $ % ^ & * _)

So, although *bifurcation* might be a nice 11-letter word that most people don't use often, it's a terrible password—it contains only one of the four character types. Windows XP would reject this password if enforcement is enabled. Far better would be *Bi4cation*, which is easy to remember because it's pronounced the same way and uses three of the four character types, even though it's shorter. Best would be *Bi4Kshunn*, which is pronounced the same but is further still from the original word. Even if good passwords are enforced, however, users might still create bad passwords. Here are some examples of bad passwords:

- Names or nicknames of spouse, partner, child, or pet
- Birthdays or anniversaries
- Phrases the person is known for using or liking (like *fuggetabouditt*)
- Social security numbers, phone numbers, license plate codes, or employee ID numbers
- Any common word, or any recognizable sequence of numbers, like 123456 or 246810

Windows can also enforce a minimum password length. The longer a password, the more difficult it is for someone to guess it in any reasonable amount of time. In general, a password should *never* be fewer than 6 characters, and 8 is an even better minimum. Some companies require 12 digits as the shortest possible password. Of course, longer passwords are harder to remember, and people will write down a password if they can't remember it. That can be a disaster, and if you're setting up a secure system for your business, it should be your policy to forbid anyone to write down a password. Each user should select a password she or he can remember without writing it down, or you've just got one more thing to worry about. A piece of paper tucked into a wallet goes where the wallet goes; passwords should stay inside the heads of their owners.

Requiring Passwords and Enforcing Good Ones

By default, Windows XP doesn't require that a password be assigned to a user account, nor does it require that passwords created be good ones. Here's how to change both of those characteristics.

Note   If you are trying this on a computer at work and you are connected to a network, these options may behave differently—if you can even access them at all.

Caution   Like the settings you'll find in the Device Manager, those you're about to explore can dramatically affect your use of Windows. They can even restrict your ability to log on. Never change any setting until you know what it does, and always keep your finger near the Cancel button so you can undo any change you make. Settings are saved as soon as you close the Local Security Settings so you'll have no opportunity to exit without saving changes.

Log on as Administrator, open Control Panel, click Switch To Classic View, double-click the Administrative Tools icon in Control Panel to open the Administrative Tools dialog box, and double-click to open Local Security Policy. Make sure that Account Policies is selected in the hierarchical list in the left pane, and double-click to open Password Policy at the right. First, let's make passwords mandatory. Double-click Minimum Password Length and change the setting to eight or more digits, as shown in Figure 17-1. Then click OK.

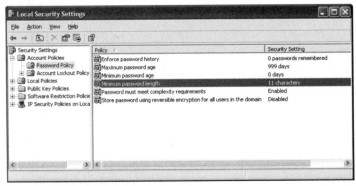

Figure 17-1 The Local Security Settings Policy window allows you to make passwords mandatory and control their length and quality, among other features.

Next, let's enforce complex passwords. Double-click Password Must Meet Complexity Requirements, click the Enable option, and then click OK. From the File menu, select Exit. Next, open the User Accounts dialog box and add a password to the account you're using or change the account's password so that it complies with the Windows complexity requirements you just turned on. Other users will be prompted to add or change their passwords the next time they log on to this PC.

The Limits of Password Protection

If you make the changes just described but change nothing else, you'll restrict local access to your PC, but that's all you'll do. Anyone who can log on to the PC will be able to open and modify any files and run any program on it. That fact can be changed, and I suggest you do so before moving on to the next section on permissions.

First, let's assume you're using Windows XP Simple File Sharing, because that's the default. It's less secure and more permissive than the alternative I'll show you in a moment, but it can still provide protection for of some of your files. By default, the files of any user of your PC are accessible to any other user. To prevent others from seeing your files, open My Computer and select the document folder that corresponds to your username. In my case, as in Figure 17-2, that folder is called Scott's Documents.

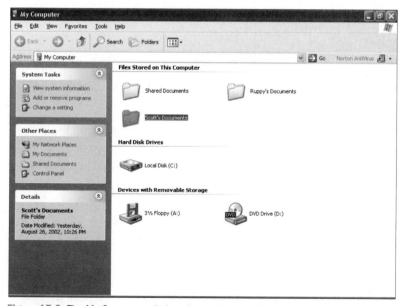

Figure 17-2 The My Computer window shows document folders belonging to each authorized user account.

Right-click the folder and select Sharing And Security from the shortcut menu. The Properties dialog box in Figure 17-3 opens. Click the Sharing tab, select the Make This Folder Private check box, and click OK. If you haven't yet created a password, Windows asks you whether you want to do it now. If you don't use a password, as I said previously, anyone who wants access to your files can simply log on as you. In the meantime, all files and folders in your document folder are made private so that only you can see them. Other users who log on with their own account will be unable to access anything except files you explicitly drag into the Shared Documents folder.

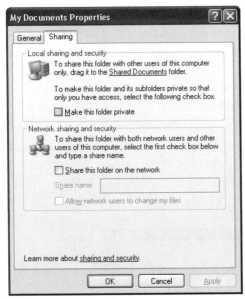

Figure 17-3 The Sharing tab of the Properties dialog box provides access to Simple File Sharing settings like folder privacy.

To protect your files further, right-click your document folder again, select Properties, and click Advanced on the General tab. Shown in Figure 17-4, this dialog box allows you to encrypt files so that their contents can't be discerned without your password, even if someone steals the drive and mounts it as a slave drive inside another PC—a common trick for bypassing simple security software. Select the Encrypt Contents To Secure Data check box and click OK twice. Windows asks whether you want to apply the change to all folders inside your document folder. You do—select the Apply Changes To This Folder, Subfolders And Files option and click OK. It might take a moment for Windows to change all the files if you have a large number of documents, but when Windows is done, your documents are private to anyone who doesn't have your password.

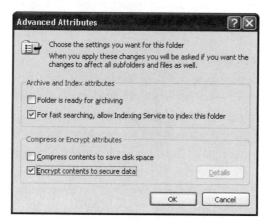

Figure 17-4 Encrypting files keeps their content private even if your PC hardware is stolen.

Simple File Sharing is good, as far as it goes, but if you're working with a business PC, you might want even more control. Permissions will give you that control, but they're off by default. To turn permissions on, you just need to turn Simple File Sharing off. From My Computer, select Folder Options from the Tools menu. Select the View tab, scroll down to Use Simple File Sharing (Recommended), and click to clear the box, as shown below. Click OK, and you're ready to enter the world of permissions.

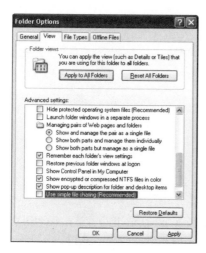

Permissions

Permissions establish whether a user (or a group of users) has permission to use a resource. Resources include devices like network printers as well as files. With Simple File Sharing disabled, some of the power of Windows XP is revealed—you're now using the same access control provided under Windows 2000. Things look a little different, like the Sharing tab of your document folder, shown in Figure 17-5. This highlights one of the big differences between Simple File Sharing and regular file sharing.

With this type of file sharing, the whole concept is split: file sharing now consists of files that are shared by users of this specific PC (which I'll call the *local* PC) and files that are shared by users on a network. They do not, by any means, have to be the same files. When you disabled Simple File Sharing, Windows checked to see whether any of the user document folders were set to Private. Those that were are automatically converted to the regular file sharing version of privacy, in which only the owner has access to the files inside. That's convenient; you won't have to tell each user to reset document privacy. However, it also means that the system administrator no longer has access. That might not be what you want, particularly if you're the administrator, so we'll add Administrator access to a folder in the next section and see how permissions work at the same time.

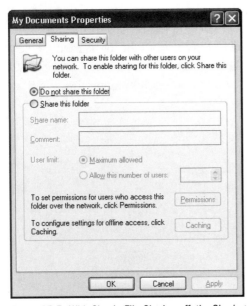

Figure 17-5 With Simple File Sharing off, the Sharing tab now controls network sharing, not local sharing.

The Sharing tab, meanwhile, is now exclusively responsible for network sharing. Folders that shouldn't be accessible over the network should have their Do Not Share This Folder option selected (the default). By contrast, folders you want to share can be shared easily by selecting Share This Folder and entering a share name by which people on the network can identify the folder. You might want to enter a comment to explain the folder's contents, but you don't have to. By default, everyone on the network is given full access to a shared folder. Because restricting network shares and local shares is the same process, let's look at how permissions work.

Working with Permissions

Back in Figure 17-5, you saw that the Sharing tab looks different under regular file sharing; you can see that there's a new tab, too: Security. The Security tab, shown in Figure 17-6, is the realm of permissions. Permissions determine which users, or groups of users, can access certain resources. Access in this case is broken down into a number of categories, seven of which are enabled by default: Full Control, Modify, Read & Execute, List Folder Contents, Read, Write, and Special Permissions. Selecting Full Control in the Allow column automatically sets the other permissions, as you might expect.

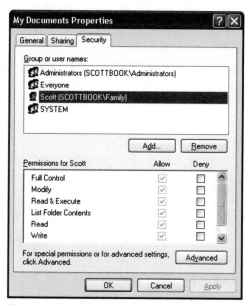

Figure 17-6 The Security tab now controls individual users' access to files and folders.

The meaning of each bit of access is fairly obvious, but let me highlight a few points:

- Read & Execute access makes it possible for a user to run a program. If a program is stored in a folder for which a given user has only Read access, that user won't be able to run it.

- Sometimes it's useful for people to be able to see all the files in a shared folder even though they might not have access to all the files. The List Folder Contents setting makes it possible to implement this.

■   Granting Write access to a folder allows a user to save files in that
    folder, but not delete the folder.

Caution   Granting Write access to a file doesn't allow the user to delete the file—
only Modify access does that. But because the user could open the file, select and
erase the file contents (of, say, a text, spreadsheet, or graphic document), and then
save the file, I advise you to think of granting Write access as granting the ability to
destroy a file's contents.

Setting permissions is really quite easy, and some are preset for you. By
default, whichever user first creates a file is considered the file's owner. That
person will always have full control by default, although you can change permissions later. The user named SYSTEM also always has full control; SYSTEM is
another way of saying Windows. I advise you never to modify any SYSTEM permissions unless you're an expert systems administrator. Also, an object—a file or
a subfolder—automatically inherits permissions from the folder that contains it.
So if you save a file into a folder that another person can't access, the person
won't be able to access that file, either. Most of the time, this is exactly what you
want.

To change a user's access, just select his or her name in the Group Or User
Names list, and then click to change check marks appropriately. To deny access
entirely, you can select a user's name and simply remove it from the list. You can
do this to deny access to a specific file or to an entire folder and all of its files
and subfolders. Similarly, to grant access to a user not listed, click Add. In the
Select Users Or Groups dialog box, shown in Figure 17-7, type the user's name
or click Advanced and then Find Now in the Advanced dialog box to search for
usernames.

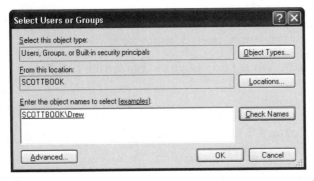

Figure 17-7 Add users or user groups to the list to set access permissions.

Select the username in the list that appears, and click OK. To select more than one name, just hold down the Ctrl key and click additional names, and then click OK. The username or names appear in the Select dialog box. Click OK to return to the Security tab, where you'll see the new users in the list. Click to modify the check boxes to grant or deny access as you want.

Note   You might be wondering why there's a Deny column at all. Isn't not checking to allow access the same as denying it? No, because of the inherited permissions I mentioned earlier. If you store a file in a folder to which a user has some access, the file automatically inherits that folder's permissions. Selecting an access level's Deny box restricts access, regardless of the parent folder's settings. In this way, you can set aside a folder for a group of users' work and still control access to individual files or subfolders that might contain sensitive information.

A Permissions Example

An obvious use of permissions, even in the home office, is to restrict access to sensitive data. For example, you might not want your kids to be able to see everything you do. Creating a username for each child is a great way to make her or him feel special and important; the benefit to you is security and protection. If you don't want a child to have to remember a password, that's probably fine, too. Just go back and change the minimum password length to zero, and make sure your own account is password-protected. Of course, make sure a child's account is of the Limited type, *not* an Administrator account.

Unless you started out using Simple File Sharing and set your document folder to Private, everyone who uses the PC will still have access after you enable file sharing and create usernames for your kids. So open the folder properties and delete the Everyone user, which you see in Figure 17-8. If you want to be the only administrator who can access your files, remove the Administrators account as well. (Keep in mind that, in a business environment, you might not be able to or allowed to remove Administrator access; it might even be a violation of policy to do so.)

Figure 17-8 If the Everyone user group is present, everyone probably has access to the selected resource.

Incidentally, if your kids' files are set to Private under Simple File Sharing, you, as the Administrator, won't have access to them under regular file sharing. The easiest solution is to turn Simple File Sharing back on, clear the Private Files box, and then disable Simple File Sharing again. Both Administrators and Everyone will have access to the files. (You might want to remove Everyone from the list so that a little one doesn't delete your valedictorian's senior thesis.)

Note   Any files you place in the Shared Files folder under Simple File Sharing will be accessible to the Everyone user group after you enable regular file sharing. If this is what you want, fantastic. If it's not, move the files to a different folder to restrict access to them. Files in your Shared Files folder are *not* automatically accessible when your PC is connected to a network. The Shared Files folder must be explicitly shared.

You can go further, however. You might not want your kids to start a program like Microsoft Money, which you use to maintain your finances, or Project, where you manage work. Just right-click the program name on the Start menu, select Properties, and click Find Target. This opens the folder containing the program and selects the file that actually starts the application. Right-click the highlighted file, and select the Security tab. Find your kids' names in the User list, select each, one at a time, and select Full Control in the Deny column. Click OK and close the open folders. If any of those users tries to start the application, they'll simply be told that access is denied.

Tip   This technique is a great way to protect a program's data even when you're not certain where that data is stored. It's certainly not foolproof, because someone else might know where to find the data and know how to import it into a PC with a second copy of the program. However, most children aren't trying to be malicious, so an Access Denied message when they try to start the program will most likely just lead them to find something else to do.

Permissions for User Groups

You can deny access to the World Wide Web in a similar way. Open My Computer, double-click to open Program Files, and then double-click to open the folder called Internet Explorer. Locate the file called IEXPLORE, right-click to select Properties, and select the Security tab, as in Figure 17-9. Notice that the Group Or User Names list contains a group of users named Users. You can tell it's a group because of the little two-headed icon to the left of the name. You don't want to deny access to this group because then only Administrators would be able to use Microsoft Internet Explorer. (On the other hand, if you and your partner or spouse are both Administrators and the kids are the only other users of the PC, just delete the Users group, and you're done!)

Alternatively, click Add and search to add each child's username to the Group Or User Names list; then select each child's account and select the Read & Execute box in the Deny column. Windows reminds you that Deny settings take precedence over Allow settings; click Yes to continue.

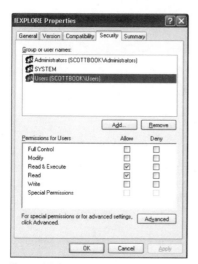

Figure 17-9 Restricting access to a program is as easy as restricting access to a data file.

Note   The way Windows works, giving precedence to Deny permissions, is exactly what you want. This way, you can allow most users to have access to a resource while denying access to just a few—even if those few users are members of the same user group. The users whom you deny access will be denied even though other users in the group have access.

So what's with this whole *user group* thing, anyway? Groups are just a way to organize user accounts so that you can quickly grant or deny access to everyone in the group. Windows creates a few groups by default, including the Administrators and Users groups that you've already seen. Creating new groups is easy. From the Performance And Maintenance option on Control Panel, select Administrative Tools, and double-click to open Computer Management. Double-click Local Users And Groups, and then click Groups in the left pane. The right pane shows a list of extant groups, as in Figure 17-10.

Right-click in the right pane and select New Group from the shortcut menu. In the New Group dialog box that opens, give the group a name, and click Add to go through the process of selecting the users who will be part of it. (It's the same process you went through to locate a user account to add it to the Group Or User Names list.) After adding users to the list, click Close to return to the Computer Management window. Choose Exit from the File menu, and you're done! You can now open the permissions for folders, files, or other resources, and add a user group to the Group Or User Names list.

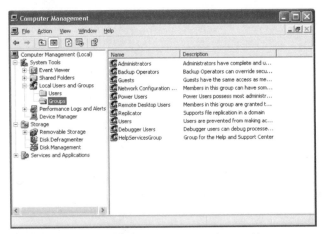

Figure 17-10 The Computer Management window provides access to review and modify users and user groups.

If you want to remove a user from a group, just select the group's name in the Computer Management window and right-click to select Properties. Select User Names from the list, and click Remove to finish the job. Any permissions that you've specifically set for the users you remove will be retained. Any permissions the removed users inherited as group members will be thrown away.

Protecting Your Computer from Outsiders

Having taken a good look at keeping your local PC's hardware and files safe, it remains for us to consider security threats from outside. If your computer resides on a network or has any connection with the Internet, it can be vulnerable to outside interference ranging from accidental deletion of data files to malicious destruction of your entire disk drive. Here's how to protect all your valuable data.

Network Security

Being part of a local area network (LAN) can be a threat to your data security. With Simple File Sharing disabled, any folder you share will provide Full Control access to the Everyone user group—that is, to anyone on the network. (You can't share individual files across the network. To share a single file, you must create a new folder, place the file inside it, and then share the folder.)

To retain better control over the files you share, you'll need to open the Sharing tab in the Properties dialog box for each shared folder, and then click the Permissions button. You'll see the dialog box shown in Figure 17-11, which looks rather like a file or folder's local Security tab.

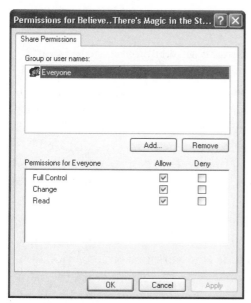

Figure 17-11 Setting permissions for a resource shared over the network is similar to setting local permissions.

Over the network, you can select whether a folder's contents can have the Read permission or the Change permission. Change access includes the ability to delete files and folders. Full Control allows network users to change file attributes.

Of course, the chances are good that you're sharing only resources on your network that you want others to access, and that you know you can trust the people with whom you share. However, there's no particular reason to trust the world at large, even if you're generally well disposed to people. So a key aspect of network security is protecting the network as a whole from outside influence. At the moment, there's nothing quite as influential as the Internet.

Internet Security

Regrettably, short of disconnecting your PC from any kind of network and keeping it locked up, there's no such thing as "so safe, you no longer have to think about security." The only real safety comes from constant vigilance, as anyone named Mad-Eye Moody will tell you. The one-two punch I'm going to describe in this section simply provides constant vigilance when you're away or busy with other things, and it provides vigilance at the code level where you can't go, anyway. There are ways to implement it in hardware or in software, although almost all of us use software for at least the second punch. Windows XP comes with all the software you need for the first punch, and third-party software and hardware are inexpensive.

One Punch: Internet Firewalls

In a building, a "firewall" is simply a wall made of inflammable material. It's designed so that a roaring fire will hit the wall and be unable to pass and spread to the rest of the building. *Internet firewalls* are aptly named. They keep malicious users from electronically bursting in and either taking charge of or damaging your PC. The threat here is real, although certainly exaggerated by the media with such high-profile happenings as distributed denial of service (DDOS) attacks, in which hundreds or thousands of unprotected PCs are taken over and caused to send so much Internet traffic to a specific server, the server is overpowered and disabled.

An Internet firewall is essentially a filter. It uses a tool called a *proxy server* to perform two tasks. First, it can absolutely stop outsiders from connecting to your network or the PCs and servers on it. If you work in a large corporation, you might have started Internet Explorer, only to be asked for a proxy username password. If you don't have one, you won't be allowed to connect to the outside Internet at all.

More commonly, rather than totally blocking such external access, the proxy server is set up by an experienced administrator to allow certain types of nonthreatening external communications, while totally blocking all others. For technical reasons, your PC's overall connection to the Internet is divided into several different *logical ports*, each of which is set up to facilitate a given type of data traffic.

Lingo A *logical port* is simply a pathway over which data flows. Network ports are called logical because they're not physical entities, like your PC's serial or USB port is. Networking ports are just ways that packets of data are electronically labeled so that each computer that must deal with the data knows how to handle it.

Each logical port has a number. Port 25, for example, is part of the protocol normally used to send Internet-based e-mail, the Simple Mail Transfer Protocol (SMTP). (You first encountered protocols back in Chapter 9.) By using a firewall to block access to port 25, it's possible to prevent an unscrupulous person from using certain e-mail spamming techniques that cause people to receive trash Internet e-mail that appears to be sent by you. Other ports are commonly used for a variety of dedicated purposes, from moving Web content to making chat possible.

A firewall can be part of the networking hub you purchase to connect your PCs together as a network or to bridge between your PC and a broadband Internet connection, like DSL. If so, the hardware comes with detailed instructions on how to configure each aspect of its proxy server so that you get the protection you need. Setting up a hardware firewall isn't exactly hard, but neither is it a job for a true beginner. If you're comfortable with networking PCs together and are somewhat knowledgeable about the technical side of the Internet, you should have no problems configuring a basic hardware firewall.

On the other hand, a software firewall most often provides the expertise necessary to protect you in minutes, if not seconds. The firewall software that's part of Windows XP, the Internet Connection Firewall, is almost embarrassingly easy to use. In Control Panel, select Network and Internet Connections, select Network Connections, and right-click the Local Area Connection you want to protect. Select Properties, select the Advanced tab, and select the Protect My Computer And Network check box. Click OK, and that's it. You're done. The Internet Connection Firewall scans all external signals coming in from the Internet and simply throws away those that originate from a computer other than your own.

Except for a few cases, you should never find your computer being con-
tacted by an outside source without you knowing about it first. One such exception might be chat software that allows a remote user to see that you're online
and say hello to you. In some cases, this software is crafted to work with the
firewall. In others, the firewall prevents it from working.

You should have a firewall of some kind, either software or hardware, on
any computer that's connected to the Internet, with one exception: PCs on your
local network that use Windows XP Internet Connection Sharing as clients (that
is, they connect to another computer which is, itself, connected to the Internet)
shouldn't run a firewall. The firewall should either be part of the physical connection to the initial PC or should be run only on that first PC. Every computer
that shares the connection will benefit from the one firewall.

If you're unable to use certain Internet software or tools after installing your
firewall, you might need to "open holes" in the firewall to let that traffic through.
You'll find guidance on how to do that in a hardware firewall's manual. For a
software firewall, you might need assistance from the Internet software's manufacturer to find out exactly what the software is doing that's being blocked
before you can know how to modify the firewall to stop the blocking. Most of
us will never encounter any of these problems.

Two Punch: Antivirus Software

The follow-up punch that can make a dramatic difference in keeping your PC
and network safe is antivirus software. (Antivirus hardware does exist; it's just
rare outside of distributed environments like Internet service providers and Web
site hosting servers.) Several antivirus products are available, and you can get
some of them for free. One of the best ones is Norton Antivirus. It isn't free,
although the manufacturer does provide a Web-based service that can check
your PC for viruses for free.

But even if you have to pay for it, antivirus software is one of the least
expensive—and probably the best—PC purchases you'll ever make. Whichever
antivirus product you select, I strongly suggest you consider it a mandatory part
of your PC, on level with, say, a CPU. Any PC that connects, even occasionally, to
the Internet or to any network, is vulnerable to invasion from a virus, a *Trojan
horse*, or other malicious content. (I recognize that it's technically inaccurate, but

I am going to use the single word *virus* to refer to this entire class of malicious software. Otherwise, you'll be as tired reading "virus, Trojan horse, or other malicious content" as I will be of typing it.)

Lingo   A *Trojan horse* is a piece of malicious software that masquerades as some kind of harmless program, like a game or utility. When you innocently run the Trojan horse, it does its damage. Some Trojan horses even display a real game, to hold your attention while the program quietly erases file after file in the background.

Now, some people argue that not *all* viruses are malicious. I couldn't disagree more strongly. It's true that some display only a silly message on your screen, whereas some antics of other virus creators are extremely harmful. I consider them the same, and I argue that you should do likewise. The presence in your private space of something you didn't invite is threatening. Refusal to see these "friendly attacks," as if there were any such thing as a friendly attack, as crimes has only clouded the issues and made it harder to successfully prosecute those who write code that's actually destructive.

Against all viruses, antivirus software works in two ways. First, it contains an index of known threats that it uses to check every file on your PC or network. Files that contain code recognized in the index are flagged, and you have the opportunity to delete them.

Antivirus software also scans traffic coming across your network and from the Internet and can identify virus code in the data stream before anything is ever written to your disk. Incoming e-mail is scanned so that messages containing malicious attachments can be deleted before you accidentally open them. (For more on e-mail issues, see the sidebar "Virus Hoaxes.")

The second way antivirus software works is to use complex investigatory methods to watch for virus-like behavior. These work like an electronic bloodhound to ask questions like, "Is it normal for a Web page to instruct my PC to erase its hard disk?" Such threatening processes can be detected and stopped before they do any harm, even if they use no previously known virus code or techniques. As new code and techniques are discovered, the maker of the antivirus software provides updates you can download to keep your software current. Failing to do so is almost as bad as running no antivirus software at all.

Virus Hoaxes If there's anything more time-wasting than a virus, it's a virus hoax. I wish I had a dollar for every minute I've lost sending the same "Relax, it's a hoax" e-mail out to the same people. Viruses are created by pathetic little people who know how to program computers and are desperate for attention. Virus hoaxes are probably created by similar, less intelligent, people. So let me give you some pointers about what a virus, Trojan horse, or other malicious content (collectively, "a virus") can and can't do:

- Under Windows XP, nothing can format the hard disk containing Windows.

- Under Windows XP, nothing can format *any* disk in your system if you aren't logged on as Administrator. This is one of the reasons Microsoft urges users to create a Limited account for general use. (You can still perform administrative functions from a Limited account if you have the right permissions and know-how.)

- There is simply *no such thing* as a virus that lurks in, or can do any harm from, an image file. If it's a JPEG, a GIF, a BMP, a TIF, or any other type of image file, it's safe. Similarly, there can be no virus in a traditional sound file like WAV or MP3 files, nor in movie files, like AVI, MPG, MPEG, or MOV files.

- There's simply *no such thing* as a text file virus. Indeed, there's no such thing as a text virus, period. That means if you receive an unformatted e-mail message that has no attachment, it doesn't have a virus in it, either. Unformatted e-mail is just plain text. It's totally harmless. If you get e-mail saying "Warning! Do not even read a message from Fintoozler because it contains a virus that will wipe out everything!" you can safely and simply ignore it. Or, better yet, send a message back to the person saying that they're spreading a hoax and annoying more people than they can even imagine.

- Viruses can lurk in document files like DOC files and spreadsheets because the programs that create those files provide macro languages that automate tasks but that can behave maliciously, too. Antivirus software catches known macro viruses, but you must apply the general rule of viruses to this kind of file.

- The type of files that most commonly contain viruses are those that are executed (run). This particularly includes EXE files, along with COM, DLL, BAT, VBX files, and others. As a matter of fact, COM files are antiquated, and you should look at any COM file you encounter as an attachment to e-mail with extreme suspicion. A few remain on your PC as part of Windows and remnants of an earlier age, but, in general, you shouldn't encounter a COM file at all. BAT files, too, are largely antiquated and you should always view their contents before running them. (To do this, right-click any BAT file, and select Open With. Then choose Notepad from the list. BAT files are simply text files that contain instructions for the operating system to carry out.)

■ E-mail messages that contain active HTML (Web) content can be dangerous because they can link to and open a Web page containing destructive code without warning you or even identifying the Web page first. To guard against these threats, always disable your e-mail program's preview pane, and never open e-mail if you don't know who sent it. (This is a great way to avoid annoying spam, too. Habitually deleting anything sent to you by any person or company you can't easily identify is a surprisingly fulfilling way to guarantee that the money these companies have spent to put their junk in your face is money wasted.)

Caution   As a general warning against viruses, the threat of which is no hoax, always apply this rule: never open a file or an e-mail attachment if you don't know for certain who created it.

I don't tell you about all these virus hoaxes to suggest that you don't need to worry about viruses. My intent is just the opposite. When you understand what viruses can and can't do, you'll behave more safely overall. You won't let your cautious behavior lapse because you've spent so much time encountering hoaxes that you've decided a genuine threat is a hoax. Neither will you give the people who create this trash the satisfaction of knowing their childish efforts have had any effect.

Surfing Safely Among the Sharks

The Web is an active, online superhighway for malicious and beneficial content, alike. You probably don't want to access a Web page that will cause destruction to your data or open you up to federal investigation because you inadvertently allowed your PC to be part of a massive Internet attack. Fortunately, Internet Explorer provides protection of two different types to address this real concern. The first level of protection, Internet Security Zones, disallows certain types of potentially harmful code, like ActiveX controls on a Web page. The second level, the Content Advisor, lets you choose which kind of Web pages will even open on your PC. (What amounts to a third level, the Internet Connection Firewall, we discussed in the section "One Punch: Internet Firewalls," earlier in this chapter.)

Internet Explorer lets you set a security level for your Web surfing. This level is maintained through a combination of settings on the Security tab and Privacy tab of the Internet Properties dialog box. On the Security tab, shown in Figure 17-12, you can enter the names of Web sites that you know to be either safe or malevolent. Internet Explorer automatically prevents you from intentionally or indirectly accessing one of the malevolent sites (because one way that crimi-nals get you to access their malicious ActiveX controls is to redirect you trans-parently from a site you intend to visit to one you don't). After you select the Restricted Sites zone, you can click the Sites button and add sites you want to avoid to the list. You can also enter trusted sites and internal sites that you know are safe into their respective zones.

Figure 17-12 The Security tab of the Internet Properties dialog box allows you to set how Internet Explorer restricts Web browsing to unsafe sites.

The Custom Level button here allows you to dissect the security behavior associated with each zone. Simply select the zone at the top of the dialog box, and then click Custom Level to change any of the defaults. You might, for exam-ple, want to enable any active Web content that's part of one of your company's own Web sites. Alternatively, you might want to be prompted before any active content of any kind is ever run. Settings such as these can be chosen and customized.

The Privacy tab, shown on the next page, makes up the second part of the whole Internet Security Zone package. This tab allows you to set a protection level for the handling of Internet *cookies*.

Lingo   A *cookie* is a small file that maintains information about you or about your use of a Web page.

Cookies are of two types. First-party cookies are those created by the Web sites you directly visit. These are commonly generated when you shop online, when you use certain online research tools, and so forth. Third-party cookies are those that are created by Web sites you visit indirectly—like the banner ads that pop up whether you want them to or not.

Your privacy setting restricts the creation and use of cookies. At the highest level, cookies are disabled. At the lowest level, all cookies are allowed. The default setting is Medium, but I personally prefer to use Medium High, which allows me to conveniently shop online and so forth, but which prevents most third-party cookies from ever being created on or read from my PC. When you encounter a site that you know is trustworthy, you can click Edit and allow it to create first-person cookies at will, regardless of your privacy level. You can also block specific sites that repeatedly annoy you by trying to create cookies you don't want.

The Content Advisor, which you'll find available at the top of the Content tab, as in Figure 17-13, restricts access to Web sites that contain certain content you might prefer to avoid. Click Enable to turn the feature on. On the Ratings tab, you can select from four levels of access in four categories—Language, Nudity, Sex, and Violence. Select the category, and then move the slider to the level you want.

Figure 17-13 Select the level of access you want to give, not what you want to restrict.

The level you select is what Web browsers are *allowed* to see, so if you want to keep your kids from viewing violent content of any kind, you want the slider set to Level 0: None, not Level 4: Wanton And Gratuitous Violence. The system is confusing to some people, because it might seem more obvious to say, "I *don't* want my kids to see wanton and gratuitous violence," than it is to say "I *do* want my kids to have access to wanton and gratuitous violence," but that's how the system works. In the Language category, Inoffensive Slang is always allowed, probably because many people feel it's harmless. As a writer, I can tell you, that just ain't so.

On the Approved Sites tab, you can list Web addresses for sites you want to allow, regardless of their content. Because content rating is voluntary, the General tab allows you to choose whether unrated sites can be visited and to select which of several rating systems you want to use. Clicking Find Rating Systems takes you to the Microsoft Web site, from which you can download different systems, and clicking Rating Systems lets you select which system is active. The General tab also makes it possible for you to create a password which, when entered, bypasses the Content Advisor and allows unrestricted access to content.

Key Points

- PC safety and security is everyone's concern.

- You can implement some simple common sense to reduce the risk of someone stealing your desktop or mobile computer.

- Data that's sensitive should be encrypted; data that's vital should be backed up.

■ User profiles are a way to manage access to your PC and its resources. Profiles also maintain customized settings for each user.

■ Passwords restrict access to a user profile and its assigned resources.

■ Passwords should never be shorter than six characters; a minimum of eight is better.

■ Passwords should be of good quality, using a variety of character types, including uppercase and lowercase letters, numerics, and symbols.

■ A password that's written down is worse than no password at all.

■ Permissions specify whether a user account or group can access, modify, or create files, folders, or other resources (including printers).

■ An Internet firewall prevents outsiders from accessing your PC or its content.

■ Antivirus software catches and eliminate viruses, Trojan horses, and other malicious content.

■ The Internet Security Zone features of Internet Explorer prevent you from surfing to malicious Web sites or compromising your privacy through cookies.

■ The Content Advisor prevents users from accessing objectionable content.

Index

Numbers and Symbols

Scott H. A. Clark

Scott H.A. Clark has been the director of Peter Norton's series of computer books for the past decade. He has written two editions of the bestselling *Inside the PC*, and is well known for his ability to make technology accessible to readers of all levels. He lives with his partner in Southern California.

The manuscript for this book was prepared and submitted to Microsoft Press in electronic form. Pages were composed by Microsoft Press using Adobe FrameMaker+SGML for Windows, with text in Garamond and display type in ITC Franklin Gothic Condensed. Composed pages were delivered to the printer as electronic pre-press files.

Cover designer:	Tim Girvin Design
Interior Graphic Designer:	James D. Kramer
Principal Compositor:	Mary Beth McDaniel
Project Manager:	Susan H. McClung
Copy Editor:	Chrisa Hotchkiss
Technical Editor:	Don Lesser
Proofreaders:	Jackie Fearer, Charlotte Maurer, Katie O'Connell
Indexer:	Edwin Durbin

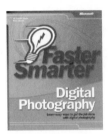   

Self-paced
training that works
as hard as you do!

Information-packed STEP BY STEP courses are the most effective way to teach yourself how to complete tasks with the Microsoft Windows operating system and Microsoft Office applications. Numbered steps and scenario-based lessons with practice files on CD-ROM make it easy to find your way while learning tasks and procedures. Work through every lesson or choose your own starting point—with STEP BY STEP'S modular design and straightforward writing style, *you* drive the instruction. And the books are constructed with lay-flat binding so you can follow the text with both hands at the keyboard. Select STEP BY STEP titles also prepare you for the Microsoft Office User Specialist (MOUS) credential. It's an excellent way for you or your organization to take a giant step toward workplace productivity.

Microsoft Press also has STEP BY STEP titles to help you use earlier versions of Microsoft software.

- **Home Networking with Microsoft® Windows® XP Step by Step**
  ISBN 0-7356-1435-0

- **Microsoft Windows XP Step by Step**
  ISBN 0-7356-1383-4

- **Microsoft Office XP Step by Step**
  ISBN 0-7356-1294-3

- **Microsoft Word Version 2002 Step by Step**
  ISBN 0-7356-1295-1

- **Microsoft Project Version 2002 Step by Step**
  ISBN 0-7356-1301-X

- **Microsoft Excel Version 2002 Step by Step**
  ISBN 0-7356-1296-X

- **Microsoft PowerPoint® Version 2002 Step by Step**
  ISBN 0-7356-1297-8

- **Microsoft Outlook® Version 2002 Step by Step**
  ISBN 0-7356-1298-6

- **Microsoft FrontPage® Version 2002 Step by Step**
  ISBN 0-7356-1300-1

- **Microsoft Access Version 2002 Step by Step**
  ISBN 0-7356-1299-4

- **Microsoft Visio® Version 2002 Step by Step**
  ISBN 0-7356-1302-8

Microsoft Press® products are available worldwide wherever quality computer books are sold. For more information, contact your book or computer retailer, software reseller, or local Microsoft Sales Office, or visit our Web site at microsoft.com/mspress. To locate your nearest source for Microsoft Press products, or to order directly, call 1-800-MSPRESS in the United States. (in Canada, call 1-800-268-2222).

Prices and availability dates are subject to change.

microsoft.com/mspress

Work smarter—
conquer your software *from the inside out!*

Hey, you know your way around a desktop. Now dig into Office XP applications and the Windows XP operating system and *really* put your PC to work! These supremely organized software reference titles pack hundreds of timesaving solutions, troubleshooting tips and tricks, and handy workarounds in a concise, fast-answer format. They're all muscle and no fluff. All this comprehensive information goes deep into the nooks and crannies of each Office application and Windows XP feature. INSIDE OUT titles also include a CD-ROM full of handy tools and utilities, sample files, an eBook links to related sites, and other help. Discover the best and fastest ways to perform everyday tasks, and challenge yourself to new levels of software mastery!

MICROSOFT® WINDOWS® XP INSIDE OUT
ISBN 0-7356-1382-6

MICROSOFT WINDOWS SECURITY INSIDE OUT FOR WINDOWS XP AND WINDOWS 2000
ISBN 0-7356-1632-9

MICROSOFT OFFICE XP INSIDE OUT
ISBN 0-7356-1277-3

MICROSOFT OFFICE v. X FOR MAC INSIDE OUT
ISBN 0-7356-1628-0

MICROSOFT WORD VERSION 2002 INSIDE OUT
ISBN 0-7356-1278-1

MICROSOFT EXCEL VERSION 2002 INSIDE OUT
ISBN 0-7356-1281-1

MICROSOFT OUTLOOK® VERSION 2002 INSIDE OUT
ISBN 0-7356-1282-X

MICROSOFT ACCESS VERSION 2002 INSIDE OUT
ISBN 0-7356-1283-8

MICROSOFT FRONTPAGE® VERSION 2002 INSIDE OUT
ISBN 0-7356-1284-6

MICROSOFT VISIO® VERSION 2002 INSIDE OUT
ISBN 0-7356-1285-4

MICROSOFT PROJECT VERSION 2002 INSIDE OUT
ISBN 0-7356-1124-6

Microsoft®
microsoft.com/mspress

Target your problem and
fix it yourself—
fast!

When you're stuck with a computer problem, you need answers right now. TROUBLESHOOTING books can help. They'll guide you to the source of the problem and show you how to solve it right away. Get ready solutions with clear, step-by-step instructions. Go to quick-access charts with *Top 20 Problems* and *Prevention Tips*. Find even more solutions with *Quick Fixes* and handy *Tips*. Walk through the remedy with plenty of screen shots. Find what you need with the extensive, easy-reference index. Get the answers you need to get back to business fast with TROUBLESHOOTING books.

Troubleshooting Microsoft® Office XP
ISBN 0-7356-1491-1

Troubleshooting Microsoft Access Databases
(Covers Access 97 and Access 2000)
ISBN 0-7356-1160-2

Troubleshooting Microsoft Access 2002
ISBN 0-7356-1488-1

Troubleshooting Microsoft Excel Spreadsheets
(Covers Excel 97 and Excel 2000)
ISBN 0-7356-1161-0

Troubleshooting Microsoft Excel 2002
ISBN 0-7356-1493-8

Troubleshooting Microsoft Outlook®
(Covers Microsoft Outlook 2000 and Outlook Express)
ISBN 0-7356-1162-9

Troubleshooting Microsoft Outlook 2002
(Covers Microsoft Outlook 2002 and Outlook Express)
ISBN 0-7356-1487-3

Troubleshooting Your Web Page
(Covers Microsoft FrontPage® 2000)
ISBN 0-7356-1164-5

Troubleshooting Microsoft FrontPage® 2002
ISBN 0-7356-1489-X

Troubleshooting Microsoft Project 2002
ISBN 0-7356-1503-9

Troubleshooting Microsoft Windows®
(Covers Windows Me, Windows 98, and Windows 95)
ISBN 0-7356-1166-1

Troubleshooting Microsoft Windows 2000 Professional
ISBN 0-7356-1165-3

Troubleshooting Microsoft Windows XP
ISBN 0-7356-1492-X

Troubleshooting Your PC, Second Edition
ISBN 0-7356-1490-3

Microsoft Press® products are available worldwide wherever quality computer books are sold. For more information, contact your book or computer retailer, software reseller, or local Microsoft Sales Office, or visit our Web site at <u>microsoft.com/mspress</u>. To locate your nearest source for Microsoft Press products, or to order directly, call 1-800-MSPRESS in the U.S. (in Canada, call 1-800-268-2222).

Prices and availability dates are subject to change.

microsoft.com/mspress

Get a **Free**
e-mail newsletter, updates,
special offers, links to related books,
and more when you

register on line!

Register your Microsoft Press® title on our Web site and you'll get a FREE subscription to our e-mail newsletter, *Microsoft Press Book Connections*. You'll find out about newly released and upcoming books and learning tools, online events, software downloads, special offers and coupons for Microsoft Press customers, and information about major Microsoft® product releases. You can also read useful additional information about all the titles we publish, such as detailed book descriptions, tables of contents and indexes, sample chapters, links to related books and book series, author biographies, and reviews by other customers.

Registration is easy. Just visit this Web page and fill in your information:

http://www.microsoft.com/mspress/register

Microsoft

Proof of Purchase

Use this page as proof of purchase if participating in a promotion or rebate offer on this title. Proof of purchase must be used in conjunction with other proof(s) of payment such as your dated sales receipt—see offer details.

Faster Smarter PCs
0-7356-1855-0

CUSTOMER NAME

Microsoft Press, PO Box 97017, Redmond, WA 98073-9830